PRAISE FOR NEAR A THOUSAND TABLES

"An appetizingly provocative book . . . Who cannot appreciate [a] superb description of the proper way to eat an oyster?"

—*Los Angeles Times*

"This survey of gastronomic lore can't be beat."

—*Publishers Weekly*

"*Near a Thousand Tables* belongs to that excellent . . . genre, the 'brief history'. . . . [A] short, lively rundown on the subject. Bright, fun, and naughty."

—*The New Yorker*

"Whether you are content with bread or your taste instead runs to snails or human flesh, you will take away from this book a new appreciation of your favorite menu."

—Jared M. Diamond, author of the Pulitzer Prize–winning
Guns, Germs, and Steel

"With gusto and analytical savvy, [Fernández-Armesto] traces the long and complex evolution of food since the Middle Ages. After reading this book, you'll never think of eating the same again. Highly recommended!"

—Douglas Brinkley, director, Eisenhower Center for American Studies

"As interesting to the hungry man in the street as it is to the austere academic."

—*The Wall Street Journal* (Europe)

"A sparkling ramble through history which scatters countless pointers to new research along the way. It is intellectual history, but not in the least arid: His opinions are strong, but supremely palatable."

—*Financial Times* (London)

Near a Thousand Tables

A History of Food

FELIPE FERNÁNDEZ-ARMESTO

FREE PRESS

NEW YORK · LONDON · TORONTO · SYDNEY · SINGAPORE

_f_P

FREE PRESS
A Division of Simon & Schuster, Inc.
1230 Avenue of the Americas
New York, NY 10020

First Free Press trade paperback edition 2004

FREE PRESS and colophon are
registered trademarks of Simon & Schuster Inc.

For information about special discounts for bulk purchases,
please contact Simon & Schuster Special Sales:
1-800-456-6798 or business@simonandschuster.com

DESIGNED BY KEVIN HANEK
SET IN ADOBE JENSON

Manufactured in the United States of America

1   3   5   7   9   10   8   6   4   2

Library of Congress Cataloging-in-Publication Data
Fernández-Armesto, Felipe
Near a thousand tables: a history of food / Felipe Fernández-Armesto.
p.   cm.
Includes bibliographical references and index.
1. Food—History. I. Title.
TX353.F437 2002
641.3'009—dc21   2002023318
ISBN 0-7432-2644-5
0-7432-2740-9 (PBK)

Contents

Il faut vivre pour manger et ne pas manger pour vivre.

— MOLIÈRE, *LE MALADE IMAGINAIRE*

What shall I tell you, my lady, of the secrets of nature I have learned while cooking? . . . One can philosophize quite well while preparing supper. I often say, when I have these little thoughts, "Had Aristotle cooked, he would have written a great deal more."

— JUANA INÉS DE LA CRUZ, *EPÍSTOLA A FILOTEA*

*And oft I thought (my fancy was so strong)
That I, at last, a resting-place had found;
"Here will I dwell," said I, "my whole life long,
Roaming the illimitable waters round;
Here will I live, of all but heaven disowned,
And end my days upon the peaceful flood."–
To break my dream the vessel reached its bound;
And homeless near a thousand homes I stood,
And near a thousand tables pined and wanted food.*

— WILLIAM WORDSWORTH, *GUILT & SORROW,*
OR INCIDENTS ON SALISBURY PLAIN

Preface

The great press baron Lord Northcliffe used to tell his journalists that four subjects could be relied on for abiding public interest: crime, love, money and food. Only the last of these is fundamental and universal. Crime is a minority interest, even in the worst-regulated societies. It is possible to imagine an economy without money and reproduction without love but not life without food. Food, moreover, has a good claim to be considered the world's most important subject. It is what matters most to most people for most of the time.

Yet food history remains relatively underappreciated. Most academic institutions still neglect it. Many of the best contributions to its study are made by amateurs and antiquarians. There is no consensus about how to approach it. For some people, it is all about nutrition and malnutrition, sustenance and sickness; for others, less anxious to avoid condemnation for frivolity, it is essentially about cuisine. Economic historians see food as a commodity to be produced and traded. When it gets to the stage of being eaten, they lose interest. For social historians, diet is an index of differentiation and changing class relations. Cultural historians are increasingly interested in how food nourishes societies as well as individual bodies—how it feeds identities, defines groups. In political history, food is the stuff of tributary relationships and its distribution and management are at the heart of power. The small but gallant and growing band of environmental historians sees food as linkage in the chain of being: the substance of the ecosystems which human beings strive to dominate. Our most intimate contact with the natural environment occurs when we eat it. Food is a subject of pleasure and peril.

Increasingly, in recent years—indeed, in some ways since before the Second World War, when the *Annales* school of French historical geography began to teach historians to take food seriously—the diversity of approaches has multiplied the scholarly output and made it harder to synthesize. Today, the materials available to a writer attempting a general conspectus are wonderful but intractable. Following the example of *Annales*, many historical periodicals carry frequent relevant articles. A specialist periodical, *Petits propos culinaires*, has appeared for more than twenty years. The Oxford Symposium on Food History, established by Alan Davidson and Theodore Zeldin, provided a focus for interested students and a steady output of published transactions. Excellent general histories include Reay Tannahill's *Food in History*, first published in 1973 and still deservedly popular, Maguelonne Toussaint-Samat's *Histoire naturelle et morale de la nourriture*, which first appeared in 1987, and the compilation edited by J.-L. Flandre and M. Montanari in 1996, *Histoire de l'alimentation*.

Yet the rate at which new material appears makes it increasingly hard even for the best works of previous decades to be satisfactorily updated by periodic revision. Tannahill's book, despite its title, is determinedly in the "how-we-got-to-where-we-are" tradition and is not much concerned with an aspect of particular interest to many readers: the relationship between food history and history in general. Toussaint-Samat's work is a wonderful quarry but a sprawling and indisciplined work, chiefly composed as a series of essays on the histories of various foodstuffs. Flandre and Montanari, who launched the most scholarly and professionally ambitious attempt up to their time, only aimed to cover the history of food in Western civilization and its ancient predecessors. Like most volumes by multiple contributors, theirs is endlessly interesting but lacks the coherence of some of its rivals. *The Cambridge World History of Food* appeared late in the year 2000, when the present book was almost finished; together with Alan Davidson's *The Oxford Companion to Food*, which preceded it by about a year, it is invaluable for reference and unbeatable for browsing. But its massive dimensions make it a work *sui generis*; and its greatest strengths are on the study of food as a source of nutrition, rather than culture.

In this book, I aim not to replace other histories of food but to offer readers a useful alternative: to take a genuinely global perspective; to treat food history as a theme of world history, inseparable from all the other interactions of human beings with one another and with the rest of nature; to treat evenhandedly the ecological, cultural and culinary concepts of the subject; to combine a broad conspectus with selectively detailed excursions into particular cases; to trace connections, at every stage, between the food of the past and the way we eat today; and to do all this briefly.

The method I have adopted is to classify the material under the headings of eight great "revolutions"—as I call them—which seem to me, between them, to provide an overview of the entire history of food. This method should have enabled me to be more concise than is possible in traditional approaches which categorize the subject product by product or place by place or period by period. By calling my divisions revolutions I do not mean to suggest they were rapid episodes, narrowly confined in time. On the contrary, though I think it is fair to say that they all began at particular moments, they all had stuttering starts, long unfoldings and enduring reverberations. The origins of some are truly lost in the vast expanses of prehistory. Some of them started at different times in different places. Some of them began long ago and are still going on. Though I have tried to give my account of them a very broad chronological structure, it should be obvious to readers that my revolutions did not happen in sequence, but overlapped in unpatterned complexity. All of them are in a special sense part of the history of food but have obvious repercussions beyond it, in other aspects of world history. To emphasize these continuities, I try to keep up a program of shifts between past and present, place and place.

The first revolution is the invention of cooking, which I see as an episode of human self-differentiation from the rest of nature, and an inaugural event in the history of social change. I deal next with the discovery that food is more than sustenance—that its production, distribution, preparation and consumption generate rites and magic, as eating becomes ritualized and irrational or suprarational. My third revolution is the "herding revolution"—the domestication and selective breeding of edible animal species: I deal with this before plant-based agriculture, which is the subject of my fourth revolution, partly for convenience and partly to draw attention to my argument that at least one kind of animal husbandry—snail farming—was an earlier innovation than is generally admitted. The fifth revolution is the use of food as a means and index of social differentiation: under this heading, I try to trace a line of continuity from the probably Paleolithic origins of privileged entitlement in competition for food, down to the courtly and bourgeois cuisines of modern times. The sixth revolution is that of long-range trade and the role of food in cultural exchanges of transforming effect. The seventh is the ecological revolution of the last five hundred years, which is now usually called the "Columbian Exchange," and the place of foodstuffs in it. Finally, I turn to industrialization in the "developing" world of the nineteenth and twentieth centuries: what food contributed to it and what were its effects on food.

The book has been written mainly as a *devoir de vacances* in the course of the calendar year 2000. Most of the work was a sort of spin-off from preparation for my previous book, *Civilizations*, a study of the relationship between civilization and environment, which appeared in the U.K. in 2000 and in the United States in 2001. A Fellowship of the Netherlands Institute of Advanced Study in the Humanities and Social Sciences and a Union Pacific Visiting Professorship at the University of Minnesota helped me to get some thoughts straight and to harry some problems. I am profoundly grateful to both institutions, which provided wonderfully exciting and rewarding environments for work.

—F.F.-A., QUEEN MARY, UNIVERSITY OF LONDON, 1ST JANUARY, 2001

The Invention of Cooking

—

The First Revolution

"A loaf of bread," the Walrus said,
"Is chiefly what we need:
Pepper and vinegar besides
Are very good indeed—
Now if you're ready, oysters dear,
We can begin to feed."

—LEWIS CARROLL, THROUGH THE LOOKING-GLASS

Thus you can see everything, the food in the raw and the chemistry of fire—
which not only stills the howl of the hygiener but adds vivacity to the room.

—WILLIAM SANSOM, BLUE SKIES, BROWN STUDIES

THE TRANSFORMING FIRE

It is no way to eat oysters. You see the fastidious eater fiddling with them in restaurants, coating them with lemon juice strained through muslin napkins, or dosing them with bizarrely flavored vinegars, or sprinkling them with glowing stains of vermilion Tabasco or some other blindingly, chokingly hot sauce. This is deliberate provocation, designed to refresh the bivalves before death, a little mild torture under which you can sometimes feel that you see the victims wriggle or flinch. Then the diner manipulates spoon and scoop, prising and sliding the oyster out of its bed onto a curl of cold silver. The sheen of the creature clashes with the shine of the cutlery as he raises the slick, slippery mollusk to his lips.

Most people like to eat them that way, but it means they forfeit the full, true oyster moment. Unless you discard the utensils, raise the half-shell to your mouth, throw back your head, scrape the creature from its lair with your teeth, taste its briny juice and squelch it slightly against the palate before swallowing it alive, you deprive yourself of a historic experience. For most of history, oyster eaters enjoyed the slightly fetid, tangy smell of the inside of the shell, undoused with the disguising dressing of aromatic acids. This was the way fourth-century poet and traveler Ausonius liked them, in "their sweet juice, mingled with a sensation of the sea." Or in the words of a modern oyster expert, your aim is to receive "some piercing intuition of the sea, and all its weeds and breezes. . . . You are eating the sea, that's it, only the sensation of a gulp of sea water has been wafted out of it by some sorcery."

For almost uniquely, in the repertoire of modern Western cuisine, the oyster is eaten uncooked and unkilled. It is the nearest thing we have to "natural" food—the only dish which deserves to be called "au naturel" without irony. Of course, when you eat it in a restaurant, its shell has been barbed and unclamped with all the panoply of civilization by a trained professional, wielding appropriate technology, an inviolable ritual and a stylish flourish. Before that, the oyster was reared underwater on a stone tile or wooden trellis, herded in an oyster bed, grown for years under expert eyes and harvested by practiced hands—not plucked from a rock pool as a prize seized from nature. Still, it is the food that unites us with all our ancestors—the dish you consume in what is recognizably the way people have encountered their nourishment since the first emergence of our species.

Even if you are one of those people who think they hear the scream of the pear or peanut as they seize it and munch it raw, you will still find virtually no food in modern Western cuisine as convincingly "natural" as the oyster, for, with very few exceptions, such as some fungi and seaweeds, the fruits and vegetables we eat—even the "wild" berry picked from the bramble—are the result of generations or eons of selective breeding by man; the oyster remains a product of little modified natural selection and varies markedly from sea to sea. Furthermore, we eat it while it is still alive. Other cultures have more foods of this kind. Australian aboriginals guzzle witjuti grubs, seized from gum trees, plump with half-digested wood pulp in their guts. Nenets chomp the living lice lifted from their own bodies "like candy." Nuer lovers are said to show mutual affection by feeding each other lice freshly plucked from their heads. Masai drink blood squeezed from wounds in live cattle. Ethiopians like honeycombs with the young larvae still alive in the chambers. And we have oysters. "There is a dreadful solemnity" in eating them, as Somerset Maugham observed, which "a sluggish fancy cannot grasp," and which would surely make the Walrus weep without hypocrisy. What is more, oysters are fairly unusual among raw foods because they are usually ruined by cooking. To put them in steak-and-kidney puddings or skewer them wrapped in bacon, as the

English do, or smother them in various kinds of cheese sauce, as in the dishes called oysters Rockefeller and oysters Musgrave, or to stuff them in an omelette, as in the signature dish of the regional cuisine of the Chinese province of Xiamen, or to chop them for stuffing Thanksgiving turkey, is to smother their taste. Inventive recipes can occasionally be more successful: I once had an impressive dish of oysters at the Athenaeum, lightly poached in wine vinegar and pasted with spinach-flavored béchamel. Such experiments are justified for fun but rarely advance the frontiers of gastronomy.

The oyster is an extreme case, but all raw food is fascinating because it is anomalous—an apparent throwback to a precivilized world and even to a prehuman phase of evolution. Cooking is one of relatively few odd practices which are peculiarly human—odd, that is, in the scales of nature, judged by the standards of common approaches to nourishment. One of history's longest and most luckless quests has been the search for the essence of humanity, the defining characteristic which makes human beings human and distinguishes them collectively from other animals. The effort has led nowhere. The only objectively verifiable fact which sets our species apart from others is that we cannot successfully mate with them. Most of the other features commonly alleged are inadmissible or unconvincing. Some are plausible but partial. We arrogate "consciousness" to ourselves without knowing quite what it is or whether other creatures have it. We claim unique powers of language—but other animals, were we able to communicate with them, might dispute this. We are relatively inventive in problem solving, relatively adaptable in our ability to inhabit varied environments, relatively dexterous in our use of tools—especially of missiles. We are relatively ambitious in our works of art and in making embodiments of our imaginations. In some respects, in these connections, the gaps between human behavior and that of other species are so enormous as to qualify, perhaps, as differences of quality. We are genuinely unique in exploiting fire: though some other primates—chimpanzees, for example—can be taught to use it, too, for limited applications like lighting a cigarette or releasing the odor of incense, or even keeping a fire alight, this only happens under human instruction and only people have ever taken the initiative in harnessing flame. Cooking is at least as good as all the other candidates as an index of the humanity of humankind—except for one serious qualification: in the vast span of human history, cooking is a late innovation. There is no possible evidence more than half a million years old, no absolutely convincing evidence from more than about 150,000 years ago.

Of course, it all depends what one means by cooking. Cultivation, in some eyes, is a form of cookery—"*terram excoquere,*" as Vergil called it—exposing clods to the baking sun, turning the earth into an oven for seeds. Animals with suitably robust stomachs prepare their food by chewing the cud: why should this not be classed as cooking? In hunting cultures, the men who make the kill often reward themselves with a meal of the partially digested contents of the stomach of their prey: instant replacement for the energy expended in the hunt. This is a kind of natural protocookery—the earliest known instance of eating processed food. Many species, including ours, make food edible for infants or the infirm by chewing and spitting it out. Warmed in the mouth, attacked by gastric juices, pounded by mastication, it acquires some of the properties of food processed by the application of heat. The moment you rinse your food in water—as some monkeys do with some nuts—you start to process it, and indeed some real raw food freaks like to leave on the dirt. Like Farmer Oak in *Far from the Madding Crowd*, they would "never fuss about dirt in its pure state."

As soon as you squirt lemon juice at your oyster you are beginning to alter it, to change texture and taste: a generous definition might call this cooking. A marinade, applied for a long time, can be as transforming in its effects as the application of heat or smoke. Hanging meat to make it gamey, or just leaving it around to rot a little, is a way of processing for texture and digestibility: it is obviously an older technique than cooking by means of fire. Wind drying, which is a specialized form of hanging, works a profound biochemical change on some foods. So does burying—a technique, once common to induce fermentation, familiar to anyone who has eaten kimchee in a Korean restaurant but rarely used in modern Western cuisine. It is, however, commemorated in the name of gravlax: literally, "grave-salmon." Burial as quasi-cookery is also recalled in the dark tint now chemically applied to cheeses of kinds which were traditionally preserved in earth. Among some horse-borne nomads, cuts of meat are rendered edible by being warmed and pressed in the horse's sweat under the saddle on a long ride (below, p. 77). Churning milk is a process of almost alchemical magic: a liquid becomes a solid, white becomes gold. Fermentation is even more magical, because it can turn a boring, staple grain into a potion that can change behavior, suppress inhibitions, conjure visions and unlock imaginary realms. Why should cooking with kindled flame be privileged among all these startling ways of transforming food?

The answer, if there is one, lies in the social effects of fire-cooked food. Cooking deserves its place as one of the great revolutionary innovations of history, not because of the way it transforms food—there are plenty of other ways of doing that—but because of the way it transformed society. Culture begins when the raw gets cooked. The campfire becomes a place of communion when people eat around it. Cooking is not just a way of preparing food but of organizing society around communal meals and predictable mealtimes. It introduces new specialized functions and shared pleasures and responsibilities. It is more creative, more constructive of social ties than mere eating together. It can even replace eating together as a ritual of social adhesion. When Bronislaw Malinowski, the pioneer of Pacific island anthropology, was at work in the Trobriand Islands, one of the ceremonies that most impressed him was the annual yam harvest festival in Kiriwina, where most ceremonies took the form of food distribution. To the accompaniment of drums and dancing, food was arranged in heaps, then carried off to the various households to be eaten in private. The climax of what most cultures think of as a feast—the actual eating—"is never reached communally. . . . But the festive element lies in the preparations."

Cooking in some cultures becomes a metaphor for the transformations of life: Californian tribes, for instance, used to put women who had just given birth and pubescent girls into ovens dug in the ground, covered with mats and hot stones. In others food dressing becomes a sacred ritual, which not only crafts society but also nourishes heaven with sacrificial emissions of smoke and steam. Amazonian peoples who see "culinary operations as mediatory activities between heaven and earth, life and death, nature and society" generalize a notion which most societies apply to at least some acts of cooking.

The normal Japanese term for a meal—gohanmono—literally means "honorable cooked rice." This reflects not only the ubiquitous and essential place of the rice staple in Japan but also the social nature—indeed, status—of feeding. Life is measured in ritual meals. At a child's birth, parents receive gifts of red rice or rice with red beans from family and neighbors; at a first birthday, they distribute fragments of a rice cake the child has stepped over. A new home is erected with a sacrifice of two fish and inaugurated with a meal for neighbors. Wedding guests take food gifts home from the reception—rice cakes on which cranes or turtles are depicted or fish paste molded into the same shapes, as talismans for longevity. Other meals mark communion with the dead, and their anniversaries.

In Hindu society, "the rules concerning food are extremely important for marking and maintaining social boundaries and distinctions. Castes rank themselves in terms of purity, and this is reflected in the kinds of food which may or may not be shared with other castes. . . . Raw food can be transferred between all castes, whereas cooked foods cannot, since they may affect the purity status of the castes concerned." Cooked foods are divided between further classifications. Those cooked in water are distinguished from those fried in clarified butter: the latter can be exchanged between a wider range of groups than the former. Apart from the rules determining what foods may be shared or exchanged, eating habits and dietary prescriptions are peculiar to groups of certain status. Vegetarianism, for instance, is proper to the highest and "purest" castes, "while meat-eating and alcohol-consumption are associated with less pure status. Certain untouchable castes are marked most obviously by the eating of beef." The Tharu, the third rank in Dang, Nepal, will not exchange food with lower castes or feed them in their houses, but will eat pork and rats. The complexity of Fijian taboos has made them popular with anthropologists as objects of study. In Fiji, when particular kinds of groups eat together, they are confined to mutually complementary foods. In the presence of warriors, chiefs eat the captured pigs, but not fish or coconuts, which are reserved to the warriors.

Today, in cultures that think of themselves as modern, most of the food we speak of as raw comes elaborately prepared to the table. It is important to specify "food we speak of as raw" because rawness is a culturally constructed, or at least culturally modified, concept. Though we commonly eat many fruits and some vegetables with minimal preparation, we take their rawness for granted because it is culturally normal. No one speaks of raw apples or raw lettuce. Only if the food in question is normally cooked, but acceptable raw, do we specify raw carrots or raw onions or whatever. When meat and fish are served raw in the West, their rawness is so exceptional that it takes on extra connotations of subversion and risk, of barbarism and primitivism. The Chinese traditionally classified barbarian tribes into "raw" and "cooked" according to the degree of civilization they saw in them; and a similar mental classification of the world comes easily in the West, where literary tradition has long equated lust for raw flesh with savagery, blood-thirst and the rage of gastric impatience.

The classic "raw" meat dish of Western cuisine is steak tartare. The name alludes to the ferocious medieval reputation of the Mongols, also known, from the particular name of one group of Mongol tribes, as Tatars. The word reminded medieval ethnographers of Tartarus, the classical hell, and made it seem especially appropriate to demonize these enemies. The dish as it is known today, however, is a focus of civilized overcompensation. The meat is ground into soft, curling, vermicular twists of bright flesh. As if to make up for its rawness, its preparation is usually turned into a table-side restaurant ritual, when the waiter ceremoniously folds in, one by one, flavor-stretching ingredients which might include seasoning, fresh herbs, spring onions and onion shoots, capers, bits of anchovy, pickled peppercorns, olives and egg. Vodka is an unorthodox but immeasurably improving addition. The other raw meat and fish dishes licensed by civilization are equally removed from nature—their nakedness heavily dressed, their savagery sanitized by elaboration. "Raw" ham is heavily cured and smoked. Carpaccio is sliced with courtly finesse into delicate slivers and no one thinks of eating it until it has been drizzled with olive oil and bedecked with pepper and Parmesan. Gravlax, though no longer buried, is layered with salt, dill and pepper and basted with its own must for several days before it is ready to eat. "If our remote ancestors ate all their meat raw," wrote Brillat-Savarin in a work of 1826, which is still the gourmet's bible and the gourmand's apologia, "we have not entirely lost the habit ourselves. The most delicate palate will respond very well to Arles and Bologna sausages, smoked Hamburg beef, anchovies, freshly salted herrings, and such other things, which have never been subjected to fire, but which stimulate the appetite for all that."

Sushi, which is now a *de rigueur* fashion accessory in the West, genuinely involves raw fish which is only very lightly dressed, if at all, with vinegar and ginger; but the main component of the dish is cooked rice. Sashimi is a reversion to a more dramatic state of rawness, but is nonetheless prepared with great elaboration. The slices of fish must be of translucent slimness, shaved with a well-tempered blade, and the presentation must be unstintingly elegant—so that the raw state of the food actually heightens the eater's sense of participation in the civilizing process. The garnishes must be chopped, teased and shredded in an ample variety of fashions and an array of nicely contrived sauces must be served. Danes like raw egg yolk as a garnish or sauce, but even this comes separated from its white. At the "endless raw meat banquets" to which Laurens van der Post was treated in Ethiopia, preparation was minimal but the formality of the proceedings was elaborate. "The raw meat was passed, bleeding and lukewarm from the living animal, from one guest to another. Each man would take the edge of the meat firmly between his teeth and then, slicing upwards with a sharp knife, would cut off a mouthful for himself—in the process narrowly missing taking the skin off his nose." The slices were not eaten undressed but dipped in berebere, a sauce so spicy that it "gives the impression of being hot enough to cook the meat"; it can also transform a stew into a mixture "so fierce that it practically makes the ears bleed." Occasionally a slice of meat would be passed over a man's shoulder to the women and children who stood in silence behind the diners. All these foods are raw only according to a very narrow definition. They are so changed from the state of nature—whatever that is—as to be unrecognizable, presumably, to the hominid ancestors we imagine for ourselves, who supposedly ate anything edible that came to hand. After the invention of cooking, in most of the world, it seems, even the raw became rarefied.

In most cultures, the origins of cooking are traced to a divine gift, Promethean fire, or to the luck of a culture hero. Fire is a secret betrayed by a defector from Olympus. In ancient Persia it was elicited from the heart of rock by a hunter's misdirected missile. For the Dakota Indians it was struck from the earth by the claws of a jaguar-god. For the Aztecs, the first fire was the sun, kindled by the gods in the primeval darkness. To the Cook Islands, it was brought by Maui after his descent into the bowels of the earth. An Australian aboriginal found it secreted in the penis of a totemic animal, while for another tribe it was an invention of women, who cooked with it during the men's absence on the hunt and hid it inside their vulvae. "Everybody has his own Prometheus" and so does almost every culture.

The real origins of the domestication of fire are unknown. All theories about it seem to have been sparked like struck flint by some sudden illumination. None occurred more memorably or endured more tenaciously than that of the "father of modern paleontology," Abbé Henri Breuil. In 1930, a young protégé of Breuil's was Pierre Teilhard de Chardin, the Jesuit anthropologist who, in his turn, would become one of the most powerful figures in the intellectual history of the century. Teilhard was working in China, combining scientific and missionary work in the best Jesuit tradition, excavating the cave dwelling of "Peking Man"—a hominid who lived half a million years ago, supposedly before tool making and fire kindling. He showed Breuil a stag's antler and asked his opinion of it. "When still fresh," Breuil replied, "it was exposed to fire. And it was worked with a crude stone implement, probably not of flint, some sort of primitive chopping tool."

"But that's impossible," Teilhard replied. "It comes from Chou Kou-tien."

"I don't care where it comes from," insisted his mentor. "It was fashioned by a man and that man knew the use of fire." As with all other theories about the date of the domestication of fire, doubts have accumulated in recent years. Breuil, however, erected on the piles of ashes excavated at Chou Kou-tien a seductive but fanciful reconstruction of hominid sophistication. In his imaginary portrait of life there, a woman makes flints, while "a Pekin Man is cutting a deer antler" and a couple nearby are making fire. The man first produces a spark by friction while the woman holds out a tuft of dry grass and leaves to catch it. "She will then carry it to the hearth which is between them surrounded by small pebbles. Behind them another fire burns brightly cooking a joint of wild boar." In reality, there is no evidence either of flint manufacture or of the kindling of fire for hundreds of thousands of years after the date of the relevant remains.

It might be supposed that cooking ensued by inevitable extension from the domestication of fire. In the modern West the commonest myth is well represented by the imaginary account of the origins of cooking in Charles Lamb's *A Dissertation upon Roast Pig*. A swineherd accidentally immolates a litter of piglets in a conflagration he caused by carelessness, and

While he was thinking what he should say to his father, and wringing his hands over the smoking remnants of one of those untimely sufferers, an odour assailed his nostrils, unlike any scent which he had before experienced. . . . A premonitory moistening at the same time overflowed his nether lip. He knew not what to think. He next stooped down to feel the pig, if there were any signs of life in it. He burnt his fingers, and to cool them he applied them in his booby fashion to his mouth. Some of the crumbs of the scorched skin had come away with his fingers, and for the first time in his life (in the world's life, indeed, for before him no man had known it) he tasted—crackling!

"The thing took wing" until "the custom of firing houses" was superseded by the intervention of a sage, "who made a discovery that the flesh of swine, or indeed of any other animal, might be cooked (burnt, as they call it) without the necessity of consuming a whole house to dress it." It is curious that Lamb traced the origins of this important technology to China, which has indeed been the world's most technically inventive country, over recorded history as a whole, but which is usually inadequately acknowledged in the West. More commonplace is Lamb's assumption that cooking must have been invented by accident. Accident has recently been rehabilitated in historical writing, because in the random world revealed by quantum physics and chaos theory, unpredictable effects indeed seem to ensue from untrackable causes. Cleopatra's nose resembles a butterfly's wing: the latter can stir up a storm; but for the former's few centimeters of adventitious elegance, there might never have been a Roman Empire. "Virtual" historians are always telling us these days that but for this or that accident the whole course of history would be different and that kingdoms are lost for the want of a nail. Really, however, accidents are only observable in the historical record if they confirm the way things are already going. The accident is our model for explaining change in "primitive" societies, which we vulgarly suppose to be static and stupid. Yet inventions are rarely, if ever, contrived by genuine accident: there is always a shaping imagination at work or a practical observer on hand.

It is possible that cooking of a sort was practiced even before fire was tamed. Many animals are attracted to the embers of naturally occurring fires, where they sift for roasted seeds and beans rendered edible by burning. Chimpanzees in the wild today can readily be observed practicing a technique which can be safely ascribed, by analogy, to hominid foragers. To a creature with enough brainpower and dexterity, some of the features of burnt-out woodland, such as the piles of ash and the partly burned trunks of fallen trees, might have appeared as natural ovens, smoldering with manageable heat, in which tough-husked seeds or tough-skinned pulses, unchewable legumes and cartilaginous flesh could be processed.

The cooking revolution was the first scientific revolution: the discovery, by experiment and observations, of the biochemical changes which transmute flavor and aid digestion. It isn't called "kitchen chemistry" for nothing. Meat—despite the disfavor it draws from modern dietitians who are minatory about saturated fats—is an unbeatable source of nutrition for human bodies but it is fibrous and muscly. Cooking makes the proteins in the muscle fibers fuse, turning collagen to jelly. If direct fire is applied, as was probably the case in the earliest cooks' techniques, the surface of meat undergoes something like caramelization as the juices are concentrated: for proteins coagulate when heated and "Maillard reaction" sets in between the amines on a protein chain and some of the natural sugars in fat. Starch has been the source of energy for most people for most of recorded history, but it is inefficient until it is cooked. Heat disintegrates it, releasing the sugar which all starch contains. At the same time, dry heat turns dextrins in starch brown, imparting the comforting look we associate with cooked food. In most cultures, for most of history, the chief alternative to dry heating is immersion in hot water: this softens muscle fibers in meat and makes carbohydrate particles swell. At about 175 degrees Fahrenheit, they break up and permeate the mixture. Sauces thicken in consequence. Heat retextures other foods so that they can be chewed or easily dissected by hand—"a primary spurt in the civilizing of eating habits, long before the introduction of chopsticks or knives and forks." Because cooking makes food more digestible, you can eat more of it: fifty tons of it in a modern lifetime. The result, up to a point, is higher human efficiency. A further consequence is the opportunity of excess, with effects on society that we shall broach in due course (below, p. 101).

As well as increasing the consumption of edible foods, cooking can work a livelier magic by making palatable what would otherwise be poisonous. Fire destroys the poisons in some potential foods. The magic which makes toxic plants comestible is particularly valuable to human beings, because poisonous food can be stored without fear of depredations by competing creatures, then detoxified for human consumption: this is the cultural advantage which made bitter manioc a staple food in ancient Amazonia and nardoo root a prized food among Australian aboriginals. Bitter manioc, the Amazonian staple, which is the usual source of tapioca, contains enough prussic acid to kill anyone who eats a meal-sized quantity, but this can be dissipated by the processes of pounding or grating, soaking and heating which are used to prepare it. How the Indians who first cultivated this plant, and came to rely on it, discovered these peculiar properties is an intriguing but insoluble problem. Most harmful infestations can be neutralized by cooking. Pig meat is often infected with a worm that causes trichinosis if ingested by humans: thorough cooking makes it harmless. Salmonella bacteria are killed by brisk and thorough cooking, listeria by intense heat. Notably exceptional is the deadliest bacterium, *Clostridium botulinum*. It is unharmed by most cooking processes and survives the range of temperatures attained in all traditional cuisine, though recipes with a high acid content can arrest its development.

As soon as the effects of heat on food began to unfold before men's eyes, the future of cooking was foreshadowed. Literally or originally "focus" means "hearth." Once fire became manageable it inevitably bound communities together, because tending the flame required division of labor and shared effort. Fire functioned as a focus, we assume, before or apart from its adaptation for cooking, because of the other functions which make people gather around it: for light and warmth, for protection from pests and predators. Cooking perfected fire's power of social magnetism by adding enhanced nourishment to these functions. It socialized eating by making it an activity practiced in a fixed place at a fixed time by a community of eaters. Formerly, it is safe to infer, there was little incentive to eat communally. Gathered foods could be consumed on the spot or secreted to be eaten at will. Though we can imagine hominids gathering around a raw carcass for communal feasting, like buzzards around a bone, eating was not necessarily a forger of community before the invention of cooking; collaborative ventures, such as the hunt and the kill and the organization of collective security, galvanized the group but fragments of beasts hunted or scavenged could be dismembered or distributed for eating apart. When fire and food combined, however, an almost irresistible focus was created for communal life. Eating became social in a unique way: communal but uncollaborative. The enhanced value cooking imparts to food elevates it above nourishment and opens up new imaginative possibilities: meals can become sacrificial sharings, love feasts, ritual acts, occasions for the magical transformations wrought by fire—one of which is the transformation of competitors into a community.

In the contemporary world, it has still been possible to recapture or reexperience a primitive sense of the power of this combination. It comes through the childhood recollections of the "peasant philosopher" of the 1930s, Gaston Bachelard:

> Fire is more a social being than a natural being. . . . I ate the fire, I ate its gold, its odor and even its crackle, while the steaming wafer crunched between my teeth. And it is always thus, with a sort of luxurious pleasure . . . that the fire proves its

humanity. It not only cooks, it makes the biscuit crisp and golden. It gives material form to man's festivities. However far back you may go in time, the gastronomical value of food always outweighs its alimentary value, and it is in joy, not in pain, that man has found his spirit. . . . From the teeth of the chain the black cauldron hung. The three-legged pot stood over the hot ashes. My grandmother would puff up her cheeks and blow through a steel pipe to reawaken the sleeping flame. Everything would be cooking at the same time: the potatoes for the pigs, the choice potatoes for the family. For me there would be a fresh egg cooking under the ashes.

FIRST FOOD TECHNOLOGIES

Ingenious imaginations were needed to cross the practical and conceptual gap that separates domestication of fire from the invention of cooking. In some climates fire can be quickly drilled. In some places, if suitable flints and kindling are to hand, it can be struck with reasonable reliability. In very remote antiquity, however, most societies did not enjoy ideal conditions for making fire. It had to be garnered and preserved, in the style of the sacred flame which even in modern societies we sometimes keep alight in memory of our honored dead or in celebration of our "Olympic ideal." For most of the past, in most places, it was easier and more reliable to keep fire alight and to carry it around than to kindle it at need. Some peoples have lost or perhaps never had the techniques for igniting it—or maybe they simply think of fire as too sacred to make themselves. This is said to be why some tribes in Tasmania, the Andaman Islands and New Guinea travel to beg fire from their neighbors, if it is extinguished, without trying to start it by means of their own. In the Easter light ceremony, with which vigil mass begins, in darkness, in Catholic and Orthodox churches, Christian tradition preserves an ancient memory of how serious it can be when a society loses fire and rekindles it from scratch.

Even if you can get fire when you want it, it is not easy to apply it to cooking. Charred in the naked flame or suspended in the smoke or baked in the embers of a fire, some foods cook satisfactorily. This is a convenient method if the fire is being kept alight anyway for another purpose: as a watchfire, say, or for warmth or to keep predators or demons at bay. Though impossible where no solid fuel is used, and inconvenient even in the best-equipped high-tech modern kitchen, this is a kind of cooking capable of achieving dishes of great sophistication. Archestratus of Gela recommended bonito wrapped in fig leaves with a pinch of marjoram, consigned to the embers until the leaves blacken and smoke. Charring seems simple, but can be made versatile by the use of pastes and marinades to coat foods before they are consigned to the flame, or by basting with well-chosen liquors or sauces. If this was the first form of cookery, it remains one of the most appetizing and surely one of the most widely practiced. An unbroken tradition unites the suburban barbecue or campfire weenie roasts with one of the most famous feasts in Western literature: the banquet with which Nestor the charioteer honored Athene in the *Odyssey*.

> The axe cut through the tendons of the heifer's neck and it collapsed. At this, the women raised their celebratory cry. . . . When the dark blood had gushed out and life had left the heifer's body, they swiftly dismembered the carcass, cut out the thigh bones in the usual way, wrapped them in folds of fat and laid raw meat above them. The venerable King burnt these on the firewood, sprinkling red wine over the flames, while the young men gathered round with five-pronged forks in their hands. When the thighs were burnt up and they had tasted the inner parts, they carved the rest into small pieces, pierced them with skewers and held the sharp ends to the fire till all was roasted.

Yet this—which can be surmised as the most primitive technology of cooking—has obvious disadvantages. It permits only a limited culinary repertoire. It cannot cope with foods which require slow cooking. It requires carcasses to be butchered raw, with unnecessary expenditure of energy; and it consumes large amounts of fuel. It has unmistakable connotations of savagery, especially if the meat is only given rudimentary butchering before the roasting. An Italian visitor to the pampa in 1910 was struck by the "utterly primitive" way the gauchos cooked their meat in the hide "so that it conserves its bloody juices" and ate it with razors while seated on tree trunks.

The early cook's solution was the invention of the hot-stone griddle: using fire to heat stones, and hot stones to cook food on. This is particularly effective for foods that come naturally wrapped by coatings which retain moisture while being permeated by heat—mollusks by their shells, for instance, or some kinds of fruits or wild grains by thick or densely fibrous husks. Alternatively, food can be leaf-wrapped, as for ember cookery. In this style of cookery, the stones can be piled in order to envelop the food in heat, though this does not mean that hot stones have the same result as embers: if they press on the food, their weight affects it. If cavities are created to avoid this, they form air pockets and the effect of all-around heat is diminished. The time-honored ways of getting around these problems are to use suitable leaves, grasses, turf or animal pelts as upper layers of insulation. It is not hard for a traveler imbued with a modest spirit of adventure to find this style of cooking today. A few years ago in the Cook Islands, Hugo Dunn-Meynell sampled leaf-wrapped parcels of manioc, breadfruit, taro, octopus, sweet potatoes, suckling pig, parrot fish and chicken marinated in guava juice, on pumice stones heated over pits of coconut husks. Some families used pits over a century and a half old. The husks were lit by rubbing banana wood sticks together.

In contemporary civilization, at least until recently, the likeliest context in which to reexperience hot-stone cuisine has been the clambake. In New England in the late-nineteenth and early-twentieth centuries, these were genuine communal or civic undertakings, perpetuating practices which early colonists learned from Indians. The town outing enacted in Rodgers and Hammerstein's *Carousel*, where "that sure was a real good clambake" and the revelers "sure had a real good time," captures the romance, ingenuous or innocent, with which traditional clambakes are remembered. So does the intent, intense concentration with which clambake eaters bend to their task in Winslow Homer's painting. The clams had to be dug from the sand while the fire was made of driftwood and seaweed to heat the stones. Because the clamshells open with heat, the upper insulators had to be impermeable: otherwise the clams' natural juices would evaporate with unpalatable effects.

A refinement of great importance in the history of hot-stone cookery was the cooking pit. This innovation took ingenuity to devise, but no tools except a digging implement to fashion. A dry pit could be heated with stones to make an oven. A pit dug below the water table, heated by the same means, made a boiler or poacher. This represented an innovation of enormous importance—unequaled by any subsequent technical innovation in the history of cooking until our own day: it facilitated boiling, a new method of cooking or, at least, one which previously could only be approximated by using a tripe or skin filled with water, suspended over the fire, as a cooking pot. Late but representative examples were discovered in Ireland at Ballyvourney, County Cork, in 1952, where the water table was high enough to keep water from seeping away. In the second millennium B.C., a trough had been opened in a peat bog and lined with timber. Nearby an oven had been made in piled-up dry soil by scooping out a cavity and lining it with stone. There are at least four thousand similar sites in Ireland alone. Experiments conducted on the spot showed that large joints cooked satisfactorily in a few hours if hot stones were regularly replaced under a turf lid. About seventy gallons of water can be brought to boiling point in about half an hour by this method. In clay soil, the inner lining of the pit would tend to bake into earthenware, making the sides watertight enough for water to be poured into pits in which it did not occur naturally. Alternatively, the inside of any pit could be smeared with clay and fired to hardness.

Pit-cooked food is not easily obtained in the modern Western world, except by experiment in the field (or, occasionally, at a traditional open pit barbecue in the American Southwest). In his cowboy days, which extended into the early decades of this century, James H. Cook considered it a treat to enjoy a hog's head "Indian style": buried among live coals for several hours in a pit two and a half feet deep. It "came from the hole resembling a lump of charcoal, but the flavor appealed greatly to such epicures of the brush country as usually feasted on it." Cooking pits are still favored by traditional cooks in rural locations in much of the Pacific and parts of the Indian Ocean. It must be admitted, however, that civilization tends to crowd them out. Their great disadvantage is that for all but a few small or simple dishes which demand little heat, it is necessary, even for dry cookery, to kindle fire outside the pit and heat it by transferring hot stones. Nevertheless, an effect similar or identical to that of pit cookery can be procured by using the clay oven usually called "tandoor," or by some such name, in India and the Middle East. Tandoori cuisine is surely a development from pit cookery. In essence, the tandoor is a cooking pit, elevated above ground. Fire is kindled inside it: the aperture at the top has to be broad enough to keep the fire supplied with oxygen but narrow enough to be conveniently sealed with a heavy lid without much temperature loss once the fire has been allowed to die down. While the structure heats up, dough can be slapped onto the outer walls to make flat bread. After the fire dies, the heat-retaining properties of the oven can be used to bake meat, fish and vegetables or to stew casseroles.

All these technologies—of cooking with embers, naked flames and heated stones, in pits or over open fires—certainly predated specialized cookware. Though shells may have made good stock pots, in antiquity, there are few places in the world with shells large enough for economical cooking. Only those of turtles and similar creatures can have preempted the manufactured pot. Yet pots—even those hewn from wood—must be supposed to have been relatively late inventions in the history of humankind; those of clay or metal, of course, arose later still. Weaving fronds or grasses is a simpler technology to master and if the right kinds of plants are available can produce entirely watertight vessels, such as are still in use among peoples of Northwest America. A frequently asserted explanation for the invention of earthenware pottery in remote antiquity is that wicker vessels were smeared with clay as insulation to enable them to be suspended over fire.

Because of the perishable nature of basketware, it is impossible to date the origins of cookery in manufactured pots. A simpler option, however, was called into use earlier: filling skins, tripes, cauls or stomachs of animals for cooking in. The skin is of limited usefulness as a sealant in most species and is frequently more valuable if it is stripped off the carcass before cooking and tanned for garments, pouches and awnings. The internal organs, however, are nature's cooking vessels—reliably impermeable and elastic enough, in most quadrupeds, to contain all the other edible parts of the animal and more. Because they can be filled with water, they can function as boilers and—if, say, a small intestine is packed and placed inside a large one—they make serviceable bains-marie, as long as the cook has some method of shielding them from damage by excessive direct heat. Nowadays, surviving traces of this early style of cookery can be found even in the most sophisticated cuisines. The best sausages are still stuffed in strips and tubes of innards. No respectable blood pudding comes packed in anything but a length of intestine. In many popular sweet puddings nowadays a muslin cloth (to hold the contents together while cooking) does duty for the outer casing which a stomach or bladder formerly supplied. Bag puddings are a way of using offal (or, in cognate dishes, blood), which would perish quickly if left uncooked. For this reason, they occur frequently in the cookery of transhumant herders. Haggis, the "chieftain o' the puddin' race," is an example easily attainable today wherever the Scots diaspora has reached. The recipe does not really evoke a very primitive age because it calls for a large admixture of oatmeal, which is a sedentary cultivator's food. But the other ingredients—chopped lungs, liver, heart—are typical. In purer herdsmen's food, blood and fat might fill the cavities which in the haggis are stuffed with oatmeal.

Nomad lives would be encumbered by *batteries de cuisine* and it is therefore among nomads that one should expect to find enduring examples of the use of innards as cooking pots. At least, manufactured pots have never entirely replaced their primitive predecessors in nomadic cuisines, although even nomads seem to appreciate metal vessels, provided they can be made easily transportable: culinary variety is, within limits, a form of luxury almost universally esteemed and, in any event, a pot is a convenient container to cook a stuffed gut or stomach in. Turkic peoples have a curious range of cookware. The qazan, which literally means "hollowed-out thing," is a capacious tin vessel with built-in feet designed to be easily lashed to a horse. The Turks also consider it indispensable to carry a rack for steaming dumplings over an open fire. Their former use of shields as cooking trays is perpetuated in the broad, shieldlike shallow dish known as a saj. The spear can be a toasting fork. In some cultures, it is tempting to imagine the brochette evolving from the use of sticks as skewers. In most of the Eurasian steppe there are no trees and sticks are rare and precious. The shish kebab—the universal gift of Central Asian cuisine—is more likely to have been cooked in antiquity on a dagger.

At their most solemn feasts, however, most peoples tend to eat their most traditional foods and among the steppeland nomads this means reverting to cooking
in skins and stomachs and guts. Sharon Hudgins is the author of the most vivid
modern accounts of steppeland dining experiences. She was served with a sheep's
head in its skin, wool intact, at a Buriat banquet in 1994. Her husband was
exempted from need to sing a sheep's head song—the relic of the propitiatory
ritual which seems inseparable from solemn meals in most traditions. Libations
were poured and scraps of fat flung into fire. Toasts, which the Buriats like to
make in grain spirit imported from their sedentary neighbors, were accompanied
by songs. The next course was a sheep's stomach filled with cow's milk, sheep's
blood, garlic and spring onions, tied with intestines.

> All the Buriats around the table waited expectantly for me to take the first bite.
> But I didn't know where to begin. Finally our hostess leaned over and sliced the
> top off the stomach. The contents had not been fully cooked and blood oozed
> out onto my plate. She took a large spoon, scraped out some of the semi-
> coagulated mass, and handed the spoonful to me. . . . The other guests waited
> for me to make the next move. And suddenly it occurred to me: pass the dish
> around. That's exactly what they wanted.

Irrationally, some meals made by stuffing intestines still command a certain
prestige in Western gastronomy, whereas puddings cooked in stomachs are now
regarded as food unfit for gourmets—rustic dishes which betray primitive origins.
In some versions of andouilles and andouillettes, a pig's large intestine is stuffed
mainly with chopped bits of the small intestine, without sacrifice of cachet.
Boudins blancs are tidbits of great delicacy. A gourmet might relish a melting
morcilla but think a goat's paunch gross, such as the roasted one stuffed with
blood and fat with which Odysseus was rewarded for his prowess in wrestling.

Lévi-Strauss was right to suppose that boiling "requires the use of a receptacle, a cultural object," since a skin or tripe used as a boiler has really been transformed into an artifact by human imagination, and a boiling pit is a substantial
contrivance, which has to be dug and lined. But by the same standard the spit or
the skewer, and even the kindled fire, are cultural objects, too, and roasting or
grilling must be classed as "cultural" or "civilized" no less than other methods. In
the transition to culture, or the early "civilizing process," a bigger step than boiling
was therefore taken by frying: this required manufactured vessels, because,
although you can use innards as boilers, you cannot use them as fry pans. The
sequence of evidence begins with the first earthenware shards. In Japan, the oldest

examples which recognizably belonged to pots date from the eleventh millennium B.C., in Africa and the Middle East from about three thousand years later. In Greece and Southeast Asia they date from c 6,000 B.C. This technical advance made the modern *batterie de cuisine* essentially complete. When cooks had earthenware pots, which were resistant to fire and impenetrable by water, they could add frying to the repertoire of roasting, boiling and grilling. We like to congratulate ourselves on the accelerating pace of modern technological change; but since the invention of earthenware, nothing else we have devised to cook with has had such an enriching effect, and none, until the microwave, opened up the possibility of any genuinely new method of cooking. In the meantime, we have acquired tools and gadgets which made culinary processes easier, without extending their range.

THE ERODING WAVES

Cooking has done individuals and societies so much good that it seems unsurprising that the cooking revolution has been sustained to our own days. Yet no practice is so beneficent as to disarm distrust. Cooking today is condemned by critics; and its socializing effects are said to be under threat from technological change.

The end of cooking has been tearfully predicted and ardently desired. What might loosely be called the anti-cooking movement is now more than a hundred years old: it started among feminists and socialists, who wanted to liberate women from the kitchen and replace the family with a wider community. Charlotte Perkins Gilman wanted to make cookery "scientific," as she said: in effect, this meant eliminating it from most people's lives, secluding it from the sights and sounds and smells of the larder and the range and confining them to kitchenless apartments, while professionals in meal-making factories saw to it that energy levels were maintained for a world of work. "It is impossible," she wrote, "that half the world, acting as amateur cooks for the other half, can attain any high degree of scientific accuracy or technical skill." As well as from progressive critics, cooking came under attack from primitivist prejudices. Gandhi despised it. He tried fruits and nuts, goat's milk and dates, in a search for a satisfactory diet which could be eaten without it. Underlying his preferences, perhaps, was the same kind of brahminical vanity which made Professor Godbole, in *A Passage to India*, affect indifference to all food, of which he ate copiously but abstractedly, encountering it "as if by accident." Today, the prejudice in favor of what is "natural"—and therefore supposedly precultural—makes raw food attractive to modern urbanites repelled by our overcontrived lifeways, seeking readmission to Eden. Civilization seems ossified and one way of transcending its limitations is to reach for the recovery of the raw. Romantic primitivism allies with ecological anxiety. The new soul food favored by many middle-class African-Americans dumps the fat-rich dishes of Dixie tradition—collard greens suppurating with pork fat, pigs' feet with black-eyed peas and the like—in favor of raw or marinated vegetables. The fashion for crudités in smart restaurants and for repulsive "salad bars" in popular eateries, where dog-eared leaves and sad shreds of salad vegetables lie exposed to contamination, are evidence of how far the taste for raw refreshment now reaches.

The popularity of raw food does not mean that cooking is going to stop. But it may be unrecognizably changed by other pressures. Cooking was a precious invention because of the way it forged community. Contemporary eating habits threaten to unpick this achievement. Food on the fly feeds the values of hustle, nourishes the anomie of postindustrial society. People eat while they are doing other things, with eyes averted from company. They are on the streets, hurrying between appointments or sauntering between pleasures. They are at their desks, with their gazes riven to the computer monitor. They are at lectures and seminars, looking at the whiteboard or the screen. Before they left home in the morning they did not share breakfast with the rest of their household, either because modern working hours are staggered or because leisure for breakfast has been crowded out of the daily routine. When they get home in the evening, there may be no meal to share—or if there is, there may be a shortage of sharers. Sandwich shops can be sociable: the old-fashioned kind, where you waited in a potentially companionable queue before ordering your sandwich from the person who made it, buzzed, at a low level, with dialogue and encounters; but the big market in the industrialized West today is for impersonal sandwiches, grabbed ready-made from refrigerated shelves and bolted down in isolation.

The loneliness of the fast food eater is uncivilizing. Food is being desocialized. In the microwave household, home cooking looks doomed. Family life must fragment if people stop having shared meals, for as Carlyle once said, "If the soul is a kind of stomach, what is spiritual communion but an eating together?" The microwave should not be underestimated as a device with the power to change society. Its rise has been startlingly rapid. In 1989, fewer than 20 percent of French respondents to a survey had microwaves and defrosters at home; a year later the figure had risen to nearly a quarter; by 1995 it was over half. I suspect that some, at least, of the alarm this trend arouses is justified. Technically, of course, microwave technology is just one form of cooking; it uses electromagnetic rays to penetrate the food instead of the infrared radiation generated by fire. It is the first innovation since the frying pan genuinely to have opened up a new cooking method: to food lovers, its arrival ought to have been an auspicious occasion but it cannot fairly be said that the results have been very exciting. Most microwaved dishes look unappetizing because electromagnetic radiation cannot brown food on the outside. The texture of what is served is boring because the process cannot deliver crisp effects or, indeed, any great variety of texture. In most kitchens, the device is used only to heat up a réchauffé: this may work well for the relatively limited range of dishes which benefit from reheating, such as curries and casseroles, but most dishes on reheating acquire a tired appearance and a distinctive flavor—slightly earthy, slightly acrid.

Despite these deficiencies, people like microwave ovens for two reasons, neither of them good. First, for "convenience": it is a quick, clean way to heat up precooked, prepacked meals. In partial consequence, the fastest growing market in the modern West is for boring, overprocessed pap. Of course, this is not entirely the microwave's fault, for the irresistibility of pap is as marked in food literature as in food. Readers who could have Brillat-Savarin settle for the Williams-Sonoma catalogue. The microwave oven is part of what might be called pap culture. Ready-prepared meals in various forms have tended to be demanded, throughout history, in highly urbanized societies. The rise of the microwave is a consequence as well as a cause of their renewed popularity today (see below, pp. 216–22). The second great virtue of the microwave in its admirers' eyes is that it is liberating. Eaters can choose to heat up whatever ready-mades are to hand—which in modern Western cities means that a huge choice is on offer. No reference to community of taste needs to be made. No matriarch or paterfamilias has an opportunity to arbitrate for a family. No one in a household has to defer to anyone else. Moreover, no two people need to eat at the same time or table. This new way of cooking is staggeringly counterrevolutionary. It reverses the cooking revolution, which made eating sociable, and returns us, in this respect, to a presocial phase of evolution.

Food nourishes: the cooking revolution extended this effect by increasing the range of edible foods and easing digestion. Food gives pleasure, which cooking can enhance. It forges society, especially when cooking provides focus and structure. After the invention of cooking the next great revolution was the discovery that food has other virtues and vices: it can encode meanings. It can do the eater good of kinds which transcend sustenance and evils which are worse than poison. It not only maintains life but also enhances it and sometimes degrades it. It can change the eater for the better or worse. It has spiritual and metaphysical, moral and transmutative effects. Curiously, perhaps, the people who best exemplify this discovery—and who therefore introduce the next chapter—are cannibals.

The Meaning of Eating

—

Food as Rite and Magic

Cannibalism is a problem. In many cases the practice is rooted in ritual and superstition rather than gastronomy, but not always. A French Dominican in the seventeenth century observed that the Caribs had most decided notions of the relative merits of their enemies. As one would expect, the French were delicious, by far the best. This is no surprise, even allowing for nationalism. The English came next, I'm glad to say. The Dutch were dull and stodgy and the Spaniards so stringy, they were hardly a meal at all, even boiled. All this sounds sadly like gluttony.

—PATRICK LEIGH FERMOR

I've always gotten my strength from two books—my cookbook and the Bible.

—HELEN HAYES IN THE 1952 MOVIE MY SON JOHN

THE LOGIC OF CANNIBALISM

It was official. The anthropophagi, humans who fed on human flesh, really existed. Long fabled, and long supported by hearsay, they were now reported as fact, backed by an incontrovertible weight of eyewitness corroboration from virtually the entire crew of Columbus's second transatlantic expedition. The shipboard physician wrote home with an account of Arawak prisoners, liberated from the man-eaters' power on the island now known as Guadeloupe.

We inquired of the women who were prisoners of the inhabitants what sort of people these islanders were and they answered, "Caribs." As soon as they learned that we abhor such kind of people because of their evil practice of eating human flesh they felt delighted. . . . They told us that the Carib men use them with such cruelty as would scarcely be believed; and that they eat the children which they bear them, only bringing up those whom they have by their native wives. Such of their male enemies as they can take away alive they bring here to their homes to make a feast of them and those who are killed in battle they eat up after the fighting is over. They declare that the flesh of man is so good to eat that nothing can compare with it in the world; and this is quite evident, for of the human bones we found in the houses, everything that could be gnawed had already been gnawed so that nothing remained but what was too tough to eat. In one of the houses we found a man's neck cooking in a pot. . . . When the Caribs take away boys as prisoners of war they remove their sexual organs, fatten them until they grow up and then, when they wish to make a great feast, they kill and eat them, for they say the flesh of women and youngsters is not good to eat. Three boys thus mutilated came fleeing to us when we visited the houses.

On his previous voyage, Columbus had misheard the Arawak word "Cariba," and rendered it "Caniba." The terms "cannibal" and "Caribbean" both derive from the same name.

Many similar accounts followed and as European exploration spread, reports of cannibalism multiplied. The cannibals encountered by Odysseus or reported by Herodotus, Aristotle, Strabo and Pliny gained credibility with each new find. The "Renaissance Discovery of Man" included the discovery of man as man-eater. The earliest editions of Vespucci's *Voyages* were illustrated with woodcuts of cannibal barbecues. The Aztecs, according to a sympathetic observer, who made strenuous efforts to gather his information at first hand, had feasts specially supplied with slaves purchased for the purpose and fattened "so that their flesh should be tastier." The bellies of the Chichimeca were a "sepulchre of human flesh." The Tupinamba were said to consume their enemies "down to the last fingernail." Hans Staden's account of his captivity among them in the 1550s was a best-selling spine-chiller and cliff-hanger because of the way the author's own immolation at a cannibal feast kept getting postponed. His description of the cannibal ritual was menacingly memorable. The victim had to endure the women's boasts and tend the fire on which he was to cook. He was slaughtered by a blow which dashed out his brains. Then the women

scrape his skin thoroughly and make him quite white and stop up his arse with a bit of wood so that nothing may be lost. Then a man . . . cuts off the arms and the legs above the knee. Then four women carry away the severed pieces and run with them round the huts with shouts of joy. . . . The entrails are kept by the women who boil them and make a thick broth called "mingau." This they and the children drink. They devour the bowels and the flesh from the head. The brains, tongue and whatever else is edible is given to the children. When this is done all go home, taking their share with them. . . . I was there and have seen all this with my own eyes.

Toward the end of the century, scenes of human limbs butchered for the grill, or of cannibal women supping blood and biting entrails, enlivened many of Theodore De Bry's popular engravings of scenes from American travels. The seventeenth century produced little that was new in the tradition, for the horror was familiar and no major new cannibal peoples or customs came to light. Eighteenth-century Europeans, however, found their fascination revived, as more cannibals were encountered and philosophy strove to reconcile the practice with the emerging theory of the nobility of savagery. Even in the highly civilized Christian empire of Ethiopia, Europeans imagined specialist vendors of human butcher meat. In the Indian wars of eighteenth-century North America, a soldier of the Massachusetts militia was alarmed to discover that his adversaries roasted their enemies bit by bit "at a most doleful rate." The greatest concentration of new cases arose during the exploration of the South Seas by ever more ambitious voyages. Melanesian cannibalism, of which many stories accumulated in the eighteenth century, seemed more practical than most: no edible organ of a captive foe was untasted, and the bones made good needles for sewing sailcloth. When Captain Cook first met Maoris, they mimed how to pick clean a human bone. His account was doubted by skeptics in Europe, but confirmed at the cost of captives' lives. Fijian cannibalism, in accounts made familiar in Europe by missionaries' reports in the early nineteenth century, seemed to exceed all previously known cases in depravity because of the scale on which it was reported and the routine nature of cannibal repasts, bereft of any culturally extenuating context, "not indulged in from a species of horrid revenge," as Methodists averred in 1836, "but from an absolute preference for human flesh over other food."

Taken one by one, the veracity of all these reports was open to question. Cannibalism can be a useful source of the comfortable horrors which boost sales of an otherwise boring travelogue. In the late Middle Ages and, with diminishing force, in the sixteenth and seventeenth centuries, it was an extremely useful attribute to ascribe to one's enemies; for cannibalism, like buggery and blasphemy, was classed as an offense against natural law. Those who committed it put themselves beyond the law's protection. With impunity, Europeans could attack them, enslave them, forcibly subject them and sequester property from them. Sometimes, the "man-eating myth" was a reciprocal fantasy: white enquirers were surprised to find themselves suspected of cannibalism by "natives" who also regarded it with horror. Raleigh in Guiana was mistaken for a cannibal by his Arawak hosts. The Mani of the Gambia supposed that the apparently insatiable Portuguese demand for slaves was caused by their inordinate anthropophagous appetites. When George Vancouver entertained inhabitants of Dalco Passage to dinner in 1792, they refused his venison on the suspicion that it was human flesh. The Ku Waru of highland New Guinea assumed that their Australian "discoverers" were "people who eat other people. They must have come around here in order to kill us and eat us. People said not to go walking around at night." Allegations of cannibalism should be discounted like any other crime statistic: some of them must be supposed to have been invented and others to have gained horror in the telling.

Nevertheless, the numbers of well-authenticated cases put the general question beyond a peradventure. Cannibalism existed. The reality of cannibalism as a social practice is not in any genuine doubt. To judge from archaeological evidence, moreover, it has been extremely widespread: human bones snapped for marrow seem to lie under the stones of every civilization. And as the tally of observed cases grew, the assumption that cannibalism was an inherently aberrant activity, abnormal or unnatural, became ever harder to sustain.

Of course, many stories concerned rogue cases which have arisen in Western society contrary to the accepted norms: what might be called "criminal" cannibalism, practiced with a conscious commitment to outrage. Here "Demon" barbers double as pie-men. Maniacal tyrants, seeking exquisite extremes of sadism, serve enemies at table with concoctions of the flesh and blood of their wives and children. There are even practitioners of cannibalism for kicks: individuals who get intellectual pleasure from transgressing convention, perverts who get sexual thrills from ingesting flesh. The most bizarre and ghoulish story is of the Rocky Mountain prospector who called himself "Alferd" Packer. In a notorious case in 1874, he split his companions' skulls open while they slept—except for one whom he shot in the back—before robbing their corpses and feeding on their remains: after eighteen years' imprisonment, he was released into a changed world, where he was welcome as a curiosity and even honored as "an old mountaineer." Pilgrims still visit his grave and, with a kind of irony which some find appetizing, the Alferd Packer Memorial Grill at the University of Colorado in Boulder is named after him. Hannibal Lecter has other real-life predecessors, including "Liver-eating Johnson," who targeted Crow Indians in revenge for the murder of his wife in 1847, and Isse Sagawa, "the cannibal of the Bois de Boulogne," who disposed of an unwanted girlfriend by eating her in 1981. In 1991 in Milwaukee, Jeffrey Dahmer, whose tastes comprised gay necrophilia and sadism as well as cannibalism, had a fridge full of human body parts when the police came to call.

Even in the modern history of the Western world, a form of social cannibalism has been recognized, practiced and, for a long time, licensed in law. In the extremities of siege or retreat, the quick feed off the dead. Not infrequently, living victims of shipwrecks and air crashes stay alive on the strength of dead comrades' flesh and sometimes end up, *in extremis*, drawing lots to sacrifice their lives to their comrades' hunger. In the early modern era, the age of long and perilous sea journeys under sail, survival cannibalism became a "socially accepted practice among seamen," the "custom of the sea." In 1710, for instance, survivors of the wreck of the *Nottingham Galley* turned "fierce and barbarous" after nourishing themselves from the corpse of the dead ship's carpenter. Further cases were reported at intervals during the nineteenth century. Géricault included scenes of cannibalism in sketches for the most famous of all images of nautical disaster, *The Raft of the Medusa*, though in this instance the evidence was not conclusive. Fiction strove to exceed fact. Captain Ahab's obsession with Moby Dick was motivated by memories of the demoralizing experiences which followed the lash of the whale's tail: his story was based on the real-life saga of the wreck of the *Essex*, whose men drew lots to determine the order in which they ate each other after a similar incident in 1820. In 1835 the homonymous captain of the capsized *Francis Spaight* was rescued, allegedly "in the act of eating the liver and brains of his apprentice." In 1874 a boat from the abandoned collier *Euxine* was rescued in the Indian Ocean, with the remains of the butchered carcass of a crewman in its locker. Conrad's sinister hero Falk had plenty of real-life counterparts. In 1884 "the custom of the sea" was at last outlawed when two survivors of the foundering of the yacht *Mignonette* were sentenced, to their genuine surprise, for killing a shipmate for food during twenty-four days without succor in an open boat.

The custom of the sea had its landward parallels, though conventional morality has never been unequivocal about it. In 1752, for instance, a party of deserters from the colonial militia fled New York for French territory; lost on the way, they ran out of provisions. Four or five of them were eaten by the others. In 1823, Alexander Pearce, a convict in Tasmania, admitted killing a comrade for food, not to survive but to satisfy an appetite acquired during an earlier attempted escape, when he alone of eight companions returned alive from the bush. Apart from depraved cases like Alferd Packer's, practical or opportunistic cannibalism accounted for many dead among lost miners and wagoners of the North American frontier in the nineteenth century, satirized by Mark Twain's story of respectable passengers' recourse to cannibalism on a delayed railway journey between St. Louis and Chicago. The most recent recorded instance of this sort occurred in 1972, when an aircraft carrying the Old Christians rugby team from Uruguay crashed in the Andes. The survivors stayed alive by eating those who died.

It has never been enough simply to assert that "eating people is wrong." Being "contrary to nature" does not seem a strong enough sanction when people are really hungry. Any more than sanctions against homosexuality on board ship (or in prison) or onanism when alone . . . and no one ever died from a lack of sex. If it seems abnormal to some, it represents normalcy for others. Cannibalism has always had apologists. Sometimes, as in the case of defenders of the custom of the sea, they appeal to necessity: in other words, they explain cannibalism by representing human flesh as a source of food, ultimately morally indistinguishable from other food sources. In other contexts, the defense is based on cultural relativism and the recognition that, in some cultures, human flesh is more than food: its consumption is justified not because it sustains individual lives, but because it nourishes the community, invokes the gods or harnesses magic.

In the early modern period, when Western thought was obliged to come to terms with social cannibalism, reformers intent on saving "primitives" from exploitation and victimization produced ingenious defenses. Bartolomé de Las Casas, who plagued the conquerors of the New World with denunciations of their injustice, argued that cannibalism was merely a phase of development which virtually all societies went through: he cited convincing evidence of it in the remote past of Greece, Carthage, England, Germany, Ireland and Spain. Jean de Léry, who survived captivity among cannibals in Brazil, thought their sensibilities would be offended to hear of the massacre of St. Bartholomew. Montaigne's essay *On Cannibals* is often cited as an example of how Western self-perceptions were revolutionized by the cultural encounters of the conquest of America and the "Renaissance Discovery of Man." He suggested that the morality of cannibalism was no worse than the cant which enabled Europeans to butcher one another with every conviction of self-righteousness, despite the advantages of Christian education and philosophical tradition. The tortures and burnings which confessional foes inflicted on one another in France "ate men alive" and "I consider it more barbarous to eat a man alive than dead. . . . We are justified in calling these people barbarians by reference to the laws of reason but not in comparison with ourselves, who surpass them in every kind of barbarity." Robinson Crusoe was able to purge Friday of his cannibalism by kindness. His first impulse was to shoot any cannibal he encountered for "inhuman, hellish brutality" but reflection made him realize that "these people do not commit this as a crime; it is not against their own conscience's reproving, or their light reproaching them. . . . They think it no more a crime . . . to eat human flesh than we do to eat mutton."

As knowledge of cannibalism grows, the problems it poses seem increasingly acute. The really interesting question concerns not the reality or even the morality of cannibalism, but its purpose. Is it part of the *histoire de l'alimentation*—a feeding practice designed to supply eaters with protein? Or does it belong to the history of food, as presented in this chapter—a ritual practiced not for a meal but for its meaning, nourishment for more than material effect? The literature on the subject is vast. But though a practical line through it leads to a secure conclusion that cannibals may and sometimes do eat people for simple bodily nourishment—that is not why cannibal practices become enshrined in some cultures. Most cases concern other aims: self-transformation, the appropriation of power, the ritualization of the eater's relationship with the eaten. This puts human flesh on the same level as many other foods which we eat not because we need them to stay alive but because we want them to change us for the better: we want them to give us a share of their virtue. In particular, it aligns the cannibals with their real modern counterparts: those who eat "health" diets for self-improvement or worldly success or moral superiority or enhanced beauty or personal purity. Strangely, cannibals turn out to have a lot in common with vegans. The tradition which links them is the subject of this chapter.

In New Guinea, many former cannibals—and some practicing ones—still alive with memories of their raids and feasts, tell anthropologists that their enemies are "their game." In 1971 a court exonerated Gabusi tribesmen who had eaten the corpse of a neighboring villager on the grounds that it was normal practice in their culture. The fact that cannibalism can be socially functional may coexist with the exploitation of human flesh for food. "Famine cannibalism" is still—or was until recently—a regular feature of life in the islands of the Massim near New Guinea and of some other societies of Southeast Asia and the Pacific. But most peoples who tell ethnographic enquirers that they eat their enemies "for food" seem to have concealed the symbolic and ritual logic underlying the act, like the Papuan Orokaiva, for whom it is a means of "capturing spirits" in compensation for lost warriors. There were no obvious ritual features in the cannibal meals of the Onabasulu: the meat was prepared in the same way as for pig or game, except that intestines were discarded; but they ate no fellow humans except witches—an instance of discrimination which suggests that some other motive than protein acquisition was at work. The Hua of New Guinea eat their own dead to conserve nu, the vital fluids that they believe to be nonrenewable in nature.

The women of the Gimi of the Papuan highlands used to eat their dead menfolk. The practice continued until the 1960s and is still reenacted in mime with dummy corpses. Their explanation recalls the famous story of Alexander and the sages, who ate their honored dead out of respect. "We would not have left a man to rot!" protest the women. "We took pity on him!" "Come to me, so you shall not rot on the ground. Let your body dissolve inside me!" More is at stake in the ritual, however, than the decorous disposal of corpses, or the macabre recollection of sex. According to one theory, this is a classic case of protein substitution: as men have progressively monopolized the diminishing resources of the forests, women supplemented their diet by eating men. Yet, as part of the ritual, men distribute pork rations to the women in proportion to the amount of male flesh consumed. So the men seem to acknowledge the women's generosity: if they had wished to assuage their hunger, they could simply have handed over the pork without inviting the cannibalism. The cannibal feast takes place only after four or five days of collective grieving. It takes place in the men's house, where, in normal circumstances, women are excluded, and where, during the feast, the women are treated as men. The symbolic meaning of the meal therefore seems connected with the fact that women can encompass and include masculinity by bearing a male child: the immolation of dead men in women's bodies is a restoration to the womb, a magical guarantee of the cycle of fertility.

Normally—where it is normal—cannibalism occurs in the context of war. This is not like hunting for food: rather, it is a clash of rival predators. Cannibalism is not usually lightly undertaken even by its most enthusiastic practitioners; and the parts of the victims consumed at cannibal meals are often highly selective and sometimes confined to token morsels, most frequently the heart. The whole business tends to be highly ritualized. Among the Aztecs, ingesting the flesh of a captive in war was a way of possessing his prowess: in a complementary gesture, the captor also donned his victim's flayed skin, with the hands flapping at his wrists like trinkets. Even in Fiji before the coming of Christianity, when cannibalism was practiced on a scale which suggests that some people—the chiefly and warrior elites—were getting a useful dietary supplement from human flesh, the surviving bones are always marked by signs of torture and sacrifice: this distinguishes them from the remains of other animal foods, killed cleanly for speed and efficiency. A visitor in 1847 was told that Chief Ra Udreurdre of the Rakiraki district placed a stone to record each body he ate: there were nine hundred stones. But the very fact that cannibal meals were worthy of such spectacular special commemoration puts them in a category apart from that of ordinary eating. Human meat was the gods' food and cannibalism a form of divine communion. Cannibalism makes sense as part of a pattern of "metaphors symbolizing dominance."

Alternatively, it is part of a "mythical charter of society" sustained, again in Fiji, by "an elaborate cycle of exchange of raw women for cooked men."

Cannibals and their critics have always agreed about one thing. Cannibalism is not neutral: it affects the eater. Critics claim the effect is depraving, as on Sinbad's companions who began "to act like gluttonous maniacs" as soon as they tasted cannibal food and "after a few hours of guzzling" became "little better than savages." Cannibals, on the other hand, find it a means of self-improvement. In cannibal logic, cannibalism is a conspicuous instance of a universal fact: food reinterpreted as more than bodily sustenance—the replacement of nutrition by symbolic value or magic power as a reason for eating: the discovery that food has meaning. After cooking, this is, perhaps, the second great revolution in the history of food: second in importance, though, for all we know, its origins may even be more ancient than those of cooking. No people, however hungry, has escaped its effects, for there is now no society which merely eats to live. Everywhere, eating is a culturally transforming—sometimes a magically transforming—act. It has its own alchemy. It transmutes individuals into society and sickness into health. It changes personalities. It can sacralize apparently secular acts. It functions like ritual. It becomes ritual. It can make food divine or diabolic. It can release power. It can create bonds. It can signify revenge or love. It can proclaim identity. A change as revolutionary as any in the history of our species happened when eating stopped being merely practical and became ritual, too. From cannibals to homeopathists and health foodies, eaters target foods which they think will burnish their characters, extend their powers, prolong their lives.

Diet and eating habits are inseparable from the rest of culture: in particular, they interact with religion, morals and medicine. They also connect with spiritual perceptions in eating programs to "feed the soul" and with such secular ideals as health, beauty and fitness. Health foodies—or other contemporary faddists who eat for beauty or brainpower or sex drive or tranquillity or spirituality—are in the category of the cannibals. They, too, are targeting food for transcendent effect. They, too, are part of the great revolution, which is still resonating, which first ascribed meaning to eating.

SACRED AND PROFANE FOOD

Most societies have foodways which belong to the sphere of the sacred: there are substances you consume to make yourself holy or intimate with the gods or ghosts, others which interpose between the flesh and the spirit and increase divine distance. Staples are almost always sacred, because people depend on them: they possess divine power. The fact that staples in their turn usually depend on man for cultivation does not seem to compromise their sacred status. For cultivation is *cultus*—the most abject kind of worship, in which people serve the crops daily in the fields, bowing their backs to till, sow, weed, dibble and harvest. When these gods sacrifice themselves in men's mouths, it is in the sure knowledge of imminent resurrection. It is no disrespect to eat a god: it is a way of enshrining him.

Examples abound. In Christendom, only wheaten bread will do for the sacramental meal. Similarly, maize is the traditional sacred food of most of the Americas, wherever it can be grown. Not only is maize sacred to Native American peoples who eat it, its mystique spreads further afield. Even outside the maize-fed culture area which covers the tropical and semitropical zones of the hemisphere, it can be found in a place of honor, as at the high-mountain shrines of Andean peoples, where maize was traditionally cultivated in temple gardens on a small scale for ritual use, far above the altitude at which it is viable as a food crop. The mythology of maize has common elements from the St. Lawrence to the Río Negro: divine provenance and a divine covenant. According to the Huichol, highland people dispersed among several states of Mexico, maize was originally a gift of the sun—showered on man by the sun's son, its cultivation taught by his daughter. Long maturation and hard work were imposed as a punishment for human ingratitude. A favorite topic of Huichol jokes is the phallic digging stick, which forms the cavities in which maize seeds are planted, impregnating the earth. The stalks are called the "antlers of young deer," for all food sources are seen as resembling maize, or are even conceived as forms of maize, rather as in the West we speak of sustenance in general as "bread." The maize has sentience, consciousness and will. The shaman beseeches its permission to eat it at harvest time. Aztec women practiced rituals of propitiation before daring to eat maize. They picked up spilled grains in case the maize should be offended and "complain to their lord." They breathed on them before cooking so that they should not fear the fire. Even after evangelization, when maize can no longer strictly be worshipped as a god, and God must be consumed under the form of a wheaten host, the Huichol continue to regard their superior maize strains as signs of divine favor, compared with the varieties eaten by their neighbors. Corn kernels are still used for divination, as they are among the Maya, because of the grain's special access to the transcendent world.

In other societies, it is rarely eaten foods which acquire the mystique of sacred status. Not all ceremonial meats are necessarily sacred: the fact that goose and turkey are popular at Christmas in Europe and America invests neither bird with holiness. Paschal lamb makes a metaphorical allusion to the self-sacrifice of God, but is never confused with the sacramental body of Christ. At the Passover Seder, the annual meal at which Jews retell the story of the Exodus from Egypt, the central plate is filled with ritually significant foods that are, in other circumstances, rarely eaten: matzoh, the unleavened bread, commemorating the departure of the Israelites under conditions that did not permit allowing bread to rise; bitter greens, in acknowledgment of the acrimony of slavery; the nut, apple and wine paste called haroset, intended to resemble the bricks, in tradition if not fact, of Egyptian buildings. When the Ogallala of the North American prairie eat puppies, the meal is considered as essentially spiritual food. The dog feast is an enactment of divine order, the slaughter preceded by a lament for the loss of a friend. Anointed with a line of red paint to symbolize "the red road . . . which . . . represents all that is beneficent in the world," the dog is made to face west, to be garroted by women who stand on either side of him, pulling a rope around his neck, while the medicine man administers a blow from behind. "The act of killing the dog is likened to being struck by lightning and guarantees that the spirit of the dog will be released in order to go to the west where it will join the thunder people, those spirits who have power over life and death, and who themselves are symbolized by lightning." The meat is boiled without seasonings: this is a cross-cultural feature of sacred food, which is not eaten for savor but for salvation.

Though foods of high repute are commonly sacred, and food hallowed by sacrifice is eaten in almost every known culture, there is no connection between sacrality and comestibility. Hindus above the lowest caste respect the sacredness of cows by abstaining from their flesh. This exemption puts sacred meat in the same class as impure meat, which is also forbidden: that of carnivores, insects and rodents. Rational or scientific explanations have always been sought to explain why certain foods are proscribed. Cicero was first in a long line of theorists who have explained prohibitions as economically motivated—bovines, for instance, are too valuable to eat and the societies which sacralize them are practicing a conservation measure. Yet this must be false, as beef is eaten in many places where bovines are vital for plowing, transport and dairying; and in communities where they are sacralized, as among Hindus, their practical value is much diminished in consequence. Alternatively, revulsion from some creatures is explained on grounds of their intimacy with man; yet dogs and cats are treated as foodstuffs in some societies. Another popular claim is made on behalf of hygiene as the basis of at least some taboos, especially in connection with the puzzlingly selective prohibitions enjoined on the Jews in Leviticus. "I maintain that the food which is forbidden by the Law is unwholesome," wrote Maimonides. "Pork contains more moisture than necessary and too much superfluous matter. . . . [The swine's] habits and its food are very dirty and loathsome." This is good-intentioned nonsense, on a par with Maimonides's contention that women had two wombs, corresponding to their number of breasts, because there is little or no difference in cleanliness to distinguish most of the forbidden meats of Moses from most of those allowed. The nearest thing available to a convincing version of a rational explanation is the view of the anthropologist Mary Douglas, who argued that the prohibited creatures are anomalous in their own classes and that integrity, necessary for holiness, is offended by terrestrial creatures that wriggle, or airborne ones with four feet, or those that are cloven-hoofed but nonruminant, like the pig and camel.

It is pointless to seek rational and material explanations for dietary restrictions, because they are essentially suprarational and metaphysical. Meanings ascribed to foods are, like all meanings, agreed conventions about usage: ultimately, they are arbitrary. This does not mean that food taboos are not socially functional. They are, because all of them are totemic: they bind those who respect them and brand those who do not. Permitted foods feed identity, excluded foods help to define it. The taboos are usually related to, and supportive of, the collective beliefs which help a society keep going. It is common for dietary restrictions to outlaw foods which are thought to impede access to the sacred world by conveying "impurities." There are even devil's foods, like the apple of Eden, which are seemingly wholesome but which degrade men or alienate deities, and dishes which can be polluted by association, or which can be either good to eat or fatal, depending on the circumstances. In Fiji, no one may eat the plant or creature which is his totem—though a neighbor may eat of it freely—or plants which grow near a shrine—though the same plant may be eaten if harvested elsewhere—or fruit which grows in graveyards: these will cause mouth ulcers. Taboos imposed on pregnant women are given medical justifications: crab and octopus would cause rashes and warts. Coconut liquids, if consumed by mother, might give the infant a cough. Bemba women must be alert to protect their cooking hearths from anyone who may have had sex without ritual purification—otherwise a child who eats the food will die. Aztecs said that if meat stuck to the side of the stewpot, the diner's spear thrust would be skewed or, if the eater was a woman, that her baby would cling to the womb. The supposed effects are magical, in the sense that they are expected in ignorance or defiance of evidence; and many of them are bound up with the most widespread belief in food's magical properties—which occurs in societies of every level of sophistication: the belief in the interdependence of food and sex.

Although eating and sex seem to be complementary, mutually lubricating forms of sensuality, every particular aphrodisiac is a kiss in the dark. None has anything that could remotely be called scientific endorsement. Truffles are widely fancied as having erotic properties. One of Brillat-Savarin's anecdotes was of his inquiries into the validity of their reputation. "An investigation of this sort is no doubt somewhat indelicate and likely to provoke cynical laughter. But *honi soit qui mal y pense*: the pursuit of truth is always praiseworthy." One of his interviewees confessed that a supper of "superb truffled fowl from Perigord" had been followed by uncharacteristic importunities from her guest. "What can I say, Monsieur? I put it all down to the truffles." His informal committee of inquiry found however, that "the truffle is not a true aphrodisiac; but in certain circumstances it can make women more affectionate and men more attentive." Yet faith in aphrodisiacs has been maintained by food magicians in every society. It has been invoked to explain the enormous quantity of threshed borax seeds found in a Paleolithic cave. Every seducer needs a larder of

> ... *manna and dates, in argosy transferr'd*
> *From Fez, and spicéd dainties, every one,*
> *From silken Samarkand to cedar'd Lebanon,*

or something of the sort. Pythagoras, mythicized in Western tradition as a mathematician and protoscientist, was really a magus whose followers believed he had divine parents and golden body parts: one of his cries was, "Thou wretch, abstain from beans!"—a recipe for food magic which suggests that he shared the convictions of the sandwich man who used to roam London's main shopping street, distributing leaflets against "passion proteins." Most dietary prescriptions blame beans for no malady except flatulence. Foods which are supposed to be suggestive—asparagus tips or mussels, say, because they resemble, in suitably fervid eyes, the male and female sexual parts, or viscous tidbits, which recall squelching organs and sexual fluids to a suitably disposed mind—are no more than that. They are most unlikely to initiate arousal. Just as there are foods credited with inducing lust, others have been adopted as promoters of chastity. Again, it is usually only by a doctrine of sympathetic magic that such recommendations can be justified. On a visit to Canterbury in the late twelfth century Giraldus Cambrensis vindicated barnacle geese as Lenten food for clergymen on the false assumption that they reproduced without sex and therefore might be expected to nourish without exciting inappropriate lusts. As we shall see in a moment, modern dietetics were founded, in part, in the early nineteenth century, as a result of an attempt to create a diet conducive to chastity.

CURATIVE FOOD MAGIC

The fact that many food taboos are enforced by the threat of sickness or deformity puts them, considered from one aspect, in the same category as the health regimens which are found in almost every society but which are particularly characteristic of the modern West. The only surviving recipes from ancient Egypt are for invalid food and come from medical treatises. Chicory was added for liver trouble, iris for bad blood, fennel for colitis. The theory of humors dominated Greek and Roman medical dietetics: indeed, it has been the most enduring and thoroughgoing influence on dietary tradition in the Western world. Menu planners for the sick in classical antiquity tried to correct an excess of cold and moist "humor" by providing hot, dry foods and vice versa. Galen recommended instances of food combining which seem as unscientific as anything in the Beverly Hills Diet: pastries made with flour and butter would be injurious unless served with plenty of honey. Fruit was unsuitable for children and even for nursing mothers.

The notion that foods have a range of properties which must be balanced for perfect health has appealed to many other cultures. Humoral dietary theory is a traditional framework for the pharmacopoeia of many societies, but the details always differ and often contradict each other. In Iran all foods except salt, water, tea and some fungi are classified as "hot" or "cold." The terminology is reminiscent of Galen but, as with all such schemes, there seems to be no coherence in the categories and no relationship to the way foods are classified in other parts of the world. Beef is cold, as are cucumbers, starchy vegetables and cereals, including rice; mutton and sugar, however, are hot, as are dry vegetables and chestnuts, hemp seed, chick peas, melon and millet. In a system traditional in India, sugar is cold, rice hot. In Malaya, rice is neutral. Chinese cuisine, even in circles where Taoism is mistrusted as magical, remains influenced by the ideal of achieving balance between yin and yang: most food is classed as one or the other. Additionally, traditional Chinese medicine had a theory of humors, now fallen into disuse, which was, perhaps, of Western origin. There was an ineluctable common sense about the way foods were assigned to the classes: ginger, pepper, meat and blood were hot; Chinese cabbage, watercress and other green vegetables were cold. Sometimes the results of the theory were disastrous for patients: diarrhea sufferers, for instance, would be denied vegetables on the grounds that their sickness was "cold" and could best be treated with meats and strong spices. In the Malay system, constipation is treated by the avoidance of cold foods, including okra, eggplant, pumpkin and papaya.

Traditional dietetics depends, in most cultures, on arbitrary categories. It is therefore unscientific or, at least, not scientific in the usual sense of the word. It is more readily understood as a kind of transformative magic similar to the magic of cannibalism: you acquire the qualities of what you eat. You, too, can have a figure like Jack Spratt's, a "hot" temper, a "cool" disposition. On the other hand, a commonsense assumption links food and health. What is cooking, "if not medicine?" asked a pseudo-Hippocratic treatise of antiquity. Indeed, food is medicine in a sense, despite the efforts governments make to distinguish between them for purposes of taxation and regulation. Damien Hirst, who founded a restaurant unappetizingly called Pharmacy, painted canny satires, in which foodstuffs appeared packaged as drugstore merchandise. In a similar sense, food is also poison. Universal observation reveals that too much food or too little is injurious and sometimes fatal. Some other correspondences are too obvious to be called scientific but too well justified to be called superstitious. Galen proscribed fish from sewer water and indigestible substances, like cartilaginous meat, for the elderly. Much of the history both of food and of medicine could be written in terms of the search for a more exact tabulation of the correspondences between particular foods and particular physical conditions.

The connection between food and health is at its most obvious in cases where specific diseases are caused by dietary deficiencies and, therefore, can be remedied by dietary adjustments. Beriberi occurs in eaters who overrely on polished rice, which lacks thiamin; vitamin A deficiency—which in rare cases can arise from strangely selective diets—causes dry eye and even blindness. Shortage of vitamin D causes rickets. Lack of niacin leads to pellagra. Among mineral components of food, iodine is needed to keep goiter at bay, calcium against osteoporosis and iron against anemia. The most conspicuous case in history is that of scurvy, which is a deficiency disease pure and simple, caused by lack of the vitamin C in ascorbic acid. In most societies, for most of the time, it has been a very marginal phenomenon, but it acquired unaccustomed significance in world history in the sixteenth, seventeenth and eighteenth centuries, when it debilitated and killed large numbers of European seamen engaged in unprecedentedly long voyages of ocean-spanning exploration and trade.

Most animals can synthesize ascorbic acid readily enough from glucose. Like monkeys and guinea pigs, however, humans cannot do this and must get vitamin C supplies directly from diet. The body's natural reserves generally get depleted to dangerous levels after six to twelve weeks without replenishment. Though ascorbic acid is active in many biological processes, its most important function is maintaining the body's supply of collagen, a cement that binds cells together. Lack of vitamin C affects the amount of two amino acids in collagen, resulting in a lower melting temperature of the collagen. This, in turn, causes the capillary walls to break down and cells to hemorrhage throughout the body; when capillaries lose the "glue" that holds them together, symptoms of scurvy appear. They begin with fatigue and depression and continue with pustules, bleeding and swollen joints. The worst suffering tends to be concentrated around the mouth. Gingivitis sets in, and the gums swell, blacken, soften and engulf the teeth and become so painful that mastication is impossible. The description of the sufferings of Samuel de Champlain's men, icebound on the St. Lawrence in 1535–36 after their Atlantic crossing, is typical: legs bloated and inflamed, "sinews contracted and black as coal," and "mouths so tainted that the gums rotted to the roots." After ninety days, the disease can be fatal.

The new oceanic routes opened up from Atlantic-side Europe to cross the world in the sixteenth century regularly imposed much longer open-sea voyages on the seafarers. Travelers to the Indian Ocean normally spent at least ninety days without calling at an intermediate port and usually much more: 150 to 180 days constituted a normal run. No two major places on transpacific routes were normally less than ninety days apart. It was not unusual to spend six months at sea. Even transatlantic routes, which were shorter and faster, could involve journeys which exceeded the threshold period for scurvy, especially if they led straight across the Caribbean or were executed in convoy. A hundred or 130 days was within the normal range for a voyage from Seville to Veracruz. Voyages of such long duration were unprecedented and unanticipated. No one knew what the problems would be, let alone how to respond to them. In the early stages of this history, expeditions regularly ran out of food. Nor was it normal, or even possible, to carry antiscorbutics aboard ship. Of foods which can be classed as reasonably accessible in the modern West, blackcurrants are easily the best source: four times as rich in the vitamin as oranges or lemons, eight times richer than limes. None of these fruits, nor most other richly ascorbic fruits, had ever been classed as ship's stores, nor, even had seamen known of their properties, could they be successfully stored for long on board. The problem of obtaining vitamin C on long voyages is compounded by the fact that it is destroyed by heat—and therefore by most preserving processes—and dwindles rapidly in fruit that has been kept stored for a few days. Any oxidation—exposure to the air, slicing with an iron knife—increases the rate of loss.

In 1497–99, Vasco da Gama's first voyage to India and back, which involved two spells of fully ninety days on the open sea, was the occasion of the first great visitation of scurvy, which probably claimed the lives of most of the hundred men lost to sickness in the course of the expedition. Meanwhile, the explorers tried to relieve their swollen gums, on the commanders' orders, by washing their mouths with their own urine. By the time Magellan's men reached Guam, on the first recorded crossing of the Pacific in 1520, they were reduced to eating weevily biscuit, sodden with rat's urine, and gnawing helplessly at leather casings off the yardarms with gums spongy from scurvy. Few of the men remained unaffected; twenty-one died. Scurvy was an unremitting enemy to long-haul navigators for the next 250 years.

Although other cases were known—among siege victims and soldiers on long campaigns—the fact that the incidence of scurvy was so commonly associated with long sea voyages turned physicians' speculations toward humidity and salinity in their search for the causes of the disease. Association with crowded shipboard conditions encouraged belief that it was an infectious or contagious affliction. The notion that fresh victuals might help was first suggested in the late sixteenth century, probably by readings in Galen, who had a strong prejudice against fruit but whose system of health emphasized the importance of a balance of humors in patients of cold and phlegmatic disposition; in particular, in a modification of his usual categories, Galen admitted lemons as a "warm" fruit for "cold" diseases. Scurvy was classified as a "cold" disease; even so, it was thought inadvisable to administer fruit to patients unless their temperaments were suited to it.

Meanwhile, the best progress in finding suitable treatments was made by physicians in Spanish America, who saw relatively large numbers of cases and had the pharmacopoeia of ethnobotany—the native knowledge of the properties of plants—at their disposal. The best account of both symptoms and remedies was published by an outstanding Franciscan writer, Fray Juan de Torquemada, in the 1560s. He described vividly the horror of treating men in agony, who could not bear to be touched or clothed, and who wasted with the want of solid food. The wonder cure he recommended was a kind of wild pineapple which he called by the native name, xocohuitzle,

> and God gave this fruit such virtue that it reverses the swelling of the gums, and
> makes them grip the teeth, and cleans them, and expels all the putrescence and
> pus from the gums, and after a couple of ingestions of this fruit the patient
> recovers sufficiently to be able to eat properly again and try any sort of food
> without trouble or pain.

As early as 1569, the Pacific explorer Sebastián Vizcaíno was taking care to reprovision with fresh produce at every opportunity to cure scurvy or keep it at bay. As soon as he got back on shore in Mexico after a grueling transpacific voyage,

> the general ordered fresh food to be brought to the men on board ship, such as chickens, hens, kids, bread, papaya, bananas, oranges, lemons, squash and berries . . . so that in the nine or ten days they spent in port they all recovered their health and strength and rose from their beds so that by the time the ship sailed again, they could man the rigging and the helm and take their watches and do guard duty . . . for there was no medicine nor apothecary's drug, nor remedy nor doctor's prescription nor any other human cure against this disease; or if there was such a cure it was fresh food alone and plenty of it.

In 1592, a friar apothecary, Agustín Farfán, recommended the juice of half a lemon and half a sour orange with a little burnt alum. By that date, the effectiveness of such remedies had become widely known. English and Dutch navigators tried to get lemons, oranges or other fruit for their men where they could, but the problems of supply, storage and—from the point of view of naval administrators—expense all remained insuperable.

A crisis in the history of the disease occurred in 1740–44, when George Anson lost almost 1,400 out of a complement of over 1,900 men during his round-the-world voyage. Scurvy was only the worst of a plague of deficiency diseases, including beriberi, blindness, "idiotism, lunacy, convulsions," but the Anson voyage provoked at last a systematic inquiry into how to treat it. James Lind, a naval surgeon who had seen service in the West Indies, tried out a large selection of the remedies previously proposed on a sample of twelve patients at sea, including such unpromising suggestions as seawater, "gutts of elixir of vitriol"—drops of a solution of sulfuric acid—and an ominous mixture of garlic, mustard, radish, quinine and myrrh.

> Their cases were as similar as I could have them. They all in general had putrid gums, the spots and lassitude, with weakness of the knees. They lay together in one place . . . and had one diet common to all, viz., water-gruel sweetened with sugar in the morning; fresh mutton-broth oftentimes for dinner; at other times puddings, boiled biscuit with sugar, etc., and for supper, barley and raisins, rice and currants, sago and wine, or the like. Two of these were ordered each a quart of cider a day. Two others took twenty-five gutts of elixir of vitriol three times a day, upon an empty stomach, using a gargle strongly acidulated with it for their mouths. Two others took two spoonfuls of vinegar three times a day, upon an

empty stomach, having their gruels and other foods well acidulated with it, as also the gargle for their mouth. Two of the worst patients . . . were put under a course of sea-water. Of this they drank half a pint every day, and sometimes more or less as it operated by way of gentle physic. Two other had each two oranges and one lemon given to them every day. These they ate with greediness, at different times, upon an empty stomach. They continued but six days under this course, having consumed the quantity that could be spared. The two remaining patients took the bigness of a nutmeg three times a day of an electuary recommended by an hospital surgeon, made of garlic, mustard seed, *radix raphana*, balsam of Peru and gum myrrh; using for common drink, barley water well acidulated with tamarinds; by a decoction of which, with the addition of cream of tartar, they were gently purged three or four times during the course. The consequence was that the most sudden and visible good effects were perceived from the use of the oranges and lemons; one of those who had taken them, being at the end of six days fit for duty.

The cider drinkers showed a slight improvement. Everybody else got worse.

Lind had discovered a cure, but not a preventive; for there was still no way of preserving oranges and lemons at sea for long enough to secure the health of the crews. Nor was it clear from his work that citrus fruits would work for all patients: the theory of humors retained a residual hold on physicians' minds and universal cures were distrusted as quackery. During the 1750s and early 1760s, at least forty publications appeared in Britain alone with proposals for dealing with the disease. Richard Mead, who studied Anson's records and recollections, despaired of a solution: he concluded that sea air was irremediably unhealthful. Lind's own proposal was to issue rations of concentrated lemon juice; but the process destroyed the ascorbic acid and cost more than the Admiralty was willing to pay. John Huxham advocated the addition of cider to ships' rations, but the modest beneficial effects of this beverage vanished when it was stored aboard ship. Gilbert Blane realized that the therapeutic properties of fruit juice needed to be fortified to endure at sea and suggested adding alcohol: this kept the decoction drinkable but did not restore its effectiveness. David MacBride advocated unfermented malt, which, recommended by its cheapness, was adopted by the Royal Navy but was utterly inefficacious. It had the enthusiastic endorsement of Johann Reinhold Forster, the shipboard physician of Cook's voyage of 1772–75, though for the printed edition of his journal the recommendation was deleted. A surgeon with experience of Russian Arctic exploration advised "warm reindeer blood, raw frozen fish, exercise" with any edible greenstuff that might come to hand. During his Pacific odyssey from 1785 to 1788 Jean-François de La Pérouse put his faith in breathing "land air," and mixing molasses, "wort, spruce beer and an infusion of quinine in the crew's drinking water." "Spruce beer" was an invention of Cook's, made of an extract from the Newfoundland spruce, mixed with molasses and pine sap and laced with spirits. It contained virtually no vitamin C.

The only vegetable food which retains reasonable quantities of ascorbic acid in a pickled state is sauerkraut, a food peculiar to Dutch ships among the navies of the early eighteenth century, but one which seemed to do good. In the 1760s and early 1770s Captain Cook's experiments convinced him of the virtues of this nostrum, which, thanks to Cook's matchless reputation, became standard-issue rations for long voyages. Cook virtually eliminated deaths from scurvy, after zealous trials of all the recommended remedies. His success was assisted by his regime of cleanliness, enforced by iron discipline. But until a way was discovered to preserve the juice of citrus fruits cheaply and without destroying the ascorbic acid, every substitute was of limited value. The only effective remedy was to replenish with fresh supplies at every opportunity and to eat as much greenstuff as could be encountered wherever a ship could land, ravaging desert islands for the barely edible weeds sailors called "scurvy grass." By the time of the voyage of Alessandro Malaspina, the most ambitious scientific expedition of the eighteenth century, from 1789 to 1794, scurvy was virtually banished from the fleet, thanks to the conviction of the medical officer, Pedro González, that fresh fruits—especially oranges and lemons—were the essential remedies. Only one outbreak occurred in the entire course of the journey, during a voyage of fifty-six days between Acapulco and the Marianas islands. Five men, who were weakened by dysentery contracted in Mexico, went down with the disease and only one exhibited serious symptoms. After three days ashore on Guam on a diet rich in vegetables, oranges and lemons, he was up and about. Yet other navies, which lacked the Spaniards' advantage of a large colonial empire with frequent ports of call, remained desperate for alternative diagnoses and easier cures. As late as 1795, when Spanish crews were getting the benefit of assiduous treatment with citrus fruits, George Vancouver attributed an outbreak of scurvy aboard his ship to the men's "pernicious" practice of eating fat with their beans, though he took the opportunity of feeding grapes, apples and onions to the crews when they reached Valparáiso. The issue of lemon juice rations to English sailors began the following year.

DIETETIC SORCERY

Success in the treatment of scurvy reinforced the notion that food could be elevated, above its commonplace role as a nourisher, to the ranks of a healer. Food health became a quest in which rising science met abiding religion. It was both a pseudo-science and a mystic vocation: pseudo-scientific because of the new prestige of science in the nineteenth-century West; mystical because it was developed beyond evidence by visionaries who, in many cases, were religiously inspired: if food was the key to physical health, why not moral health, too? The ancient sages, who formulated character-forming taboos of abstinence and restraint, had nineteenth- and twentieth-century successors.

Traditionally, to command prestige, medicinal foods had to be rare and costly. Readily available remedies tend to work poorly, because patients are disinclined to believe in them; part of every affliction is mental and cures have to be psychologically convincing to register mental effects. The great Jesuit traveler of the seventeenth century, Jeronimo Lobo, admitted that he had no medical knowledge outside the handbook he carried with him; but he found that he was much valued for consultations wherever he went: this was the common experience of deracinated "holy men." On one occasion, during a spell when Catholics were persecuted, he was in hiding in Ethiopia, "surrounding ourselves with brambles in order to avoid attacks by thieves and wild animals, since the land had an abundance of both." It was Lent and he wanted little food, but to get wheat for mass and lamb for Easter he treated a farmer's asthma in exchange. With difficulty, he persuaded his patient that an emetic would do no good. "Although there was a dearth of many of the things that could be of use to him, there was one item in abundance and very much available, namely, syrup of goat's urine taken in the morning on an empty stomach . . . which could not fail to bring him the desired result." Lobo never found out whether the remedy worked: "I only know the payments did not continue." Modern Western practice in healthy eating is in Lobo's tradition, because, instead of privileging rarities, it ranks commonplace foods and entire diets and "styles" of eating in order of healthiness.

Among all such schemes, vegetarianism has the longest-standing claims and the most prestigious adherents to back it. All-vegetable diets have received endorsements, since antiquity, among sages convinced of the improving effects of all kinds of austerity, and among critics of human arrogance which claims dominion over beasts. These two strands came together in the plea Plutarch attributed to a potential dish, "Kill to eat if you must or will, but do not slay me that you may feed luxuriously." In the past, however, outside utopian fiction, despite persuasive advocates, vegetarianism captured whole societies or whole religious traditions only as part of a system of taboos, recommended by religious sanctions. Pythagoras and the Buddha were credited by early followers with vegetarian messages, but they were also believers in the transmigration of souls: all meat-eating might be cannibalism and parricide in a world where "the soul of my grandam might haply inhabit a bird." Now, in the modern, secular West, vegetarianism is recommended by a different kind of magic as a means to health (though never entirely without concomitant appeals to morality and, increasingly, to ecological anxiety).

The contemporary vegetarian movement can be traced back to specific origins in the late eighteenth century. Its sources of inspiration were, in part, traditional: the cumulative effect of classical and medieval vegetarian tracts, disseminated by an increasingly active press, and reflected in the gradually accelerating output by vegetarian writers in Europe in the previous two centuries. But it thrived because of new contexts which sustained it. Its beginnings are inseparable from the context of early Romanticism and the new sensibility toward the natural world evinced in the arts and letters of Europe and the New World at the time. It may not be fanciful, too, to locate it in the context of the rapid growth of Europe's population, which alerted economists to a genuine advantage of vegetable foods: they are cheaper to produce than edible livestock, which consumes disproportionate amounts of cereals. Adam Smith, who was a canny capitalist modestly susceptible to romanticism, omitted meat from his description of "the most plentiful, the most wholesome, the most invigorating diet."

Most other advocates of the new vegetarianism were more softhearted or less hardheaded. John Oswald was a sucker for bizarre and radical causes: a self-converted, self-proclaimed Hindu, who died fighting counterrevolutionaries in Jacobin France. His vegetarian tract, *The Cry of Nature* (1791), demanded inviolability for animal life. Critics were not slow to denounce "a wretch who would not kill a tiger but died unsated in his thirst for human blood!" The radical printer George Nicholson appealed to a classical topos: meatless "feasts of primeval innocence" in the presumed "golden age" which preceded competition between species. Flesh was "matter for corruption." Vegetarians who felt uneasy about the paganism or secularism of this classical imagery could turn to the Bible and find that God had summoned his chosen to lands of manna, milk and honey. The fact that the original manna was probably an insect secretion rather than a vegetable food was not yet known.

The early apostles of vegetarianism believed—or claimed they did—that food forms character. (A lot of food magic is sympathetic: in some cultures, women who tread rice grains must be bare-breasted because of the "ancient belief that the less they wear, the thinner the rice husks will be.") For early vegetarians, more than bodily health was at stake. Carnivores, insisted Joseph Ritson, in one of English vegetarianism's first sacred texts, *An Essay on Abstinence from Animal Food as* a *Moral Duty* (1802), were cruel, choleric and bad-tempered. Meat eating led to robbery, sycophancy and tyranny. It encouraged the predatory instinct. Shelley became one of the most vociferous converts to this creed. "The slave trade," he claimed, "that abominable violation of the rights of nature, is, most probably, owing to the same cause; as well as a variety of violent acts, both national and personal, which are usually attributed to other motives." Meat food was the "root of all evil," and animal diet "the original and mortal sin," as if flesh grew on the tree of Eden. When man took to meat, "his vitals were devoured by the vulture of disease." If Napoleon had descended from "a race of vegetable-eaters," he would never have had "the inclination or the power to ascend the throne of the Bourbons." Shelley's friends were inclined to mock his vegetable appetite. Scythrop—the satirical shadow Thomas Love Peacock invented for him—was saved from suicide by the restorative effects of a boiled fowl and some madeira. Shelley's sister, however, shared the vegetarian creed. Frankenstein's monster refused the food of man and declined to "destroy the lamb and the kid, to glut my appetite; acorns and berries afford me sufficient nourishment."

Vegetarianism could never attain mass popularity on moral grounds—certainly not, in the nineteenth century, in competition with conventional religion. Good health, however, was salable in a way that good conduct could never be. Morality joined marketability in the whole wheat flour cult founded by a revivalist clergyman, Sylvester Graham, in the 1830s: his was the first American doctrine of global appeal since the Declaration of Independence. Graham was not just the "prophet of bran bread and pumpkins"; he was part of the bourgeois revolution in prudery, the revulsion the nineteenth century felt from the louche sexual habits of the preceding age. He believed that sex was not only immoral: it was unhealthy. Moreover, it was immoral most of the time but it was unhealthy all of the time, because sexual emissions were debilitating. Society was threatened by the indiscipline of an unrestrained sex drive. Consciousness of one's sexual organs was a sign of disease. Sex was paroxysm and orgasm resembled an attack of diarrhea. Graham agreed with the vegetarian warriors of the previous generation that flesh eaters were "despotic, vehement and impatient." An abstemious, vegetable diet would naturally cause and complement the minimal expenditure of semen, contributing to what Graham called a "physiology of subsistence."

At the same time he contrived to appeal to many wisps in the zeitgeist: antiindustrial rural romanticism; the idealism that called for the "return to the plough" and the reembodiment of Cincinnatus in American life. These blended in Graham's work with the rhetoric of "manifest destiny" and the economics of American imperialism, which looked to the settlement of the prairie and the conversion of the grasslands to wheatlands—an ambition that could only be fulfilled if there were a massive increase in cereal consumption. Sylvester Graham wanted it to happen in unfertilized, undebauched, virgin soil. His kind of bread, made from the whole wheat flour he formulated, would be baked lovingly at home by mothers. The unsuccessful part of his campaign was his effort to make Americans eat less: "Every individual," he declared, "should, as a general rule, restrain himself to the smallest quantity, which he finds from careful investigation and enlightened experience and observation, will fully meet the alimentary wants of the vital economy of his system—knowing that whatsoever is more than this is evil." That message was ignored. America was and remained a land of overeaters. Graham's flour, however, found a huge niche in the booming food market. James Caleb Jackson (1814–95) made a fortune from marketing Graham products, including the first cold breakfast cereal, which he called Granula.

Graham inspired imitators: a sequence of low-protein fanatics whose homespun philosophy came to displace science and to dominate mainstream thinking on nutrition for a century. By the 1890s, idealists and charlatans were competing for the huge profits generated by the markup on patent cereal products. The result was the start of the "Corn Flake Crusades," which soon became a civil war, as writs flew to protect the copyright in rival products which were all suspiciously similar. J. H. Kellogg's first cereal pirated the name Granula. He was a typical mixture of moralism and materialism, capitalism and Christianity. He came from an Adventist background: his sect had long espoused low-protein principles similar to Graham's. Unlike most of the food gurus of the time, he had studied medicine and supplemented his religious impulse with scientific ambitions: he wanted to eliminate the hundreds of millions of bacteria which, he believed, meat introduced to the colon—exterminating them with yogurt or expelling them with roughage. Eventually, the adrenaline of the arena seemed to take him over and his main ambition became to outdo all the other breakfast cereals on the market.

In part, the likes of Kellogg communicated successfully with the public because they were great showmen, with evangelists' instincts for playing an audience, creating a congregation. In part, too, they relied on mediation by ill-educated, self-styled "experts" in the science of nutrition, which still lacked a professional structure and standards. Sallie Rorer was highly typical and highly influential. She had no qualifications for her job—indeed, no educational qualifications of any kind. She was suddenly elevated to the administration of the Philadelphia School of Cooking because she was the star pupil when the first principal unexpectedly resigned. "Two-thirds of all the intemperance in the land," she believed, was due to "unscientific feeding." As a teacher she was charismatic, as a lecturer, magnetic, and she rose to be the acknowledged "Queen of the Kitchen" in the 1890s. Her demonstrations impressed audiences, if not with her food, with the radiance of the silks she wore to show that cooking could be clean. She was also a robust emotional bully. She tyrannized her biddable husband into the role of amanuensis for her cookbooks. She made her rich pupils clean their own utensils. Like many kitchen apostles she claimed to be a self-cured dyspeptic. Her claim to promote a "science" of "educated cooking" was sustained despite her collusion with advertisers and her endorsements of indifferent products, including proprietary cottonseed oil and corn flour. But she promoted good culinary causes: modest rates of consumption, salad every day, diets individually tailored to the needs of the sick.

Like all self-made nutritionists she had her *bêtes noires*: mustard and pickles should be banned, puddings avoided and the use of vinegar minimized: "If salt and vinegar will eat away copper, what must it do to the delicate mucus lining of the stomach?" She eschewed pork and veal on the grounds that they "took five hours to digest" and was proud of never eating fried food. "Banish the frying pan and there will not be much sickness either in city or country." Her early prescriptions for breakfasts were heartily in the American tradition but she later developed the theory that "stomach mucus" accumulated overnight and should not be disturbed by more than a little fruit, milky coffee or patent cereal. This was the only matter on which she ever admitted changing her mind. All but contagious disease could be eliminated by a healthy regimen.

Above all, one should eat to live, not live to eat. "Every pound of flesh more than necessary," she wrote, "is a pound of disease." To eat three meals a day was "unrefined." Rorer advocated smaller, simple, dainty meals for the urban age. She disguised meanness as "daintiness." Like so many dietitians, she did not really like food. She excoriated waste, recycled leftovers. The day's routine should begin, she said, by salvaging the leftovers the maid might throw away. A sortie into the larder might produce some strips of suet, the tough trimmings from the breakfast steak, stale cheese, stale bread, cream gone sour, a boiled potato, some celery leaves and a cupful each of leftover fish and peas. She pureed the peas and celery for soup, combined the cheese and bread in a savory rarebit, minced the beef, rendered the suet, put the sour cream into gingerbread, creamed the fish and piped the potato around it.

Rorer and Kellogg both fell under the spell of the most showmanlike of all the health food crusaders of the *fin de siècle*. Horace Fletcher was an obsessive in the tradition of Sylvester Graham. He advocated low protein intake with the same passion but in a more secular vein, stressing always his scientific claims, which were bogus, and the priority of bodily health—the one good about which everyone agreed in America's contentious and plural society. He took one of the shibboleths of the Victorian nursery—food should be chewed—and turned it into a creed. From his palazzo in Venice he urged eaters to masticate until food loses its taste. Liquids should be swished around in one's mouth for at least thirty seconds before swallowing. Most of what he represented as "pure" laboratory science was opinionated nonsense. He insisted, for instance, that "digestion took place in the rear of the mouth." By adopting Fletcher's methods, his doctor claimed to have cured his own "gout, incapacitating headaches, frequent colds, boils on the neck and acne, chronic eczema of the toes . . . frequent acid dyspepsia" and loss of interest "in my life and work": the typical testimonial of a barker at a medicine show. But despite what he claimed was his stunningly low protein intake of forty-five grams a day, Fletcher astonished all observers by his extraordinary physical prowess, which, when he was fifty-five years old, rivaled that of Yale University oarsmen and West Point cadets in trials of strength. It should be said that Fletcher left out of account the copious amounts of chocolate he ate between meals.

Thanks in part to Fletcher's fame, the claims of the low-protein cult began to be investigated by intrigued scientists in the early years of the twentieth century. Russel H. Chittenden of Yale was converted to Fletcherism and became a zealous apostle for eating less. Although Fletcher died of a heart attack aged sixty-eight, Chittenden lived to eighty-seven, while Kellogg died at ninety-one. The balance of scientific opinion, however, continued to uphold protein. This is not surprising, as one of the few verifiable laws of dietetics is that the experts always disagree. Protein had, moreover, a respectable tradition on its side. The first really serious program of systematic inquiry into the problems of nutrition had been launched in the 1830s by one of the outstanding heroes of the history of food science, Baron Justus von Liebig: his classification of the nutritional components of foods into carbohydrates, proteins and fats was the basis of all further work on the subject. He boiled, pressed, infused and pulped meat in a search for a purified form of protein. The work suggests an alchemist intent on a transmutation or perhaps, more justly, a refiner purifying ore. He admired the nutritional qualities of fat, which, "by the quantity of carbon it contains, stands nearest to coal. We heat our body, exactly as we heat a stove, with a fuel which, containing the same elements as wood and coal, differs essentially, however, from the latter substances, by being soluble in the juices of the body." Meat "contains the nutritive constituents of plants, stored up in concentrated form." This notion was not original to Liebig: he set out to prove a commonly held fallacy, well expressed many times over in the 1820s by the first great amateur of food science, Jean-Anthelme Brillat-Savarin. Envying an English party's roast mutton at an inn, that irrepressible gourmet, by his own account, "inflicted a dozen deep wounds on the forbidden joint, so that its juices should escape down to the last drop" and then scrambled a dozen eggs in the gravy. "There we made a feast of them, laughing uproariously to think that we were in fact swallowing all the substance of the mutton, leaving our English friends to chew the residue."

Liebig's was an enterprise typical of an age which tried to reduce everything to science: at about the same time, Constable claimed that painting was science; Laplace convinced readers that love was mere chemistry; Darwin conceived the notion that aesthetics and morals were produced by biological processes. Food, like most of what is worthwhile in life, is intractable to such reductionism. Meat products in fact gain no nutritional value by "extraction"; but rival firms vied to improve on Liebig's efforts. Meat extract wars, comparable to the corn flake crusades, followed in the 1870s (below, p. 200–201). Diets high in protein, or consecrated to meat, were propounded as vigorously as those of the vegetarians and Fletcherites. The most eloquent spokesman was James H. Salisbury, author of *The Relation of Alimentation and Disease* (1888). He was an adept of what he called "nerve force" and an exponent of hot-water libations to "wash out the digestive organs like an old vinegar-barrel." His experiments on himself—subsisting on an exclusive diet of one kind of food after another—left him with a revulsion of vegetables. Baked beans and oatmeal had tortured him with flatulence. Too many greens caused "vegetable dyspepsia" or chronic diarrhea. They filled

> the stomach with carbonic acid gas, sugar, alcohol, acid and alcoholic and acid yeast plants. These products of fermentation soon begin to paralyze the follicles and muscular walls of the stomach, so that it becomes flabby and baggy, and will hold an unusual amount of trashy foods and fluids. The organ has been turned into a veritable sour "yeast pot."

Vegetables, Salisbury thought, should be forbidden to invalids and strictly controlled for everybody else. Man, he argued, is by nature "two-thirds carnivorous," with teeth and stomach designed by evolution to tear and digest meat. Starch, the staple of the cereal-mongers, was

> the enemy of health. . . . Eat the muscle pulp of lean beef made into cakes and broiled. This pulp should be as free as possible from connective or glue tissue, fat and cartilage. . . . The pulp should not be pressed too firmly together before

broiling or it will taste livery. Simply press it sufficiently to hold it together. Make the cakes from half an inch to an inch thick. Broil slowly and moderately well over a fire free from blaze and smoke. When cooked, put it on a hot plate and season to taste with butter, pepper and salt; also use either Worcestershire or Halford sauce, mustard, horseradish or lemon juice on the meat if desired.

This recipe, devised by Salisbury for consumptives but recommended for virtually every condition, was evidently the type or epitype of the "hamburger steak," which was then just beginning its career as the world's future favorite dish. Salisbury's theories are forgotten and almost every informed eater today would repudiate them. But their curse lives on in nearly 46,000 McDonald's, Burger King and Wendy's restaurants worldwide.

In the early years of the twentieth century, as the debate over protein stalled and palled, "purity" became the new priority: dirt was one danger on which almost all dietitians were agreed. Hygienic preparation was part of the public image on which all the great early food giants of America—Heinz, Kellogg's, Franco-American—built their business. "Stacey's Forkdipt Chocolates were fork-dipped because 'the fork is cleaner than the hand'" and "Bishop's California Preserves were 'the only fruits in the world with a $1,000 purity guarantee on every jar.'" Yet the nutritionists' world was rife with corruption. Lack of niacin caused pellagra, one of the few deficiency diseases actually current in America when the vitamin craze took over after the First World War; but it was confined to urban black poor who lived off cornmeal and the connection was effectively suppressed until the 1930s. Until then, producers of quack remedies with impressive names—"Stream of Life," "Pellagracide"—defended their markets, while employers of the pellagra-prone blamed heredity, immorality, "bad blood": anything to justify low wages and unhealthy food doles. Elmer McCollum was one of the most influential nutritionists of all times. His experiments with rodents at Yale convinced the world that vitamin-rich foods were good for general health—promoting the big physiques habitually overvalued in America. He spent years decrying white bread's "deficiency in dietary factors." Yet when he joined General Mills as a consultant he appeared before a committee of Congress to denounce "the pernicious teachings of food faddists who have sought to make people afraid of white-flour bread." Dr. Harvey Wiley, campaigner against processed foods, became the health columnist of *Good Housekeeping* magazine and endorsed advertisers' mush, like Jell-O and Cream of Wheat. Appropriate industries proselytized for the coffee-and-donuts diet; a crash diet of fruit and raw vegetables was promoted by Californian fruit interests; the United Fruit Company backed the "bananas and skim milk" diet of the Johns Hopkins University researcher Dr. George Harrop. This became Americans' favorite, just ahead of the "Grapefruit-juice Diet."

Some of the dietary gurus were dazzled or self-deluded. Some were mere cranks. Some were charlatans. Among the breadlines of the early Depression and Dust Bowl, the overnourished of America were morally beleaguered. They wanted food to give them more than sustenance. This represented an opportunity for a new brand of grand-scale snake-oil hucksters. None was greater than Gaylord Hauser. With his advice, you could "gargle your fat away" at reducing parties. His laxative diet—one of many which imperiled dieters' health, tortured their bodies and flushed their guilt—was followed by the Duchess of Windsor. His "Be More Beautiful" diet was "a one-day house-cleaning regimen. . . . You will be amazed at how the fat rolls off." Dr. William Hay, creator of "Fountain of Youth Salad," insisted on separating proteins from carbohydrates and both from what he called "alkalines": many people continue to be suckered by the scientific sound of his nostrums. Lewis Wolberg's language was typical of the exploitative nutritionists—pretentious, sententious, didactic:

> Human eating is rich in tradition. It is cloaked in glamorous adornments, customs and taboos. It is disguised by convention and adorned with numerous social embellishments. These often corrupt nutritional efficiency and frequently lead to gastronomic sins. . . . Civilized people live on foods which are pitifully devitalized and improperly balanced.

He opposed sauces, variety ("too much variety breeds gastric discontent") and midnight snacks. He recommended milk, mastication, bananas and the "splendid physiques" produced by the diets of "the pre-European Maori, the savage Samoan, the African native and the Greenland Eskimo." His scale of progress was phony and the assumptions on which it is based were false. He characterized those at the bottom of the scale as "tribes whose methods of food pursuit and cookery are reminiscent of the Stone Age." His description of such peoples, as far as I can judge, was fantastic in every particular:

> At the bottom of the eating scale are the African Pygmies and the Brazilian forest men. The Pygmy subsists on an unadorned diet of fruits, nuts, insects, grubs, honey and shellfish. He eats his food raw and he frequently starves. Like his ancestor, the Eocene lemur-monkey-man, he is content to gather food in

times of plenty without bothering to make provision for times of dearth. The Brazilian forest-man is a barbarous creature whose eating habits are disgusting and who, when hunger grips him, is wont to poke a stick into an ant hole in order to allow ants to crawl into his mouth.

In a climate dominated by nonsense, each scientific discovery passed instantly into the hands of shysters. Vitamins were the twentieth century's new obsession—the discovery which impacted on dietary doctrines in the Western world in the new century with a force similar to that exerted by proteins and carbohydrates in the nineteenth. The vitamin could almost be classed not as a discovery but an invention, postulated just before the First World War by scientists engaged in an alchemical quest for the "life principle"—the essential ingredient that made food sustain life. Rats fed on "pure," isolated carbohydrates, fats, proteins and minerals did not survive unless they were also given real food. Frederick Gowland Hopkins, the Cambridge professor who demonstrated that milk was such a food, called it an "accessory food factor." This was a better name than vitamins, which are not amines—hydrocarbon compounds produced by rotting. They are, however, vital, though not all are diet-dependent. Most people rely on sunlight for vitamin D and there is a vitamin called K which is synthesized by bacteria in the intestine.

Vitamins began as science and became a craze. Vitamin A—the retinol natural in offal, butter and animal fat—or beta-carotene, which abounds in carrots, had to be added to margarine, even though deficiency in it was virtually unknown in the countries which adopted the measure. In Britain and America, food processing which reduced the vitamins in comestibles became a focus of anxiety in the 1930s, even though there was no evidence that it caused diet-deficient disease. In 1939 the American Medical Association recommended reinjecting processed foods with enough nutrients to bring them up to their "high natural levels." Before the Second World War, America was swept by a craze for thiamin—the so-called "morale vitamin"; Dr. Russell Wilder declared that a policy of thiamin deprivation of subject peoples was "Hitler' secret weapon." Vice President Henry Wallace endorsed the jingle "What puts the sparkle in your eye, the spring in your step, the zip in your soul? The oomph vitamin." "Vitamins will win the war" was a slogan of the U.S. Food Agency. An army nutritionist claimed he could turn five thousand draftees into supermen—invincible shock troops—with vitamin pills. In the civilian world, cafeteria food was officially judged "poor" if it missed any two of the following: an eight-ounce glass of milk or equivalent, three quarters of a cup of a green or yellow vegetable, one "serving" of meat, cheese, fish or eggs, two slices of whole grain or vitamin-enriched bread, one pat of butter or vitamin-enriched fortified margarine, and four to five ounces of raw fresh fruit or vegetables. While servicemen supposedly learned about "balanced meals" from compartmentalized trays, the president of the American Dietetic Association believed the return of demobilized "apostles of good eating . . . would save the country's undernourished from themselves." "I've got my vitamins," sang Ethel Merman, "A-B-C-D-E-F-G-H-I-I-I-I've still got my health so what do I care?" This appropriate satire was wasted on a public probably disposed to believe that vitamins F, G, H, if not known to exist, would surely be discovered.

War or the prospect of war stimulated and warped governments' appetites for nutritional research. Wartime efforts to get "food for children" had to be concealed under the slogan "Eat more food and kill more Japs." Healthy armies would guarantee victory. Sir Robert McCarrison, Britain's most influential nutritionist on the eve of the war, proved to his own satisfaction the advantages of "a perfectly constituted diet" by feeding it to "some dozens of healthy monkeys from the jungles of Madras." Those he deprived of vitamins and mineral elements developed conditions ranging from gastritis and ulcer to colitis and dysentery. Meanwhile, three or four years' nurture transformed slum children in Deptford from invalids "rickety and bronchitic . . . with adenoids and dental caries . . . [and] inflammatory states of eyes, nose, ears and throat" into specimens of the "well made child, with clean skin, alert, sociable, eager for life and new experiences." Four hundred tuberculosis sufferers' children at Papworth Settlement were made healthy by "adequate food." McCarrison's grand strategy was to "build an Al nation." Hence the medical profession's campaigns in the 1930s to "bring the nation's diet up to the optimum" with milk, butter, eggs and meat. This menu reflected the prejudices of another food Tartuffe, John Boyd Orr, who during colonial service was impressed by the Masai of Kenya, eaters of meat and drinkers of milk and blood, who towered over their high-fiber, low-fat Kikuyu neighbors.

The experience of war, when it came, seemed to belie all the dietary theory which preceded it. British fruit consumption went down by nearly 50 percent, though this was offset by potato eating, which rose by 45 percent, and consumption of vegetables, which rose by a third. Loss of meat and fish had to be made up by milk and cereals, unrefined flour products and vitamin additives. The result was a new nutritionists' craze—which endures to this day—for a wartime diet and, in particular, the elevation of coarse flour to the ranks of a panacea. Yet there may have been other explanations for the paradox of a war which was good for public health. Rationing redistributed food to the less well off, while mothers got more contact with health agencies. Children were evacuated out of heavily bombed slums to healthy, rural areas. Conditions in heavily bombed parts of post-war Germany were more extreme and therefore, perhaps, better fields for research. Nutritionists' experiments in Wuppertal established that the degree of refinement of flour made no difference: all children who got extra bread of any kind gained height and weight equally.

THE DIETETICS OF ABUNDANCE

The game has now changed. Though distribution problems still cause famines, scientific agronomy has given us the means of conquering starvation and deprivation. In partial consequence, people in the prosperous West, at least, seem to have undergone a strange historical reversion, scouring the world for magic like the cannibals'—food that will build character or deflect adversity. You can live "disease-free with the Tao," according to Jolan Chang, on "cooked raw rice, fresh fruits and vegetables." "Civilization diseases" can be eliminated by a selective diet and the "harmony of natural forces" restored. "Food is Brahman," declare Ayurvedic cooks. "When you look at a banana or a glass of orange juice, you may not fully grasp that there is prana, or universal energy there, or that the same spirit that animates everything that lives, moves or breathes exists in food, but it's there all the same."

Eating can acquire associations with other forms of sensuality, and food can be sexually suggestive: phallic asparagus felt between fingers, the squelch and softness of the vulva-shaped mussel. Still, it is hard to know whether to take seriously people who claim to believe in aphrodisiacs. "Truffles contain the male pheromones," claims a writer who is surely teasing us, "and sexologists attribute their aphrodisiac virtues to these hormones which are identical to those contained in the male boar's saliva at the time of mating." The same source recommends lecithin, sprouts, kelp and cider vinegar as "miracle beauty foods." Celery, it is said, contains the same hormones and is best as an infusion: boil for thirty minutes and "the effects are amazing." It is hard to reconcile this recommendation with the claim that "celery has been proven to be effective for reducing blood pressure among the Chinese for many centuries."

Except by being adequately nourished there is no way to "eat to think." Yet "brain food" is seriously recommended, for instance, by a French expert in nutrition, who advises "two grams of alphalinolenic acid and ten grams of linolenic acid every day. Get to your oils and fats! . . . For apes to become humans, nature may have helped the Creator by bringing the first humans—or the last apes—close to the sea, where the alphalinolenic family is very abundant" and "for the brain you should eat brain." These nostrums are reminiscent of Bertie Wooster's conviction that phosphorus was brain food and could be found in sardines.

Abundance, perhaps because it liberates us from dependence on food for nourishment, seems to have brought about a new age of food magic. Kava—the source of the favorite ceremonial libation of the South Pacific—has a proven record as a soporific, analgesic and diuretic. Its effectiveness in these respects is consistent with its pharmacological composition. Claims that it can treat chills, promote lactation, aid convalescence, relieve gonorrhea and help with a score of other complaints have no basis except in ethnobotany. It might be thought a fair assumption that islanders who recommend it medicinally in Hawaii and Fiji know what they are talking about; yet their views are contradictory and authorize no reason to suppose that kava is generally effective or superior to other prophylactics. On the contrary, it has had a health-wrecking effect on Australian aboriginal communities where its introduction has been recent and its effects monitored, apparently contributing to short breath, weight loss, scaly complexions and increased cholesterol. Yet this substance has become one of the ingredients of the cosmetic magic kit of contemporary Western women.

Can one take seriously the nostrums of Chinese dietetics, such as celery, peanuts, garlic, jellyfish and seaweed for hypertension or, for hepatitis, malt, pork gall bladder, tea and common button mushrooms? The same source on "foods to stay young with" recommends soya to cure water retention and treat "common colds, skin diseases, beriberi, diarrhea, toxemia of pregnancy, habitual constipation, anemia and leg ulcers." The author explains that sweet potatoes can cure both constipation and diarrhea "because they are full of yin energy, which can lubricate the intestine," while figs cure dysentery and hemorrhoids and, in a recommendation baffling to scientific medicine, "tea prevents scurvy." The notion that diet should serve to preserve a balance between yin and yang is, essentially, a humoral theory: we have rejected humoral theories of Western origin, but those which come clouded with emanations of the "mystic East" manage to retain their Western adherents.

It is hard to say where quack nostrums end and science begins. Ultimately, a scientific remedy is surely only one which works, and because food is produced naturally, so that its composition and properties vary from moment to moment and place to place, scientific conditions for testing its qualities can never be guaranteed, except by a level of technical intervention repugnant to anyone who wants food from the soil rather than from the lab. Bizarre and unbalanced diets can cause disease. But most societies have eons of experience behind them and except in circumstances of convulsive social change, when traditional wisdom is forgotten or abandoned, it is most unlikely that diet causes disease. The scourge of mainstream dietetics, Dr. James LeFanu, derides a World Health Organization report of 1982: by stoking the fat scare, it actually defied the experimental results of tests which showed no link between fat consumption and heart disease. LeFanu amusingly targeted consequences in busybody dietetics: "at the Christmas buffet dance for hospital staff at Hove Town Hall in 1985, Christmas puddings, pastries, gateaux, cheese crisps and meat pies were all banned. Instead, guests could choose from a variety of pulses, salads and low-fat crisps washed down with a non-alcoholic punch." A classic study of gluttony in 1967 showed that feeding eight student volunteers more than the recommended daily intake of calories only fattened them by less than one kilogram each; and after a few days, when they had adjusted to their new diet, there was no weight gain at all. The long-term Framingham study shows that there is no difference in the fat consumption of Americans who get heart disease and those who do not. Cholesterol clogs the arteries, but two individuals will eat the same amount of cholesterol-rich food with contrasting effects. Experiments, especially the Oslo trials of 1981–84 and the Lipid Research Clinics trials, the results of which were announced in 1984, did show that a low-fat diet could lower high cholesterol levels and reduce the risk of heart disease—but most people do not have a high cholesterol level, regardless of their diet, and more than 50 percent of those with afflicted hearts do not have high cholesterol counts.

It is true that most high fat-consuming cultures, especially those where saturated fats are popular, register high levels of heart disease, whereas low consumers do not. But the exceptions are sufficient to suggest that we should be doing more work, rather than shotgunning fat. Eskimos get one hundred percent of their diet from meat and fish, most of it fat. Bushmen and pygmies get about one third of theirs from meat. Yet they have blood pressure and cholesterol levels similar to those of other foraging cultures. It is hard to resist the impression that research has slowed or stopped prematurely, because a cheap culprit has been found. The prejudices induced by the modern health cult are social as well as—perhaps, rather than—scientific: they profile an identity and constitute a common creed. To anyone independent-minded, these are grounds to question, rather than to conform.

The revolution which began with the discovery that food is for more than eating is still going on. We continually devise ways to feed for social effect: to bond with the like-minded, who eat alike; to differentiate ourselves from the outsiders who ignore our food taboos; to recraft ourselves, reshape our bodies, recast our relations with people, nature, gods. Dietitians like to cultivate a "scientific" self-image, stripped of any cultural context. But they are children of their times and legatees of long tradition: dietary obsession is a fluctuation of cultural history, a modern disease, of which no health food can cure us.

Breeding to Eat

—

The Herding Revolution:
From "Collecting" Food to "Producing" It

Mexican Armadillo (for 4) $100.00

Beaver and Beaver Tail 27.00

South American Boar................................. 18.00

Caribou 75.00

Australian Kangaroo 50.00

Muskrat.. 62.00

Porcupine.. 55.00

Ostrich Eggs.. 35.00

Water Buffalo....................................... 13.00

—MENU OF THE SPORTS AFIELD CLUB, NEW YORK, C. 1953

THE VANGUARD OF SNAILS

Snails have an established place in contemporary haute cuisine "alongside lobster and foie gras"; but their reputation with gastronomes has been checkered and their rise to their present eminence is relatively recent. It was probably only in the last century, as a result of promotion of the delights of certain rustic "regional cuisines" by Parisian restaurateurs of provincial provenance, that snails began to be rehabilitated as a delicacy after centuries of marginalization and contempt. Until the era of short rations in the Second World War, it was said that no top chef would have served them. Even now, they are underappreciated in the modern West outside France, Catalonia and some regions of Italy. Yet, together with a few other similar mollusks, they have—or ought to have—an honored place in the history of food. For they represent the key and perhaps the solution to one of the greatest mysteries of our story: why and how did the human animal begin to herd and breed other animals for food?

Snails are relatively easy to cultivate. The escargots de Bourgogne, the variety most esteemed in recent times, are bred in escargotières and carefully fed on choice herbs and milky porridge. They are an efficient food, self-packaged in a shell which serves at table as a receptacle for the garlic butter with which the dish is usually sauced. The waste is small, the nutrition excellent. Compared with the large and intractable quadrupeds who are usually claimed as the first domesticated animal food sources, snails are readily managed. Marine varieties can be gathered in a natural rock pool. Land varieties can be isolated in a designated breeding ground by enclosing a snail-rich spot with a ditch. By culling small or unfavored types by hand the primitive snail farmer would soon enjoy the benefits of selective breeding. Snails are grazers and do not need to be fed with foods which would otherwise be wanted for human consumption. They can be raised in abundance and herded without the use of fire, without any special equipment, without personal danger and without the need to select and train lead animals or dogs to help. They are close to being a complete food, useful as rations for traders' journeys, pilgrimages and campaigns. Some varieties, such as eremina, contain water for several days' travel as well as plenty of meat.

In some cultures of antiquity, snail cultivation was certainly a big business. The ancestors of our escargots de Bourgogne were packed into breeding cages in ancient Rome and stuffed with milk until they were too big for their shells. The result was a luxury specialty, available in limited quantities for gourmets and—according to the medical treatise which goes under the name of Celsus—for invalids. Snail shells are so abundant at some Mesopotamian sites that it is evident that the cultivated snail was a common item on the tables of ancient Sumer. What look like the remains of a mollusk farm about three thousand years old have been unearthed under the heart of Boston.

How much earlier can we imagine this history starting? Paleolithic shell mounds contain snail varieties bigger on average than today's equivalents. It therefore looks as though the snail eaters of the late ice age were already selecting for size. Mounds of this age and kind are so common and in some cases so large that only scholarly inhibitions stop us from assuming that they are evidence of systematic food production. It is hard to break out of the confines of a developmental, progressive model of food history which makes it unthinkable that any kind of food was farmed so early; but snail farming is so simple, so technically undemanding and so close conceptually to the habitual food-garnering methods of gatherers that it seems pigheadedly doctrinaire to exclude the possibility. The practice may be some millennia older than traditionally thought. In places where shell middens form part of a stratigraphic sequence, it is apparent that societies of snail eaters preceded settlers who relied on the more complex technologies of the hunt. At Frankhthi Cave, a precious site in the southern Argolid, a huge dump of snail shells dating from about 10,700 B.C. is overlaid by others in which the bones first of red deer predominate, then, nearly four thousand years later, tuna bones.

The importance of mollusks as probably the first creatures herded and bred by men has never been broached, much less investigated or acknowledged. So what little can be said about it has to be tentative, commended as much by reason as evidence. Snails are only part of the story, for the residue of shellfish of many kinds lies alongside them in ancient refuse heaps scattered across the world. In the history of the exploitation of marine creatures for food, it is obviously reasonable to propose that herding may have preceded hunting, for fishing is a kind of hunting which demands highly inventive technology, adjusted to an unfamiliar medium. Mollusk farming, by contrast, seems a natural extension of gathering and can be done by hand. In the great shell middens of ancient Denmark, oyster, cockle, mussel and periwinkle are the main species but there are many others, among which snails abound. A great increase in the occurrence of mollusk shells occurs in Mesolithic middens. They are scattered densely on the western shores of Europe, especially in Scandinavia, where they have survived undisturbed, and along almost the entire length of the Pacific shores of the Americas. There are particularly spectacular concentrations in Scotland (at Oban and Larne), in Brittany, at sites associated with the North African culture known as Capsian, in California and near the Iberian coast in Asturias and the Tagus valley. The shells are piled beside freshwater breeding grounds all over the world. Oysters have a conspicuous place in this context. Oyster beds are not necessarily associated with anything one could reasonably call "oyster domestication" and even artificial beds do not necessarily imply selective breeding: but there seem to have been big increases in oyster consumption and therefore, presumably, impressive improvements in oyster-gathering techniques in the Mesolithic era. Off the coast of Senegal, at Lake Diana in Corsica and at Saint-Michel-en-l'Herme in the Vendée, there are islands formed entirely of discarded oyster shells, which are still growing in a sea rich in natural oyster beds. A mound of shells in Maine is estimated at seven million bushels.

The increase in the rate of accumulation at many of these sites, usually between about six and eight thousand years ago, represents an undetected revolution in the history of food. The assumption usually made by historians is that an increase in the consumption of mollusks can only be explained by a shortage of bigger game. But small, easily managed creatures had considerable advantages over big game, provided they could be supplied in large quantities. Archaeologists label mollusks as a "gathered" food, but where they were eaten in huge quantities it will make better sense, in some cases, to think of them as being systematically farmed.

It offends heroic and romantic sensibilities to imagine a great revolution led by snails. Yet, after cooking, the beginnings of systematic food production surely constitute the biggest food-connected innovation in the history of our species. The story of how it happened has traditionally been divided into two strands, both characterized by a progressive model: agriculture and the scientific improvement of plant food species are conventionally classed as growths from gathering; while herding and stock breeding are treated as developments from hunting. These are marginally misleading traditions: some kinds of farming and stock breeding are probably older than some kinds of hunting; mollusk farming is a kind of herding which is closer to gathering practices than anything which can fairly be called hunting. And sedentary farming communities can acquire domestic animals by means unconnected with the hunt: by weaning strays or by attracting scavengers to their settlements. Farmers may then develop the breeds which suit sedentarists' purposes: some species might be refined for pest control. Others are useful as natural "food processors": ruminants and foragers can turn energy sources which humans cannot consume directly—such as tough or unpalatable leaves and kitchen waste—into the human food we call meat. They could be used as a "walking larder" for times of crop failure. Still the traditional classifications make sense, because they split foods into two recognizably distinct categories, which, on the understanding that their stories are interdependent, can be tackled in turn: first, creatures; then, in the next chapter, plants.

TO BREED OR NOT TO BREED?

The origins of herding and of its almost invariable consequence—selective stock breeding—have been shrouded in myth and false assumptions. Herding has been classified as an extraordinary development in historical ecology, which could not have happened independently in more than a very few places. If it is now found almost everywhere in the world, that must—according to traditional reasoning—be a result of diffusion: a practice initiated in one place, or a very limited number of places, by a stroke of accident or genius, then radiated across the world, transmitted by migration or war or trade. This kind of reasoning is still popular in scholarship but it really belongs to the mental tool kit of a bygone age. Diffusionism as a philosophy arose among intellectual elites committed to hierarchical models of the world. Only people peculiarly favored by God or nature could initiate great ideas. Other people—less intelligent or less evolved—could only progress by learning from their betters. The idea appealed in a world dominated, in the late nineteenth and early twentieth centuries, by white men's empires, whose justification was that they were spreading the benefits of their own innovations to lesser breeds. It seemed convincing in a world of scholarship dominated by traditions of classical humanism and schooled in the tracing of the transmission of texts. Since cultural developments really do spread by diffusion from a single original source and the same models, the same techniques of research got transferred to other disciplines.

Yet there is an alternative way of approaching problems like the one before us. The fact that herding is commonplace might equally well be seen as evidence that it is not extraordinary at all, but something which comes easily, almost, one might say, naturally, as humans and other animals coevolve. The species we domesticate are those with which we have a relationship of interdependence. We use them for food, for suppression of vermin or for entertainment or help in the hunt, work or war. In exchange, we feed them and protect them from predators. These are relationships as intimate and, in a sense, natural, as those which link lice or macrobial parasites with their hosts, or seagulls with fishermen or, as we shall see in the next chapter, cultivars with cultivators. Gathering, hunting and herding, which are usually arranged progressively—placed one after the other in our conventional chronologies of prehistoric change—were really complementary techniques of obtaining food, which developed together.

Many hunting cultures do not just accept the bounty of nature. They drive herds where they want them, sometimes constructing drive lanes for the purpose and penning or corraling the catch: this is already a form of herding. Or they produce food by wielding fire to manage the environment. This was the method by which most Native American peoples of the Northeastern woodlands supplied their larders before European settlers arrived. In woodland thinned by periodic blazes, hunters could move freely and the species they favored for the pot, such as elk, deer, beaver, hare, porcupine, turkey, quail and grouse were encouraged. For the same reason, early European beholders of Australia were astonished by the vast fires they saw rising from the shore: over most of the continent, the aborigines managed the habitat of the kangaroo by this means. Although some hunting communities prefer not to pursue such techniques to the point where they become the permanent custodians of the herds, these hunting methods clearly belong to a continuum which includes pastoralism. Whether to take the process further and become full-time managers of flocks is a decision which depends on a balance of considerations: if the supply of animals for the hunt is plentiful, the extra trouble of undertaking pastoralism may not be worthwhile. The great benefit of undertaking that extra trouble is that it facilitates selective breeding and gives the community disposal of animals of the exact description to meet their requirements or their tastes, though a similar, if slower, effect, can be achieved by culling unfavored specimens during the hunt. Once herding happens, selective breeding follows.

Charles Darwin pondered these problems while he was working toward the theory of evolution. His studies of stockbreeders' methods gave him the key to how nature might work, analogously to a breeder, selecting specimens with appropriate qualities for the competition to survive. At an early stage of his work, he assumed that systematic breeding was a late development of a progressive past: the ascent of man to an ever-higher state of civilization. Partly, this assumption arose from his conviction—the orthodoxy, indeed, of his times—that all history is progressive and that human "primitives" were of modest capacities. Partly, too, it was because he revered that stockbreeders' craft and thought of it as arcane and hard of access—conceptually elusive, practically demanding. Darwin did not expect what he called "semi-civilized and savage peoples" to be well versed in breeding technique. Yet many examples arose to surprise him in the course of his researches. The Tuaregs' camels, he acknowledged, "can boast a genealogy far longer than the descendants of the Darley Arabian." Mongols bred white-tailed yaks for sale to China as providers of fly whisks. The Ostyaks and some Eskimos favored dogs with uniform coats and the Damara in Southern Africa bred their cattle for the same effect. Generally in Southern Africa, Darwin found, "the power of discrimination which these savages possess is wonderful, and they can recognize to which tribe any cattle belong." The Turuma Indians of Guiana jealously selected the best bitches to mate with the best of their dogs and kept two varieties of purely ornamental fowl. "Hardly any nation," according to Darwin, "is more barbarous than the Fuegians, but I hear from Mr. Bridges, the catechist to the Mission, that when these savages have a large, strong and active bitch, they take care to put her to a fine dog, and even take care to feed her well, that her young may be strong and well favored." "The most curious case" which came to Darwin's attention was recorded by the Inca Garcilaso de la Vega, who claimed that the Inca regularly selected the best specimens from their deer hunts to release back into the wild with the aim of improving the breed, "so that the Incas followed exactly the reverse system of that which our Scottish sportsmen are accused of following, namely, of steadily killing the finest stags, thus causing the whole race to degenerate."

This evidence compelled Darwin to revise his estimate of the place of systematic stock breeding in history. It was an early and very widespread innovation.

The commonest purpose for stock breeding is as food production. It can start in a number of ways; but hunting is certainly one of them. It is tempting to imagine a phase of human history prior to hunting, when hominids and early humans fed like vultures, gathered around the detritus of better predators' meals, or around the bones of animals dead from disease or senectitude. But the debate in food historiography over the difference between hunting and scavenging has been ill conceived. Most predatory animals do both. The significant distinction is between seeking live prey and dead. Only from live specimens can food be bred. Some easily garnered species are seized alive as they crawl the earth or get trapped in rock pools. Others can be drawn into a close relationship with people by mutual attraction. Some can be trapped in the course of the hunt, but this is certainly an unusual way for domestication to begin. Stock breeding rarely, if ever, develops in cultures which depend on hunting unless an intermediate herding phase occurs—which happens frequently, though not universally. In some respects, it is surprising that it ever happens at all.

Hunting is an attractive way of life, which still exercises a romantic appeal for some people in sedentary and even urban societies: thousands of years of civilization seem insufficient to scratch out the savage under the skin of executives, for instance, whose leisure is best spent on a big-game hunt or remote trout stream, or of their employees who go bass fishing or deer hunting. The exhilaration of the chase was expressed by a J. M. Barrie character—a pampered aristocrat liberated by a shipwreck which forced her back to "nature":

> LADY MARY: . . . I sighted a herd near Penguin's Creek, but had to creep
> round Silver Lake to get windward of them. However, they spotted me
> and then the fun began. There was nothing for it but to try and run them
> down, so I singled out a fat buck and away we went down the shore of the
> lake, up the valley of rolling stones; he . . . took to the water, but I swam
> after him; the river is only a mile broad there, but it runs strong. He went
> spinning down the rapids, down I went in pursuit; he clambered ashore, I
> clambered ashore; away we tore helter-skelter up the hill and down again.
> I lost him in the marshes, got on his track again . . . and brought him
> down with an arrow in Firefly Grove.
> TWEENY (staring at her): Aren't you tired?
> LADY MARY: Tired! It was gorgeous.

The fact that people in hunting cultures depend on it for their livelihood never seems to reduce the hunt to the level of routine work. Its challenges are relished, its magic magnetic, even where it is utterly familiar. The inspiration it has provided for rock art shows how it dominates imaginations in societies which live by it. In some ways, it is a highly efficient way of getting food. Effective hunting delivers abundance. "How I should love to be the jaguar's daughter!" exclaims a heroine in a myth of the Opaye of the Matto Grosso. "I should get all the meat I wanted."

Hunting economizes on the costs of rearing animals and laboring in fields. It directs effort efficiently by exploiting the relatively few and modest skills men are naturally good at compared with other species: using brainpower to anticipate and even influence the behavior of victim-species, taking aim, hurling a missile. Throwing power can be hugely enhanced by relatively simple technologies, like those of the boomerang, blowgun, spear-thrower and—at a relatively sophisticated stage of technical change, probably not more than twenty thousand years ago—the bow. Controlled fire can be used to stampede and channel prey. Funnel-shaped lanes—of the kind depicted in Paleolithic art and replicated in modern times in Australia, Siberia and America—can be formed from cairns or posts to maneuver animals into traps. Cliffsides or artificial pits can be used as lethal chutes down which creatures are harried to death or bogs exploited to bring them to a sticky end. Or strong or swift creatures can be trained to compensate for the physical inadequacies of the huntsman: dogs, leopards, hawks. In the right conditions of balance between the availability of game and the numbers of mouths to be fed, hunting cultures of the past found entirely satisfactory ways of keeping people well nourished, without adopting pastoral or agricultural methods of food production. Analysis of Paleolithic remains shows impressive nutritional profiles: intakes typically of three thousand calories a day, of which meat supplied about a third. Hunter-gatherers of the ice age ate about five pounds of food a day, of which nearly two pounds were meat. Though most of them enjoyed little salt, their diets were generally high in calcium; because of the nature of the plant foods they ate— few starchy grains, relatively large amounts of fruits and wild tubers—and because of the concentration of ascorbic acid in organ meats, they had five times a modern American's average intake of vitamin C.

Yet in some ways hunting is a costly and wasteful way of getting food. Even the apparently simple tools of the hunt are harder to devise and costlier to make than the ditches, swiddens, fences, dibbling sticks and panniers which were all that early pastoralists and agriculturists needed. Trained animals can be very demanding. Except for dogs, they are troublesome to acquire and time-consuming to train. And while dogs are, no doubt, worthy of their hire, they still have to be "paid" with food doles. Sometimes, they rival humans for status. This is apparent, for instance, in the graveyard of a hunting community of the end of the last great ice age. They followed the herds of deer and aurochs north to Skateholm on the Baltic, where their bones now lie. Their dogs occupy adjoining graves: burly, wolflike hunters, buried with the spoils of their careers, including antlers and boars' tusks, sometimes with more signs of honor than attend human burials. These dogs were full members of societies in which status was determined by hunting prowess: dogs who were leaders of men. Today such real-life animal heroes are only encountered in children's storybooks.

Weapons and dogs are the investment capital of hunters. When these ensure worthwhile returns, another set of problems intrudes. Overexploitation is a common hazard of hunting, because hunting cultures tend to be competitive: there is no point in conserving game to be killed by a rival. In any case, even where the need for conservation is pressing, it is hard to calculate the right levels of prey to maintain. Although a popular, romantic and primitivist view of hunting peoples credits them with ecological sensitivity and conservation strategies, these are really rather unusual. In most hunting cultures, the habit of overkill recurs. It is extremely hard to kill just what you need; large quadrupeds with the big fat resources hunters most need only come in one size: big. The hunting methods available at most times and in most places in the course of history have involved immolating large numbers of them in falls or pits. Ironically, the high kill rates are the result of the difficulty of hunting formidable creatures: the harder they are to fell individually, the more likely they are to end up in hecatombs. This generates more food than is needed and wastes the breeding stock of the creatures the huntsman relies on. Whole herds can get wiped out in one swoop. The bones of ten thousand horses lie where Paleolithic hunters drove them over a cliff near Solutré. Remains of a hundred mammoths have turned up in pits at a site in the Czech Republic. Big species are more vulnerable to extinction by hunters because they reproduce slowly and, above all, because they are hard to manage. It is difficult to be selective with creatures so elusive or dangerous that any chance of a kill seems irresistible.

The myth of Native Americans' talent for conservationism before the arrival of the white man is belied by the evidence of the scale of their slaughters. In fact, in much of North America, their methods were outrageously wasteful. Puzzlingly underused kills of American bison lie heaped where prehistoric hunters drove them over cliffs, with only bits and pieces of them butchered for food. This suggests that waste was acceptable to the hunters on a scale so enormous that it might have threatened long-term supply. At caribou hunts of the Hudson Bay Inuit, observed in the late nineteenth century, the hunters deliberately set out to slaughter whole herds, leaving, on occasion, hundreds of carcasses to rot—presumably with the intention of denying them to their enemies. Some tribes, who depended on other, frailer species did adopt self-imposed quotas. The Shoshone conserved their deer stocks. If bison survived, it was not because they were rationally conserved but because they were too abundant to exterminate. They were saved by the hunters' inefficiency and the inadequacy of the available technology: in part, this was because the hunters had no horses, which had disappeared from the New World some ten thousand years ago, during an extinction in which human depredations probably played a big part.

Indeed, in many parts of the world, the disappearance of numerous species which were the prey of man in the "great Pleistocene extinction" probably owed something, at least, to hunters' prodigality: most of the large fauna of the Western Hemisphere and Australia disappeared completely, while the Old World lost its biggest elephants—partly, perhaps, to hunters hungry for fat. Remains of mammoths killed in this era are still found with spearheads imbedded—up to eight spearheads to a beast. Numerous kinds of deer vanished, presumably to overkill. Lack of restraint in hunting species to extinction is not a peculiar vice of peoples afflicted with improvidence: it is a human characteristic. In all sorts of environments, the arrival of humans has been followed by species extinctions. The megafauna of Australasia vanished soon after the arrival of human hunters: the diprodont and the giant kangaroo, flightless birds four times as big as a man, a one-ton lizard. Later victims include the moa of New Zealand, which the Maori hunted to extinction, the Hawaiian goose, the dodo.

Hunters who forgo the technology of overkill are left pursuing a laborious quest, singling out target animals, tracking them at great cost in time and effort in the manner Barrie imagined for Lady Mary Lasenby. The energy expended by Bushmen in the hunt seems so terrible that it appears impossible that the meal which awaits at the end of the process could be worthwhile: it seems at odds with the "optimal foraging strategy" which hunting peoples are supposed to pursue to minimize the waste of energy on elusive game. Laurens van der Post accompanied a band of hunters in search of eland. One morning, they found the tracks of a herd just after sunrise. By three in the afternoon, after a nonstop pursuit at the trot, they came on the herd and loosed their arrows. The real hunt had not yet begun. To fell large game at a venture is almost impossible with a Bushman's bow. His preferred method is to wound the beast with a poisoned barb and follow it, until it drops with exhaustion and the effects of the drug, before administering a coup de grâce. The arrows are made in two stages: the tip sticks in the target; the haft falls to the ground to tell the marksman that he has scored a hit, even if no blood is shed. The wound slows the beast down so that the hunters can track it but it may be a long, arduous chase, with the hunters on short rations, before the contest ends. On the occasion van der Post described, the prey ran off so fast that there was no time to check whether a shot had gone home. The Bushmen resumed the chase, this time at a fast run. "Their minds were entirely enclosed in the chase and impervious to fatigue or other claims on their senses." They ran for twelve miles without stopping "and the final mile was an all-out sprint." The next time they made contact with the herd, one bull was seen to be tiring. It still took another full hour to harry him to a halt. "Hardly was he dead than Nxou and Bauxhau started skinning the bull. That was the amazing part of the chase: without pause or break for rest they were fresh enough at the end to plunge straight away into the formidable task of skinning and cutting up the heavy animal." And they still had to trek home before the feast and the dance could begin. Bushmen who persist with this taxing way of life to this day are obviously pursuing a commitment which has grown out of generations of invested emotion. Cultural capital is tied down in practices that would be heart-wrenching to change for the mere sake of material gain.

Most hunting communities try to control or eliminate these problems by devising ways of managing their game. A number of means of management fall short of herding. The simplest recourse is to make hunting seasonal, selecting the times when flocks are fattest or most prolific or when breeding will be undisturbed. In some cases, the seasonal rhythm of hunting is determined by the life cycle of the victim: there is little point, for instance, in killing caribou except at the approach of winter when their coats are thickest and their meat most thickly layered with fat. In others, the determining factor is the ecology of the animals' environment: when they are most densely concentrated for feeding the yield from the hunt is likely to be most bountiful. Occasionally, the annual cycle of human activity may be paramount. The Piute of the American West hunt antelope, sheep and deer in the fall, when they gather for the harvest, because their communal hunting methods demand concentrated labor. Commonly, the incidence of rain decides the frequency of the hunt, where grass fires are used to drive and direct animals to the killing grounds. The use of fire is a further and frequent method of game control. Fire promotes grazing in places selected for hunters' convenience and concentrates prey in accessible areas. This is not far removed conceptually from herding. Game reserves and, in societies with state organizations strong enough to enforce them, royal parks and forests can be preserved as privileged hunting environments. Here the kingly and aristocratic hunt was performed, not for food but as a rite of social differentiation, a display of conspicuous consumption and a reminder, perhaps, of the right of dominance of the man on horseback.

THE HERDING INSTINCT

Some animals are naturally gregarious and the hunter has no need to become a professional herdsman. All he has to do is follow the flocks. Who, in these cases, is the herder and who the herded? The flocks lead men, not the other way around. The first European invaders of the American prairie found people whose dependence on the American bison was absolute. The inhabitants ate virtually nothing but buffalo, wore buffalo hides tied with thongs of buffalo leather. They sheltered under buffalo skin tents. The earliest surviving account of life on the plains, written by one of the Spanish riders who reached Kansas in 1540, describes a classic meal of hunting cultures. When a buffalo was killed, the hunters slit the belly, squeezed out the half-digested grass and drank the juices "because they say that this contains the essence of the stomach." When they turned to the flesh they would grip a raw joint between one hand and their teeth and slice off mouthfuls, "swallowing it half-chewed, like birds. They would eat raw fat without warming it, empty a large gut and fill it with blood . . . to drink when they are thirsty." The only viable way of life was abject transhumance, the only possible culture a highly portable one. Wood was rare and precious and beasts of burden nonexistent; so transport was by light stick frames, piled with belongings and dragged by hand. Many goods had to be bundled and carried underarm.

Yet even the most slavish followers of herds intervene to direct the creatures' paths when it is time for the hunt by driving and stampeding them and channeling their movement, or cutting out specimens for slaughter. As these techniques multiply, the relationship between the species changes and men become managers of the animals' movements. Species with a herd instinct lend themselves to more intensive forms of management. Provided the terrain and other aspects of the environment are amenable, and men have means of keeping up with the herds, huntsmen can become herders and lead flocks of creatures where they wish. This becomes a particularly attractive option if dogs are available to help with the roundup or if lead animals can be trained to marshal the flocks. The most commonly herded species of cattle, sheep and goats are all distinguished from other animals by these qualities. It is not always easy to draw the line between a herding culture and a culture which hunts herds.

A middle case—midway, that is, between hunting and herding, which shows how one can be transformed into the other—is that of reindeer management in

Northern Europe. Like its American cousin, the caribou, the reindeer has been a favored food of man since the archaeological record began. Reindeer hunger drew hunting peoples north into Arctic Europe at the end of the last great ice age. Growth in the importance of reindeer as a resource can be traced over a period of more than three thousand years. In parts of the tundra, taiga and forest edge, men and reindeer between them gradually became so dominant in the ecosystem as to develop an effective duopoly, in which people had little else to live on. Various ways of exploiting the reindeer were practiced together for centuries: hunting in the wild was combined with the practice of taming selected individual beasts. At the same time the migrations of certain herds could be regulated.

What one might call controlled nomadism gradually prevailed, or a combination of a normally transhumant life, with excursions into nomadism as circumstances demanded. Like the cattle of America's Wild West, reindeer have a strong herd instinct; so they, too, can be left wild for long periods, rounded up at will and led or followed to new grazing. Compared with the big quadrupeds of the Arctic New World, European reindeer, even in the tundra, rely on relatively short migrations, usually of little more than two hundred miles. A tame male can be used as a decoy to pen an entire herd; and collaboration with man is an advantage in the search for grazing: the reindeer acquire the services of useful scouts and allies against wolves and wolverines. The herders light fires to protect their reindeer from the mosquitoes that plague them in summer. On the ocean's edge, Nenets have even been said to share their fish, for which reindeer can develop a surprising appetite. Or, in a less intense form of management, between pennings, the reindeer could be allowed to seek their seasonal haunts for themselves, with their human and canine parasites following. Large-scale herding is entirely an activity of the tundra, where the reindeer are the essential means of life; the forest dwellers breed only small numbers, which they use as draft animals and as supplementary elements in a varied diet; they move camp within only a narrow range—never more than fifty miles or so in a year; and they leave their deer to forage unsupervised, rounding them up only at need. Traditional tundra dwellers, by contrast, are inseparable from their reindeer. They have nothing else to keep them alive.

The practice of reindeer herding was well established by the ninth century A.D., when the Norwegian ambassador, Othere, boasted to King Alfred of his own herd, six hundred strong. Since then, the documented rhythms of the herding life have never varied: every year, the first migration, led by a tame stag and policed by dogs, occurs in spring. Summer is passed in breeding grounds; autumn, including the rutting season in October, is spent in an intermediate camp before the cull and the move to winter quarters. Herds thousands of head strong have been common in modern times. Only two or three herdsmen, with the help of dogs, can look after two thousand reindeer. As long as they are available in sufficient numbers, reindeer provide virtually all that is needed for life: indeed, *jil'ep,* the Nenet name for them, means "life." They bear burdens and drag sleighs—the best team leaders are castrated, preferably, according to Sami traditions, by a man who rips off their testicles with his teeth. They are slaughtered for their warm skins and their versatile bones and sinews, which make, respectively, tool heads and thongs. But their main role is as food. Their blood and marrow give instant infusions of energy; their spring horns, while young and gristly, constitute a feast. Reindeer meat, which can be preserved with ease by natural drying or freezing, is staple fare. Nowadays, it is one of the luxuries of Scandinavian city restaurants and the foundation of the fortunes of the Sami millionaires of whom stories are told around dinner tables in Helsinki and Oslo.

Compared with reindeer, the bovine herds which rolled across the American plains in the cowboy era were just one notch or so further along the scale of domestication. Writing in the early 1920s, James H. Cook described his years in the saddle, driving decoy herds to mingle with the wild cattle, riding around and around them, singing the "Texas lullaby," which, he claimed, had a calming effect on the unbroken steers. The "singing cowboy" is not an entirely monstrous invention of the entertainment industry. Stampedes were an occupational hazard and the only way to catch a cow once one had started was to trap it with a lasso; or failing that the cowboy could "catch it by the tail with his hand, and taking a turn around the saddle horse, dash suddenly ahead, causing the steer to turn a somersault." The horse then came to a sudden stop, and the rider jumped off and with one of the short "tie-ropes" which he always carried under his belt, "hog-tied the . . . brute. . . . When brought to bay by this treatment, their rage would be such that it . . . would be horns versus pistol if a strong animal regained his feet before his pursuer could tie it down." When the fallen beast's legs were thoroughly benumbed and stiffened, it could be surrounded with tame cows and released. If that didn't work, the captive would be felled again and tied by the neck to a tame old ox who would drag it to the corral.

To give up hunting in favor of herding is always a mixed blessing. Animal company can be bad for you. The herdsmen's stocks are reservoirs of infection. On Columbus's second transatlantic expedition, it was probably pigs and horses, not people in the first instance, that took, to the New World from the old, the diseases that began the precipitate collapse of Native American populations. Even in the twentieth century, the influenza virus incubated in ducks in China, "while pigs served as the 'mixing vessel' in which avian and human flu viruses exchange genes."

Nevertheless, peoples who make the transition from hunting to herding have the advantage of reliable access to food and, in some respects, an enhanced cuisine. Even herds reared by long-range transhumance, which tends to bring old, tough animals to the table, gives herders prospects of a better meal than their hunting counterparts. Not only can the herdsman breed for the table: he can pick on a particularly appetizing specimen, elevating a meal or dish to special status. He can isolate individual beasts for fattening on a milk-rich diet or the finest grasses. He can cull choice young animals for the pot and create triumphs of cruel gastronomy, like the baby beef of the gauchos or the Wyoming cattleman's sonofabitch stew based on the organ meats and brains of an unweaned calf, flavored with the milky, partially digested contents of the tube—lined with a filter of the consistency of marrow fat—which connects the beast's two stomachs.

In the gastronomy of sedentary cultures, wild game or mature animals from herdsmen's stock are always hung before cooking so that bacterial degradation can work away at the meat and soften the muscle: the process is made to last for up to three weeks in the case of venison compared with three days in the case of farmed beef. Joints can be consumed, according to need or taste, at different stages of what is best described as decomposition, though generally sold to consumers as "aging." Although accounts of the cuisine of hunting and herding cultures emphasize freshly slaughtered meat, it seems likely, in view of the prevalence of overkill in the historic profiles of hunting peoples, that the flavor of rot must always have been familiar to their palates. "Aging," as butchers now call it, begins as soon as the beast is dead. Myoglobin, which maintains oxygen in the muscles, degenerates into metamyoglobin: this process is a slow form of a similar process which continues during cooking. The meat begins to acquire a brown color, resembling its cooked state. Enzymes act on the muscles, making the meat tender. Finally, bacteria get to work, effectively devouring collagen. If "gaminess" is favored by modern gourmets it is presumably because genuinely hunted food has become an expensive rarity in urban society: a savor which would be deprecated in farmed foods is a guarantee of authenticity and a tincture of adventure when encountered in the products of the hunt. Acidic fruits have a tenderizing effect on fresh game—which is why so many recipes combine huntsman's meats with sauces based on the fruits of the animals' habitats. Reindeer is traditionally appropriate with cloudberries, boar with prunes, hare with juniper berries or in the sharp sauce Italians call agrodolce. In England, roast or grilled venison is customarily served with a wonderful concoction called Cumberland sauce, which is based on redcurrants, but succumbs to self-conscious sophistication by admitting added orange peel and port. The English habit of serving pork with applesauce perpetuates a style of serving originally devised for wild boar. As a general rule, the wilder the meat the leaner, so that most sedentarists' recipes for game or for herdsmen's stock call for barding with fat from domesticates. Among reindeer gourmets, for instance, rages an irresoluble dispute over whether pork fat should be added to stews. In other respects—except for obvious differences of emphasis that arise from the facts that most hunters and herders are transhumant and cannot be bothered with a lot of heavy cooking apparatus—there is nothing peculiar about herding and hunting cuisines.

Why are some hunted animals domesticated and not others? It is often claimed that some species simply cannot be domesticated but it seems more likely that those left to run wild are exempted for other reasons arising from the culture of the hunters or from the nature of the environment they inhabit. Kangaroos could be herded if people really wanted to manage them by that method. Some are easily tamed. A friend of mine had a pet kangaroo when he was a boy. After release into the wild, the kangaroo often returned to visit him, climbed the steps and knocked on his bedroom door. Docile specimens could be captured in their prime or reared from babyhood as breeding stock. Or the management methods traditionally used by aborigines in some parts of Australia, which include the use of fire to control the kangaroos' grazing areas, making them accessible for the hunters, could be extended or developed to the point where totally managed herds were being manipulated by man. The zebra is another creature that seems disinclined to submit to human control. Most zebras defend themselves viciously. But in medieval Abyssinia the Negus had a zebra-drawn chariot and even so rebarbative a species produces animals of varying degrees of intractability: selection of suitable specimens could, in the course of a few generations, result in a domestic breed.

Bighorn sheep were hunted in prehistoric times in what is now Wyoming by being driven into wooden catch pens, where they were clubbed to death. But this technique was never extended in full domestication, even though—to judge from their modern descendants—these animals were probably submissive on capture. The only explanation which suggests itself is that the habitat of these sheep was at a higher altitude than that of the hunters, who were willing to make seasonal forays into the mountains but not to adapt permanently to a milieu suitable for a pastoral life.

The last and biggest difference herding made was by bringing dairying into the range of food production techniques. This seems not only to have introduced a galaxy of new foodstuffs to the diets of peoples who used them but also to have had an effect on human evolution. In most hunting cultures people are not just indifferent to dairy products: they actively dislike them and in many cases the metabolism rejects them. Lactose intolerance is a condition of many cultures.

Indeed, the ability to digest animal milk is a physical peculiarity of Europeans, North Americans, Indians and peoples of Central Asia and the Middle East. Most people elsewhere in the world do not naturally produce lactase—the substance which makes milk digestible—after infancy. In many parts of the world where livestock has been herded and farmed for centuries and even millennia, it is still normal for most people to respond to dairy products with distaste or even intolerance. Dairy products do not feature in Chinese cuisine: milk, butter, cream and even such preparations as yogurt and buttermilk, which are digestible without the aid of lactase, are despised barbarian flavors. The Japanese reject them and one of the distasteful features of early European visitors to Japan was that in local nostrils they "stank of butter." In 1962, when 88 million pounds of powdered milk arrived in Brazil as American food aid, it made people feel ill. Marvin Harris, who was there at the time, found that American officials responded with resentment and blamed locals for "eating the powder raw by the fistful" or "mixing it with polluted water." Really, they were just unused to it. Brazilian ranching has always specialized in meat, not milk.

I find the very idea of drinking unmodified milk disgusting; and the way butter is prized for frying is one of the features of North European civilization to which a lifetime's effort has failed to reconcile me. For similar reasons of personal prejudice, I find it hard to understand why, in parts of the Middle East where olive oil is available, sheep's butter is regarded as the finest lubricant for dishes of boiled rice or buckwheat: this seems to me a throwback to the herdsmen's prejudices introduced centuries ago into the cuisines of the region by pastoralists of the Arabian desert and Eurasian steppe. It must be acknowledged, however, that some of the greatest triumphs of world gastronomy have been achieved in the course of the struggle to make milk digestible. They are called cheese and are produced by allowing or promoting the growth of bacteria in milk, then extracting the solids which form as the fats and proteins in the milk separate and coagulate. The flavor, color and consistency of the cheese all depend on the kinds of bacteria involved and, to a lesser extent, on the nature of the cheesemakers' interventions to promote curdling. The possible combinations are innumerable—perhaps infinite. New cheeses are being invented all the time.

When and how did the first come into being? Neither question can be answered in the present state of knowledge: cheese making is documented in rock art from the seventh millennium B.C. and in the archaeological record from the fourth at least. It can be presumed to be of greater antiquity still. I have a conceit which I find irresistible: the history of hunting and herding is reenacted in cheese. In a phase corresponding to the hunt, exposed milk is left as a trap for bacteria gathered at random. The discovery follows that certain beneficial effects can be guaranteed by regulating the conditions under which milk is left to sour: in effect, this means that particular bacteria are being "herded." Nowadays, mass production delivers a substance which hardly seems worthy of the name of cheese: pasteurization destroys the relevant bacteria at the start of the process and the desired effects are engineered instead by the introduction of selected cultures.

THE SEABORNE HUNT

Wild food is getting hard to come by. In the United States, supposedly the land of abundance, it is impossible to get game except from a handful of highly specialized shops which do not exist even in major centers of population. A German acquaintance of mine who proposed serving Hasenpfeffer to friends in Philadelphia had to travel to New York to get hare. Even game still widely hunted in the States, like wild turkey, or culled for conservation reasons, like venison and bear, can rarely be bought and, for most people, remains unsampled outside a small clutch of smart restaurants. Even in Europe, traditional wild foods like venison and rabbit have been largely replaced by domesticated versions. Grouse and pheasant moors are now so intensively managed that the gamekeepers really ought to be reclassified as farmers.

Hunting is now thought of as a primitive way of getting food, long abandoned except as an aristocratic indulgence, or leisure for those inclined to blood lust. This is an utterly mistaken view. The world's food supply still depends on hunting, almost as much today as in the era which preceded the "Neolithic revolution" and the intensification of agriculture. The amount of food yielded by the hunt has increased in the twentieth century—by an informed guess—by a factor of nearly forty and the twentieth century may go down in history not only as the last age of hunting but as the greatest. I am speaking, of course, of a relatively specialized and—today—highly mechanized form of hunt: the hunt for fish.

Fishing really is a form of hunting. The huge increase in the demand for fish in the recent history of the developed West seems to have become associated in most people's minds with the contemporary health obsessions discussed in the last chapter. I suspect, however, that the spectacular increase in demand for fish in the rich West is the result of a romantic prejudice in favor of the last major food yielded by a kind of hunt. If we fail to classify it readily as a hunt, it is only because of deceptive appearances. Fishing is obviously not hunting of the same kind as is practiced on land in the kind of agrarian and industrial societies which, overwhelmingly, prevail in the modern world. Fishing, in most cultures, is a modest occupation with none of the aristocratic savor of the chase through the forest or the shoot on the moor, the hawk's swoop or the uncaged leopard's leap. But, until recently, in traditional societies of what is now western Canada and the North-western United States, chiefly canoes, manned for the hunt, specialized in the tracking of dangerous sea creatures, including whales and large sharks. Scenes painted on ceremonial robes in the eighteenth and nineteenth centuries show speared behemoths dueling with the hunters. Among the ancient Moche of what is now Peru, the marlin hunt had enough prestige to be worth depicting in art. Today, trawling remains a form of hunting which still makes a major contribution to food resources worldwide. It has become a matter of routine, but remains steeped in its own rituals. It has become unheroic but it remains a quest. The fish have to be chased by the trawlermen. If the weather turns bad, the prey can escape. Sometimes the hunters lose their lives.

Like terrestrial hunting grounds, fisheries always tend to be overexploited. The only rational strategy for fishermen is to net as much as you can before a competitor beats you to it. The romantic image of the fisherman, most vividly and recently depicted in Sebastian Junger's bestseller *The Perfect Storm*, risking life, defying the elements, obsessive about his vocation, unremitting in the pursuit of his catch, is underlain by hardheaded realism. The impossibility of policing the seas effectively compounds the problem. The yield of the seas has increased nearly fortyfold in the twentieth century: the three billion tons landed, by John McNeill's calculations, exceed the entire catch of all previous centuries combined. The use of fish meal in fertilizers and animal feed makes fish a critical source of nourishment for the world, far in excess of the tonnage eaten by people. The litany of vanished and vanishing fisheries of the twentieth century can be explained by climatic change and the fluctuating migration patterns of fish, but overfishing is almost certainly the biggest and most pervasive cause. The Maine lobster—once so plentiful that early settlers caught them in abundance by reaching into the water at the edge of the shore—was regulated for conservation from the 1870s but the catch plunged from about 24 million pounds per annum to less than six million in 1913. The current revival is spectacular but insecure. Canada closed down its cod fishery in 1996 and Atlantic cod stocks are now believed to stand at only 10 percent of their historic average. Californian sardines and North Sea herrings have become rarities since the 1960s. The Japanese pilchard fishery was the world's largest in the 1930s—the Japanese pilchard is a variety of sardine, *Sardinops melanosticus*—but was fished almost to extinction by 1994, while the Namibian catch fell from half a million tons in 1965 to zero in 1980.

On land, when the supply of a hunted creature becomes critically low, one solution is to herd it: catch specimens, corral or concentrate them and breed from them. The corresponding method for fish is pisciculture or aquaculture: fish "farming," as it is called. It is really more closely analogous to herding terrestrial livestock than cultivating plants, though the term "farming" is justified by such usages as "pig farming" and "chicken farming," particularly as the fish producers deploy intensive practices which bring yields even more spectacular than those of the most efficient battery methods for pork or poultry. Fish farming at sea has become a focus of hopes and fears for the future. In order to be commercially viable, fishing has to be predictable and concentrated in particular places. Almost all existing fisheries are coastal, confined to continental shelves where fish can feed, and their locations are determined by migration routes the fish choose for themselves: these can change—and, indeed, are changing now as climate fluctuates. However, nearly half of the world's marine food supply is caught in five areas: in the African Atlantic off Namibia and along a stretch of coast south of the Canary Islands, in the Indian Ocean off Somalia, and in the Pacific off California and Peru. Here the continental shelves fall away rapidly or the coasts dive clifflike into the ocean. Strong, persistent prevailing winds shoo the surface water away while cold currents well up, renewing a rich supply of nutrients which attract the fish. On the coast of Peru the anchovies are sometimes so thick that women and children can scoop them up by the hatful. Conditions like these are not easy to reproduce artificially.

Nevertheless, wherever fish farming can replace fish hunting it is bound to happen, or is happening already. What was said about shellfish farming above shows how ancient a practice it is; and there are even cases where large sea fish have been farmed since a past which may be as remote as the first era of mollusk farming. In the Philippines and some other Pacific islands milkfish cultivation is of indeterminate antiquity. The farmers obtain fry by digging holes on the beach at high tide and scooping the specimens out when the tide falls. The fish feed on sea moss and grow rapidly to about three or four feet in length, when they are ready for market. Carp, varieties of which can be fed with grass cuttings and plankton too small to interest most other species, lend themselves to similar production methods in freshwater ponds of a kind documented in China from the middle of the second millennium B.C. Shrimp and salmon in offshore farms, and carp, perch, eels and pink-fleshed trout in freshwater environments are all highly amenable to the same sort of treatment on an industrial scale. These are now the dominant species in global aquaculture. Five million tons of food came from fish farms in 1980. A generation later the figure was 25 million tons. China is the world leader in the movement, accounting for more than half the total production.

Deep-sea fish farms are now technically possible. The economics of the business make it certain that they will be developed.

In the wild, it takes a million eggs to produce a fish. Artificial fertilization can ensure that 80 percent of eggs are fertilized and that 60 percent turn into fish. Hormonal treatment can be used to boost the individual fertility of the egg producers. With the aid of oxidation, controlled water temperatures and artificial plankton, the fish grow faster and bigger than in the wild. Farmed salmon yield more than 800 tons per acre of surface water—fifteen times better than the yield from beef cattle. At seventy-five degrees Fahrenheit, sea bass grows twice as fast as in the naturally varying temperatures of its usual habitat. The growth of fish farming therefore seems inevitable. The extinction of wild species will surely follow, because farmed fish are carriers of diseases which, thanks to their breeding or treatment, they can resist; but when communicated to the unimmunized populations outside the farmers' pens, they are sure to wreak havoc.

The fish farming "explosion" of our times has had a few feeble landward echoes—previously undomesticated land species, such as ostrich and some varieties of deer. Together these new efforts constitute a resumption of the herding revolution, which has been long interrupted. Herding for food on a large scale was the work of the remote antiquity of most societies, when cattle, sheep, goats, pigs and farmed fowl were brought—dare one say?—within the fold. We are reverting to truly ancient wisdom.

The Edible Earth

—

Managing Plant Life for Food

"Why, O Earth, must you be so mean?
All this digging for a grain of corn!
Gifts should be cheerful, not so grudging.
Why such sweat and labour in farming?
What harm would it do you to give for toil?"
Earth when she hears this says with a smile:
"That wouldn't increase my glory greatly,
And your pride and glory would vanish completely!"

—RABINDRANATH TAGORE, PARTICLES, JOTTINGS, SPARKS,
TRANSLATED BY WILLIAM RADICE

From his brimstone bed at break of day
A-walking the Devil is gone
To visit his snug little farm, the Earth,
And see how his stock goes on.

—COLERIDGE AND SOUTHEY, THE DEVIL'S THOUGHTS

FORAGING AND FARMING

The experience cannot be replicated in a "Mongolian barbecue" restaurant but Mongols really do cook in a firepot, made of metal, beaten thin to make the vessel light and transportable. A funnel in the middle lets smoke from the fire rise through. Water bubbles in the outer ring so fiercely that it takes only seconds to cook strips of meat—or heartwarming mutton fat, as Mongols generally prefer, in their climate of extremes, where the wind chills the steppe to forty degrees below zero in winter. Alternatively, a thin plate can be smeared with fat and laid on the fire to fry the viands. This is the food of nomads and the cuisine of the battle-ready, recalling times when the campfire was the warriors' bond, when spears were skewers and shields were pots. It is food which seems to exclude farmers: sedentary folk, whom nomads are supposed to hate and fight.

The meat comes from the companions of the Mongols' transhumant lives: the horse, on the rare occasions when surplus horses are disposable or when an old one dies, or the fat-tailed sheep, which is one of the most inventive creations of nomad stockbreeders. This grotesque beast was documented in Arabia from antiquity and is still popular today, especially in the steppelands and plateaus of the Middle East and Central Asia, wherever the nomads' culture is or has been preponderant. The sheep drags a cumbrous tail behind it, sometimes as broad as a beaver's. The loss of mobility can be serious—even to the point where a little cart has to be attached to the animal to make the tail transportable. The gain outweighs the inconvenience. For the meat of nomads' kine is journey-toughened and muscly, whereas tail fat is marvelously soft—a kind of instant oil which melts easily. Even if the nomad has no time to heat it, or no available kindling, it can be eaten raw and digested quickly. To concentrate this precious substance in a part of the animal which can be butchered without slaughter was an unbeatable blessing for people on the move.

Because there is no firewood over much of the steppeland, the Mongols traditionally cooked on fires of dung or fell back on the use of meats which could be processed without fire, by wind drying or by the characteristic method which has impressed and repelled European observers since the Middle Ages: a cut of meat is pressed under the horseman's saddle to be tenderized in the beast's sweat by the pounding of the ride. As a substitute for cooking, this procedure was recommended on good authority by a Croat captain who dined with Brillat-Savarin in 1815. "Mein Gott!" he exclaimed,

> when we are in the field and feel hungry, we shoot down the first animal that comes our way, cut off a good hunk of flesh, salt it a little (for we always carry a supply of salt in our sabretache) and put it under the saddle, next to the horse's back; then we gallop for a while, after which,

he added, "moving his jaws like a man tearing meat apart with his teeth, '*gnian gnian*, we feed like princes.'"

Most of the rest of the traditional repertoire of Mongol cuisine came from the milk of ewes and mares. The latter type of milk is literally vital: its high vitamin C content enables steppelanders to survive without access to the fruit and vegetables which are available to sedentary peoples. The herdsmen offer a vast menu of dairy products—preparations of every imaginable consistency and degree of sweetness or acridity, but the most famous product of Mongols' dairying is koumiss, their ceremonial and celebratory drink. According to the traditional recipe, mare's milk is stored in a sheepskin with a little rennet to induce fermentation, periodically shaken with a gentle motion and drunk while still slightly *pétillant*. The Masai of Kenya—another stockman nation—get 80 percent of their energy intake as milk. They are also notorious for their technique of drawing blood from their cattle on the trail and plugging the wound without having to halt. All long-range transhumance demands similar techniques. For blood, like milk, is nourishment yielded by kine on the hoof. Sedentary peoples, who prefer to cook blood before they consume it, treat as evidence of savagery or vampirism the nomad's habit of piercing a vein for a draft of blood; but it is a practical device for herdsmen on the move or for steppelanders short of fuel. For Mongol warfare it was strategic equipment: liberating raiding parties from logistical backup, contributing to the speed with which they surprised their enemies, enabling a vast empire to be cheaply policed.

On the face of it, this animal diet looks like the basis of a cuisine innocent of plant foods. It is not true, however, that nomadic herders despise the fruits of agriculture: their historic problem has been getting hold of them. Because grains and cultivated fruits and vegetables are alien in the nomads' environments, they are highly prized and often brought in at great cost, or—until the last three hundred years or so when sedentary societies have opened up a technology gap which nomad warfare could not close—they were wrested as tribute through war or the threat of war. Nomads' hostility to sedentary neighbors arises not from contempt for their culture, but greed to share its benefits. When Leo Africanus was entertained at a Targui camp in early sixteenth-century North Africa, he had a typical experience: he and his companions were served with millet bread but their hosts took only milk and meat—served roasted in slices with herbs

> and a good quantity of spices from the land of the Blacks. . . . The prince, noticing our surprise, amiably explained by saying that he was born in the desert where no grain grows and that their people ate only what the land produced. He said that they acquired enough grain to honor passing strangers.

Leo suspected, however, that this reticence was partly for show and so have most scholars ever since. Nomads need to obtain grains, if they want them, by barter or raiding or tribute, or else they must gather them wild.

The gathering strategy is not always practicable: some environments yield too little harvestable wild food. But, wherever it is possible, foraging for edible plants is popular, not only with farmers on the lookout for species to plant, but also among inveterate hunters and herders, peoples who have a strong cultural bias against agriculture, or whose habitat does not allow the wild plants to be adapted for cultivation. Many aboriginal Australian peoples exploit wild yams and assist their propagation by leaving the tuber tops in the ground or replanting them. This suggests that they could cultivate them if they so wished; but they prefer not to. When investigating the relationship between wild and cultivable grasses, Jack Harlan the agronomist, who was one of the great pioneers of historical ecology, harvested four pounds of wild wheat grain in an hour with a stone sickle: at that rate, people who had edible species available to them in antiquity had little incentive to domesticate them. The grass from Minnesota popularly known as "wild rice" which is now a prized delicacy throughout the United States was formerly the staple food of the natives, who could gather large amounts with relative economy of labor.

Somehow—we still do not know how or where—foraging began to yield to farming as a way of obtaining plant food: under this new dispensation, instead of relying on naturally occurring varieties, farmers transplanted such varieties into new locations, which they might adapt for the purpose by the sort of radical, ambitious interventions in the natural environment which we loosely call "civilization": methods of soil preparation, including, for example, turning, irrigating and fertilizing the earth; clearing natural vegetation; weeding plots; exterminating predators; refashioning the lie of the land with ditches and mounds; diverting watercourses; building fences. Farmers could then develop strains of their own by selective planting and other techniques, including hybridization and grafting. Along with stock breeding, farming was the first great human intervention in the course of evolution, producing new species not by natural selection but through manipulation—sorting and selecting by human hand. From the perspective of historical ecology, this was the biggest revolution in the history of the world, a new departure on a scale unrepeated until, perhaps, the "Columbian Exchange" of the sixteenth century, to which we shall turn in due course (below, Chapter 7), or the beginnings of "genetic modification" at the end of the twentieth century (below, p. 209–10).

This impressive intensification of ways of exploiting plant food is puzzling, partly because it happened so rapidly, crammed into a spell of about five millennia, between about ten thousand and about five thousand years ago. This seems short by comparison with the long preceding period, during which, as far as we know, gathering was the only plant-exploiting strategy practiced anywhere in the world. More curious still is that farming proved extremely popular as a way of life—so much so that the overwhelming majority of humankind eventually came to depend on it. Yet, wherever it happened, it involved sweeping social and political change, much of which can reasonably be supposed to have been unwelcome to the people who endured it. The problem of the origins of agriculture is, therefore, one of the most debated topics in recent scholarship; a survey of the relevant literature has enumerated thirty-eight distinct and competing explanations of how farming came about. No solution so far proposed seems entirely satisfactory and we are still really only refining the model proposed by Darwin:

> accustomed as we are to our excellent vegetables and luscious fruits, we can hardly persuade ourselves that the stringy roots of the wild carrot and parsnip, or the little shoots of the wild asparagus, or crabs, sloes, etc. should ever have been valued; yet, from what we know of the habits of Australian and South African savages, we need feel no doubt on this head. . . . The savage inhabitants of each land, having found out by many and hard trials what plants were useful, or could be rendered useful by various cooking processes, would, after a time take the first step in cultivation by planting them near their usual abodes. . . . The next step in cultivation, and this would require but little forethought, would be to sow the seeds of useful plants; and as the soil near the hovels of the natives would often be in some degree manured, improved varieties would sooner or later arise. Or a wild and unusually good variety of a native plant might attract the attention of some wise old savage; and he would transplant it or sow its seed. . . . Transplanting any superior variety, or sowing its seeds, hardly implies more forethought than might be expected at an early and rude period of civilisation.

Obviously, there are nigglingly unsolved problems in this model. It is never satisfying to historians to be forced back on formulations of what "would" or "might" have happened (though this recourse is inevitable in any meditation on an episode as remote and ill documented as the origins of agriculture). We want to know what really did happen and to base our findings on evidence, not on reasoning alone. The assumption that "savage" attainments must be of a kind which requires "little forethought" makes us uneasy, because it is incompatible with one of our most cherished findings about human nature: as we have not progressed in cleverness, as far as we know, since the emergence of our species, we have to acknowledge that genius occurs, uncumulatively, at every stage of history and in every type of society—as well in the Paleolithic as in postmodernity, "in New Guinea as well as in New York." Moreover, if Darwin were right, we might expect to find the earliest cases of plant domestication in areas where the wild species were deficient in quantity or nutritional value. In practice, however, the opposite seems to be the case.

Early domestications tended to happen in places where, on the face of it, there seems to have been little incentive, owing to the abundance of easily garnered wild foods. Southeast Asian river deltas, which have been proposed as the scenes of the first farming in the world, were prehistoric "seas of wild rice." All the areas commonly acknowledged to have been early nurseries of independent agriculture—in the Middle East, China, Southeast Asia, New Guinea, Mesoamerica, central Peru, Ethiopia—were characterized at the relevant time by diverse environments, rich in microclimates and specialized eco-niches, where food seems unlikely to have been in short supply. The Natufian culture in Palestine—predecessor of one of the earliest fully agrarian societies we know about—harvested wild cereals in large quantities as early as the ninth millennium B.C. Its sites are littered with grinding stones, sickles and mortars dug into bedrock. Wild barley and two types of wheat that yield kernels digestible by human beings—einkorn and emmer—seem to have been natural to the region. Actual remains of these grains, processed by the grinders' tools, have been found in Jericho (below, p. 95), Mureybit and Ali Kosh. At Çayönü the foundation of the diet of the citizens of that early experiment in urbanization included emmer, einkorn, lentil, pea and vetch.

The fact that emmer and einkorn were present at many early sites may confer a clue. Kernels of these wheats are very hard to free from the tough, inedible glumes that surround them; so people who ate large amounts of them may have had an incentive to try to breed derivatives, which were easier to process. However, if labor saving was the purpose behind the strategy, crop domestication must be reckoned a failure. In practice, it seems always to have cost early farmers more trouble than it saved. The cultivated grains on which its practitioners relied were in every case less nutritious than the wild versions they replaced, though they also yielded more volume per unit of cultivation and generally demanded less labor to prepare for eating. Prior to preparation they had to be planted and nurtured. This was a backbreaking job which absorbed more time and effort than the gathering strategies employed by harvesters of wild grains.

Furthermore, the introduction of farming frequently triggered deleterious consequences. In societies of the commonest kind—civilizations that relied on a single staple, such as rice or wheat, barley or maize—exposure to famine and disease broadened as diet narrowed. Meanwhile, instead of being a universal diversion, hunting became an elite privilege and a varied diet became the reward of power. The ensuing refinements of civilization—towering monuments built at popular expense for elite satisfaction—meant, for most people, more toil and more tyranny. Women got shackled to the food chain. Tillers of the soil became something like a caste, from which prowess could not raise them except in time of war.

I mention this with no intention of justifying romantic cant in favor of the moral superiority of spear-slingers' societies, in which hunting and gathering continued to predominate. They were and are bloodstained and riven with inequalities, just as much as those which rely on mass agriculture, only in different ways. What intensive farmers renounced was not the sylvan innocence of a golden age, but particular hardheaded advantages. In the late 1960s, the archaeologist Lewis Binford drew attention to this paradox of the evidence: farming was harmful to people in the ordinary ranks of the "original affluent societies." Shortly afterward, the richly creative, enormously influential anthropologist Marshall Sahlins published *Stone Age Economics*, in which he argued convincingly that hunter societies were the most leisured and—in relation to energy expended—among the best nourished in history. Meanwhile, evidence began to accumulate that nonfarmers are usually restrained from farming, not by lack of means or knowledge—for gatherers commonly know as much as gardeners about plants and about the principles of propagation—but by a rational preference for an easier way of life. Jack R. Harlan put it in words that can hardly be bettered: "the ethnographic evidence indicates that people who do not farm do about everything that farmers do, but they do not work as hard."

Gatherers use fire to clear ground, renew fertility and privilege or favor particular species. They often sow seeds and plant tubers. They use enclosures and scarecrows to protect plants. Sometimes they split tracts of land into proprietary plots. They have first-fruit ceremonies, rites of rain making, and prayers for the fertility of the earth. They harvest edible seeds and thresh, winnow and mill them. They are often experts on the toxic and prophylactic properties of the plants they use, processing the poison out of their own food and extracting it to stun fish or kill game. Indeed, some of the most reputedly "primitive" people in the world are expert in the control of this recondite scientific knowledge. The swamp dwellers of Frederik Hendrik Island, off New Guinea, know how to infect a fish-rich stretch of sea with poison, enabling them to gather and eat the fish without ill effect. Burke and Wills perished on their trans-Australian expedition in 1861 because, when their provisions ran out, they ate the nardoo seeds from which the aboriginals made a nourishing cake: without proper preparation, as the natives alone knew, it can be highly toxic.

"Gatherers," Harlan went on, "understand the life cycles of plants, know the seasons of the year, and when and where the natural plant food resources can be harvested in great abundance with the least effort." In the era of universal foraging, the diet—to judge from the comparative study of human remains—was better than that of early cultivators. Starvation was rare. Health was generally better, with less chronic disease and "not nearly so many cavities in their teeth. The question must be raised: Why farm? Why give up the 20-hour work week and the fun of hunting in order to toil in the sun? Why work harder for food less nutritious and a supply more capricious? Why invite famine, plague, pestilence and crowded living conditions?"

These are demanding questions. It is important, however, not to make the problem seem insoluble by exaggeration. It is all too easy now to overstate the disadvantages of agriculture, just as in the past scholarship exaggerated its benefits. Clearly, farming brought important gains for people who started to practice it: crops could be matched to convenient sites and yields increased. Agriculture multiplied muscle power, feeding more human labor for despotic projects. It created surpluses with which to sustain large, powerful animals, capable of tasks beyond human strength. The oxen plowed more land, the horses and camels helped stockpile and transport more food in a series of spiraling effects. Whatever the disadvantages for the people who had to do the work and survive on the food, agriculture added enormously to the energy reserves of the societies that practiced it. Like hunting, it could lead to forms of "fun." Early one morning in Afghanistan, Jack Harlan came across a group of men dressed in colorful embroidered jackets, balloon pants and pixie-toed shoes. They had two drums and were singing and dancing, waving sickles in the air. Women followed, shrouded in chadors, but participating in the pleasure of the occasion without undue restraint. "I stopped and asked in broken Farsee: 'Is this a wedding celebration or something?' They looked surprised and said: 'No, nothing. We are just going out to cut wheat.'"

We can acknowledge that agriculture was a mixed blessing, with some advantages. In the past we have erred too far in the opposite direction, ignoring the disadvantages, assuming that because farming happened relatively late in history it must be "progressive," or that, because we do it ourselves, it must be a more rational way of life than any which preceded it or which other people prefer. By treating it as obviously superior, we have blinded ourselves to the need to explain it. The need for open-minded inquiry can be dodged by assuming that the agricultural intensification of the Neolithic era was inevitable: part of the "course of history" or of ineluctable progress. But history has no course; nothing is inevitable, and progress, in general, is still awaited.

It may be helpful, before penetrating more deeply the controversy concerning the origins of agriculture, to set the problem in the context of other cases of great changes effected in societies in despite or defiance of crudely calculated popular interests. Great economic revolutions are often equivocal in their effects and people sometimes show amazing resilience when their standards of living fall—provided they acknowledge that the deterioration is inevitable or short-term. The case of industrialization is analogous to that of the introduction of agriculture. There seems little doubt that industrialization, for instance, normally begins with short-term damage to workers' standards of living. It wrenches them from a rural arcadia and crowds them into slums. It tears them from rooted communities and abandons them in the rat race. Some social reformers in the early nineteenth century told the victims of early industrialization that things could only get worse: capitalism was inherently exploitative and only blood could purge its evils. In retrospect, the workers who invested their labor in industry and made it work seem wiser than their advisers. Their sacrifices paid off and industrialization brought unprecedented prosperity to unpredicted numbers of people. Nevertheless, this prosperity was preceded by a period of transition when workers who suffered from the grueling living conditions of early industrial cities had to see it through, in the hope of better times or the conviction that they had no viable alternative.

A similar dilemma can be detected in the shanty dwellers who crowd around modern megacities in industrializing countries today, filling unsanitary heaps of gimcrack dwellings, beyond the reach of civic and social services. Some are drawn, some driven to the city; in some cases, their reasons for migration are a bit of both. Human beings are risk-taking creatures whose calculations of self-interest are often rationally baffling. Rationality—at least, as understood by economists— seems unable to predict mass behavior. We ought therefore to discard one of our most tenacious myths about human nature and admit that man is not an economic animal. Enlightened self-interest does not always guide our decisions, especially when we make them collectively. Anyone making an informed calculation of the ratio of effort to return would never have introduced or tolerated the agrarian systems on which the ancient civilizations of Sumer, Egypt, the Indus and the Yellow River relied. The introduction of agriculture, in early cases, may well have happened in defiance of the obvious interests of many of the people who took part in it.

The farming concept first arose in a world that was getting warmer, during the thaw that followed the last ice age. Any convincing explanation needs to take this context into account; indeed, the most popular theory, for at least twenty years from the mid-1930s, relied entirely on the "oasis hypothesis"—the assumption that higher temperatures would bring drier conditions and force animals, plants and men into ever closer contiguity and interdependence around watering holes. The thaw, however, seems to have been too slow to trigger this kind of crisis and there is no evidence which directly links agricultural origins to climatic change: indeed, farming seems to have started independently, in so many different parts of the world, in such widely contrasting climatic conditions, that it appears pointless to try to insist on any climatic prerequisites.

Since the 1950s, when confidence in the oasis hypothesis began to wither, almost every other imaginable type of explanation has been advanced. Farming, claimed one of the pioneers of modern historical geography, was a by-product of the leisure of fishermen in Southeast Asia, who devoted the spare time which abundance gave them to experimentation with plants. Or it was an invention of hill dwellers in what is now northern Iraq, whose habitat was peculiarly rich in domesticable grasses and grazing herds. Or, on the contrary, it was an invention of "marginal zones" where the need for new foods would be most acute: an equalizing device, in other words, by inhabitants of an underprivileged environment, where wild food sources were few. Or it was a process made possible not by climatic change but by the supposedly universal pattern of development of society— the "culmination of ever increasing cultural differences and specialization of human communities." Or it was a spontaneous happening—the surge of new species, springing abundantly from waste heaped where people lived. Or it was a strategy enforced by "stress," either because population was increasing or because men were hunting other food sources to extinction: pressure of growing populations or shrinking resources imposed the need to find new species to adapt for food or more intensive methods of production of existing foodstuffs.

This last hypothesis seems, perhaps, superficially convincing. It is consistent with common sense; and it is supported by impressive work by anthropologists on transitions to agriculture which have happened under scholarly scrutiny in recent times. The need for new resources can explain—beyond cavil—why some relatively unsystematic farming peoples, such as seasonal farmers or those who practice cultivation without attempting hybridization, should develop new techniques. But, as an explanation for why agriculture arose in the first place, it seems ill matched to the facts of chronology. Extinctions—or even significant diminutions—in hunters' victim-species cannot be shown to have happened in any of the right places at any of the right times. Populations certainly grew in the most dedicated farming cultures—but, in most places, more probably as a consequence than as a cause. Population pressure explains why agricultural intensification could not be reversed without catastrophe, because of the "ratchet effect" which makes it impossible, while population rises, to go back to less intensive ways of getting food; but it does not explain why it started. Intensification of agriculture, finally, was only possible in regions with abundant resources: it seems more reasonable to claim that plenty, rather than dearth, was a prerequisite of the development.

The feebleness or failure of all these theories, the uselessness—indeed—of every kind of materialism in explaining mass agriculture, drives inquirers toward religion or, more generally, culture as a source of explanations. One widely canvassed and highly persuasive explanation is rooted in studies of political culture. Food does not only sustain the body; it is also a source of social prestige. Competitive feasting in a society where power, in the form of allegiance and obligation, is bought with food can generate huge increases in demand, even if population is static and supplies are secure. Societies bound by feasting and leaders favored by conspicuous munificence will always find a use for intensive agriculture and for massive storage spaces. Monumental civilization is a function of a particular kind of conviviality.

Alongside this political context for understanding farming, it is tempting to endorse the opinions of scholars who have explained the option for agriculture in antiquity as a religious response. To plow or dibble and sow and irrigate are profoundly "cultic" actions: rites of birth and nurture of the god on whom you are going to feed; an exchange of sacrifice—labor for nourishment. The power to make food grow is represented in most cultures as a divine gift or curse or a secret stolen by a culture hero from the gods. Animals have been domesticated for sacrifice and divination as well as for food. Many societies cultivate plants which have a part at the altar but not at the table, like incense or ecstatic drugs or the sacrificial corn of some high Andean communities. Where crops are gods, tillage is worship. Planting may have originated as a fertility rite, or irrigation as libation, or enclosure as an act of reverence for a sacred plant.

If none of the proffered explanations seems wholly convincing, it may be because we have misunderstood the introduction of agriculture as a conscious process, a deliberate strategy to serve articulable ends. Farming could have been something that just happened; it might have been uncaused; or it might have been an evolutionary adaptation, or a change resembling such an adaptation, unwilled by the species involved in it. Traditionally, works on the origins of intensive agriculture have not asked why people wanted it—that has been taken for granted—but how they got the idea, as if there were something strange or extraordinary about it. It may help to shift perspective and approach the problem of farming as if it were normal. After all, we now know that the transition from gathering happened frequently and independently, in a variety of different environments, and gradually got more intensive in most of them. It can therefore no longer be represented as singular or uncharacteristic of the history of the relationship between people and plants.

In this perspective, farming and gathering reappear together, as parts of a single continuum in the management of sources of food; at the margins, they are hard to tell apart. The Papago of the Sonora Desert drift in and out of an agrarian way of life as the weather permits, using patches of surface water in fast-maturing varieties of beans. "Even the simplest hunter-gatherer society," as the archaeologist Brian Fagan has well said, "knows full well that seeds germinate when planted." The agronomy of the ancient alluvial valleys was another—but more puzzling—part of the same continuum. The process of "agrarianization" seems rapid in comparison with earlier periods but it still had plenty of time to unfold piecemeal, over several millennia, as changes in the relationships of people to other biota accumulated little by little. The terms in which the naturalist David Rindos has described early farming seem helpful. It was a phenomenon of "human-plant symbiosis" and "co-evolution," an unconscious relationship, like the cultivation of fungi by ants; strains of foodstuffs which emerged as a result of human selection and replanting needed human agency to survive and reproduce—for instance, in the case of emerging kinds of edible grasses, because their seeds would not fall to the ground without husking. Agriculture was a revolution by accident—a new mechanism intruded unintentionally into the process of evolutionary change.

Whether invented or evolved, the farming of plants did more, in the long run, to alter the world than any previous human innovation. The impact of the hunters, fishers, and stockbreeders of the last chapter could not compare—not on the landscape, or on ecological structures or even on diet. Today, all the carbohydrates people eat, and nearly three quarters of their intake of protein, come from plants. Plants are 90 percent of the world's food. Almost all the animals in the human food chain are fed, not by grazing, but by fodder grown by farmers. Plant farming still dominates the world's economy: except in terms of the numbers of people employed in producing it, food producing has not yielded its economic supremacy to any of the new activities of the industrial and postindustrial revolutions. We still depend on it absolutely. It is the basis of everything else. In the story of the spread and rise of plant farming, moreover, a few crops exert disproportionate influence and demand most attention. These are the staples—the sources of starch which, since their first development by the world's earliest agriculturists, have provided most people with most of their food. They divide naturally into two classes: grasses first, then roots and tubers.

THE GREAT GRASSES

The most influential crops prehistoric farmers developed were the seed-rich grasses that store oil, starch and protein in their grains. Despite the enormous and growing importance of a few kinds of such grasses, of which wheat is the most prominent, most of the varieties we have lived with, for most of history, have been useless for cultivation, except as adornments. If you fly over Abu Dhabi or Bahrain, and see the lawns laboriously coaxed out of the sand, or marvel from the air at the private golf course of a Lappish millionaire—as if some cosmic jeweler had mounted a vast gem in bare rock—you might feel that inedible grasses, too, can be planted in the service of the defiance of nature. But, like the wheatlands and maize plots, these are late, freakish creations. In the long term, grasslands have normally been composed of varieties inedible to man, but suitable for other animals with ruminant habits or better digestions.

The developments of rye, barley, millet, rice, maize and wheat are therefore among the most spectacular achievements of humankind: turning grasses—which nature seemed to have designated as the food of other, better-equipped species—into the staple fodder of nonruminants like ourselves. Other important plants in the repertoire include buckwheat, oats and sorghum; but the big six are special because whole civilizations have relied for sustenance on each of them. They can be ranked in global importance according to a combination of factors: their impact on history, the extent of their role as staples and the scale of their contribution to feeding the world today. We can take them in ascending order.

Wild rye still grows across a great swath of the Middle East, around the Caucasus; but, if this was where it originated, it had to travel a long way before it came into its own as a civilization-sustaining staple. Modern cultivated varieties seem to have developed from others which no longer exist but it is still easy to discern, in surviving types, the virtues which attracted early cultivators and which destined rye for other climes: hardiness, resistance to different altitudes, responsiveness to cold. Rye grows as a weed in wheatfields and sprouts when adverse weather kills the wheat. Anatolian peasants call it "wheat of Allah"—a grace which compensates farmers for the loss of the main crop. It must also have seemed heaven-sent to would-be farmers on poor soils or in cold climates, where wheat was unreliable or uncultivable. In such environments, especially along the cold northern and eastern perimeters of the Roman Empire, it arrived as a weed and became a main crop. From the first millennium B.C. onward, until potatoes rivaled or replaced it in modern times (below, p. 179), rye was the distinctive food of the fields of the North European plain—dank, cold lands cleared from the postglacial forests, zones where native grasses were sparse, puny and impossible to adapt for human use. Its main disadvantage is that it is peculiarly prone to the infestation which produces ergotism; some historians have traced the supposed frequency of mass delusions among medieval peasants to their heavy reliance on rye for food. Surprisingly, the pleasantly bitter taste of the grain and the moist, glutinous bread made from it are widely disliked. Pliny's condemnation of it as fit only for the poor has been endorsed by elites ever since. Now, however, it is undergoing a sort of upgrading as bourgeois food, with an appeal to discerning palates, to roughage-mad dieters and to enthusiasts for foods supposed to be "close to nature" because peasants make and eat them. It is also getting rarer, which, paradoxically perhaps, may help to account for its growing appeal at relatively high levels of wealth and education.

Barley has some of rye's virtues, but even more flexible habits—an even wider range of ecological tolerance. It was harvested wild in substantial quantities in Syria in the twelfth millennium B.C.; domesticated and wild varieties have been found together in silos dating from about four thousand years later. Even early varieties proved amazingly tolerant: and barley has tended to assume huge importance as a staple for human consumption wherever conditions are too hostile for other grains. But it makes poor bread and so tends to get eaten as unground grains in soups and stews, or made into an infusion for invalids, or left as fodder. Even so, it has been the basic sustenance of great civilizations. In ancient Mesopotamia, it was more important than wheat in most people's diets. It was the original sole staple of ancient Greece, where some of the earliest Athenian coins were stamped with images of barley sheaves: not much else would grow in the thin, rocky soils that Plato compared to a skeleton's skin, penetrated by bones. Gradually, commercial integration of the Mediterranean world in antiquity made it possible for wheat, grown in vast grainlands across Egypt, Sicily and the North African littoral, to become the main food of "classical" civilization. But barley still had a role to play—a new culture area to colonize, at the eastern end of its traditional area of distribution, in the heart of Asia.

In the fifth century A.D., a little understood agricultural revolution, based on barley, transformed Tibet: formerly, this isolated tableland of icy, soda-encrusted wastes was good only for nomads but once barley became available in large quantities, the advantages of a cold climate came into play. The cold protected the grains in storage. The greatness of Tibet was founded on large food surpluses. The land became a breeding ground of armies, which could march on far campaigns with "ten thousand sheep and horses in their supply trains." Barley has remained a staple crop ever since, through all the centuries when Tibet's history seems to have gone into reverse and the sometime empire became first a land of civil wars, then a victim of external aggressors. Despite the competition of other grains in modern Tibet, barley is still favored—consumed in hand-rolled balls of the toasted barley flour called tsampa, or fermented in beer.

Millet is a similarly robust type of cereal, which thrives in climates equally extreme but of the opposite character: hot and dry. It helped to make and sustain civilization in the highlands of Ethiopia, the windswept plains of the Yellow River and the fierce Sahel and savanna of West Africa, between desert and forest. Except as birdseed, or in culturally odd places, like the Vendée of northern France (where it is eaten defiantly, as a symbol of regional identity), millet has never caught on in Western civilization, perhaps because it cannot be made into leavened bread. But it is a nutritious staple, high in carbohydrates and fairly high in fat, with more protein than durum wheat. Its major role in global history was exerted via China. Conventionally, Chinese cuisine is associated with rice, but Chinese civilization would have been unthinkable without millet. Ancient songs collected in the *Shih Ching* rhapsodize on the toil of clearing weeds, brush and roots. "Why in days of old did they do this task? So that we might plant our grain, our millet, so that our millet might be abundant." Pollen finds bear out this literary source. The loess lands around the Yellow River, where Chinese civilization began, were in the process of getting steadily more arid over a period of millennia; but when agriculturists began clearing them for tillage they were still a sort of savanna, where grasslands were interspersed with trees and scrub. The alluvial plain was still partially wooded with deciduous broadleaves. The spaces where Chinese civilization bred had environments of the kind which can work magic for men: marginal environments on the frontiers between contrasting ecosystems, where a diversity of the means of life gathers, like rich ooze in a rock pool. Agriculture started at the intersection of two long processes: the very gradual increase in aridity; the favorable diversification that followed the ice age.

Both processes were still detectable thousands of years later, in a period for which the archaeological evidence is prolific and surviving written records begin. In the second millennium B.C. water buffalo were plentiful: the remains of more than a thousand of them have turned up in strata of the era, together with other creatures of marsh and forest, like the elaphure and wild boar, water deer, silver pheasants and bamboo rats and even the occasional rhinoceros. Some of this diversity must be accounted for by the power and wealth of the Shang court and cities: they could import exotica and rich foods. The most startling example is of the trade in thousands of turtle shells, an import from the Yangtze and beyond, on which the Chinese polity absolutely depended in the second millennium B.C., for these were the most favored medium of oracular divination—bearers of messages addressed to another world: questions about the future were carved on them and the shells were then heated till they cracked. The lines of the cracks led, like wrinkles on a hand under a palmist's scrutiny, to the answers of the gods. These predictors of the future have become disclosures about the past. The evidence of a more diverse environment and a wetter climate is there, among the interpretations of the oracles, scratched by diviners on bone: protracted rains, double crops of millet and even some fields of rice. In the first millennium B.C. a poetess could still be surprised by love while plucking sorrel in squelchy ground in Shansi.

Even at its wettest, however, the Yellow River valley could not sustain a rice-eating civilization. Like other civilizations of roughly the same period and environment, China's was at first dependent on mass production of a single type of food. The legendary ancestor of the most successful lineage of the time was known as Hou Chi, "the Ruler of Millet." In folk memory, when he first planted it,

> It was heavy, it was tall,
> it sprouted, it eared . . .
> it nodded, it hung. . . .
> Indeed the lucky grains were sent down to us,
> the black millet, the double-kernelled,
> millet, pink-sprouted and white.

The Shang dynasty, too, was identified with millet: when the palaces of the Shang era were abandoned toward the end of the second millennium B.C., nostalgic visitors saw it growing over the ruins.

Two varieties of millet were mentioned in the earliest known Chinese writings and both have been found in archaeological deposits of the fifth millennium B.C. Both are almost certainly indigenous to China. They are robust in droughts, tolerant of alkalines. Their earliest known cultivators grew them on plots cleared by burning and ate them with the rewards of herding and hunting—domestic pigs and dogs, wild deer and fish. Astonishingly, the rudiments of this ancient way of life survive in the mountainous interior of one of the world's most heavily industrialized and technically proficient countries, Taiwan. In 1974–75, Wayne Fogg observed and recorded the techniques: a sloping site of up to sixty degrees inclination is selected because "fire burns hotter up-slope." It is aired and sometimes dibbled before planting with seeds threshed by rubbing between hands and feet. Noisy scarecrows or magical devices—miniature wooden boats, surrounded by palms or reeds and topped with stones—are planted to ward off predators.

Each panicle is harvested by hand, tossed into a basket carried on the harvester's back and, when enough have been accumulated, they are tied in sheaves and passed from hand to hand to be collected in piles and carried home. Traditional poems capture moments in the cycle of the peasant's year: dibbling in the cold, hunting the raccoon, foxes and wild cats "to make furs for our lord" and, after the harvests, shooing crickets from under the bed and smoking out the big rats that prey on the millet stocks.

This is highly suggestive. Today, this type of agriculture is technically primitive. Yet in Shang times it could sustain what were perhaps already the densest populations in the world and keep armies of tens of thousands in the field. The best yields could be obtained only by rotation: eventually, soybeans provided the alternate crop which this system demanded, but it is not clear when—perhaps not until the mid-first millennium B.C., if any store can be set by the story that Lord Huan of Ch'i first brought it home from a campaign against the Jung barbarians of the mountains in 664. Wheat was a latecomer always tainted with foreign origins as "one that came" or mentioned in the oracle inscriptions as the harvest of neighboring tribes to be monitored and destroyed.

And rice? The problems of the origin and diffusion of rice are critical for an understanding of global history. For rice provides about 20 percent of the calories and 13 percent of the proteins people consume in today's world, where it is the main staple of more than two billion people. These figures reflect the historic trajectory of rice, but perhaps do it less than full justice; for most of history—until the scientific recrafting of wheat strains to produce today's staggeringly efficient varieties— rice was *hors de pair* the world's most efficient food: with traditional varieties, one acre of rice supports, on average, 2.28 persons, compared with 1.49 per acre of wheat and 3.65 for maize. For most of history, the rice-eating civilizations of East and South Asia were more populous, more productive, more inventive, more industrialized, more fertile in technology and more formidable in war than rivals elsewhere. The wheat eaters of the West only began to emerge from relative backwardness in the last half-millennium and, by most objective standards of judgment, did not overtake India until the eighteenth century or China until the nineteenth.

The rise of rice in Chinese culture was the result of the gradual southward displacement of China's economic and demographic center of gravity: toward the Yangtze, to regions where rice was indigenous and cultivation extremely ancient. The northern heartlands of early Chinese civilization are too cold and dry for large-scale rice production even today, except with the help of modern agronomy. Some wild varieties grew and small plots, perhaps, were laboriously cultivated for thousands of years; but rice could not rival millet as a staple or as the focus of intensive farming. Among the Yellow River people, rice was recognized as an item in a civilized larder but not grown in large amounts. As with every aspect of the early history of civilization in what is now the Chinese culture area, the origins of rice production are being pushed ever further back in time by new archaeological discoveries. Rice cultivation was practiced at least eight thousand years ago behind receding floodwaters of lakes around the middle and low Yangtze. By about five thousand years ago, "dry," rain-watered upland rice was grown on the southern margins of northern China. Unequivocal evidence coming from Shen-hsi, in the form of outlines of rice grains imprinted on pottery fragments, exists for the sixth millennium B.C. Although claims have been made for various sites in Southeast Asia and what are now India and Pakistan as the original homelands of rice farming, no conclusive evidence from any of those areas dates from before the third millennium B.C.

Meanwhile, rice became a symbol of abundance and a mainstay of the menu in a process inseparable from the making of China—a process of expansion and acculturation which fused two contrasting environments. Ancient Chinese ethnography was not based on reliable fieldwork but it was at least clear what barbarians were like: in every respect, they were mirror opposites of Chinese. They lived in caves, wore skins. They did not include people of intelligible or kindred speech. And they did not include rice growers, like the people who preceded northern colonists on the Yangtze at Ch'ing-lien-kang. The rice growers' world was the seductive frontier of the second millennium B.C., sucking settlers southward to the expanding limits of civilization, luring barbarians in, melding the natives and the newcomers into Chinese.

Crudely beheld, in what we think of as the Middle Ages, the farming cultures of Eurasia and Africa could be characterized as a patchwork of staples: rice in the east, barley in part of central Asia, wheat in the west and millet and rye around some unfavored edges. The New World, by contrast, despite the enormous diversity of the cultures it enclosed, was unified—as far as farming was concerned—by the near omnipresence of maize. To an inexpert eye, there seems little resemblance between maize and its closest relatives among surviving wild grasses. Presumably, it derived from varieties now lost, but the original feral plants certainly had no more than a single row of ill-adhering seeds. The transformation, which produced the characteristic fat cobs of the great Native American civilizations, with many rows of grains, was one of the triumphs of early agronomy. There is no evolutionary reason why maize might have acquired such a structure. It came about as the result of purposeful selection and—probably—hybridization by cultivators.

When the process started is hard to say but multikernel specimens survive entire in central Mexican sites from the mid-fourth millennium B.C. Fragmentary evidence dates from at least a thousand years earlier in both central Mexican and southern Peruvian sites. Processing, as well as production, demanded scientific flair, because without proper preparation, maize is a nutritionally deficient food, low in both two vital amino acids—lysine and tryptophan—but also in the B vitamin niacin, a lack of which causes the disease pellagra. One way of obverting this danger is to ensure that maize eaters get plenty of varied supplementary foods, and indeed, squash and beans generally formed with maize a "trinity" of divine plant foods wherever it was possible to provide all three in combination. The bottle gourd, the earliest known form of cultivated squash, was being pickled in Tamaulipas in the Sierra Madre of Mexico, and in Oaxaca (at the highly productive archaeological site of Tehuacán), as well as north of Lima in northern Peru and the Ayacucho basin, long before the earliest evidence of maize cultivation. A balanced diet, however, must have been a luxury in the most densely populated parts of ancient America. To ensure the health of the huge populations who depended on it, maize had to be soaked when the grains were ripe, and cooked with lime or wood ash, removing the transparent skin, releasing the otherwise absent amino acids and enhancing the protein value. Archaeological evidence of equipment for this process has been found on the southern coast of what is now Guatemala in sites from the mid- to late second millennium B.C.

THE WORLD CONQUEROR

"Wheat," as Darwin observed, "quickly assumes new habits of life." There is something special about wheat: in alliance with man, it is a world-beater, more "ecologically tolerant" even than the other great grasses which have spread around the world. Wheat is not quite as adaptable as man, who exceeds all other species in the range of environments in which he can survive with the aid of his unique gift for devising or appropriating technology; but it has diversified more dramatically, invaded more new habitats, multiplied faster and evolved more rapidly without extinction than any other known organism. It now covers more than 600 million acres of the surface of the planet. We think of it as an emblem of the civilizing tradition, because it represents a triumphant adaptation of nature to our own purposes—a grass we have turned into a human food, a waste product of the wilderness which science has remade to sustain civilization, a proof of the unchallengeable thoroughness with which man dominates every ecosystem of which he forms part.

No relief of the Triumph of Progress, of the kind which often decorates the tympana of our academies and museums, would be complete without some ears or sheaves. Yet I can imagine a world in which this perception will seem laughable. A few years ago, I invented creatures of fantasy whom I called Galactic Museum

Keepers, and invited the reader to picture them, as they look back at our world in a remote future, from an immense distance of time and space, where, with a degree of objectivity unattainable by us—who are enmeshed in history—they will see our past quite differently from the way we see it ourselves. They will classify us, perhaps, as puny parasites, victims of feeble self-delusion, whom wheat cleverly exploited to spread itself around the world. Or else they will see us in an almost symbiotic relationship with edible grasses, as mutual parasites, dependent on each other and colonizing the world together.

Wheat is vital in shaping our present and feeding our future; yet its place in our past can still be reconstructed only partially, tentatively. Some facts are established beyond cavil. The greatest concentration of varieties of grass classifiable as wheat is and has always been, for as far back as the archaeological record goes, in Southwest Asia. The distribution zone of wild emmer is roughly commensurate with a region where wheat was intensively cultivated by the sixth millennium B.C. Einkorn and emmer are the wild parent wheats of all the domesticates known to have been in use by that time. Almost all early cultivators of wheat also grew barley. The earliest unquestionable evidence of wheat farming available to date comes from excavations in the Jordan valley, around Jericho and Tell Aswad, in strata corresponding to the seventh or eighth millennium B.C., where varieties of both einkorn and emmer were grown. Today, the ecology of these areas looks inhospitable: desert crusted with salt and sodium. Ten thousand years ago, however, the walls which perhaps already enclosed the town of Jericho overlooked an alluvial fan, washed down from the Judean hills by trickling tributaries that fill the river as it creeps south from the Sea of Galilee. The River Jordan is thick with silt. That explains why it snakes among ancient gray deposits of marl and gypsum, left by a now shriveled lake that once occupied the valley. The banks it deposited formed the biblical "jungle of Jericho," from where lions padded to raid the sheepfolds, like God threatening Edom. Here, as a result, stood the rich wheatfields said to resemble "the garden of the Lord." Desert people, such as the Israelites of Joshua, were excluded from it and tempted to conquest.

The story of wheat's own conquest of the world—the context of ecological exchanges which carried it across the globe and smothered so much of the planet in wheatfields—belongs in a later chapter (p. 169). The problem of what makes it widely popular is, however, probably related to the problem of why people grew it in the first place. Among the great grasses, some are distinguished by hardiness, others by resistance to predators and disease, others by outstanding durability in storage, others by high yield. All of them—as well as the staple roots and tubers to which we have yet to turn—are suitable for processing in the form of alcoholic drinks. This property is worth a moment's consideration, as some authorities regard beer as the critically important product, demand for which induced people to practice agriculture in the first place. Edible grasses were presumably first gathered for seeds, which would be eaten with little preparation. But which came first: bread or beer? Beer has been proclaimed the "Ur-source of all civilization": the magic effect of fermented grain "persuaded people to settle down in companionable villages." If one subscribes to the chieftainship or "big-man" theory of the origins of agriculture, according to which farming began in order to generate surpluses for chieftainly feasts, it makes sense to assign intoxicating drinks a special role. Similarly, if religion inspired agriculture, beer as an inducer of ecstasy might well have had a special appeal.

The success of wheat, however, suggests that the critical product—if there was one—was bread. Wheat had no obvious advantage over other edible grasses for the farmers who first favored it or for the peoples subsequently seduced by it, except that it has a secret ingredient—gluten, a complex of proteins found in oats, barley and rye, but in greater concentrations than any other cereal. This makes it a peculiarly good source of bread, because gluten is the substance which combines with water to make dough malleable; its consistency contributes critically to the way the paste traps the gases released by yeast. Historically all the cultures which, at least for a time, have been indifferent or resistant to the appeal of wheat have preferred to get their starch from other confections than bread: the messes or porridge favored by millet-dependent peoples; the popcorn which presumably preceded bread in the Americas; the unleavened cakes or flatbreads, such as the tortillas of maize eaters or the oatcakes of regions beyond the range of wheat; the compressions of sticky rice which are the traditional snack of Japan, or the barley balls of the Tibetans.

Of course, other wheat products are highly palatable and some of them exploit the virtue of gluten little or not at all. Pasta is best made from durum wheat—a derivative of emmer: its naked grains, which save labor by threshing free from surrounding bracts, made it an enormously attractive variety for much of the past, before the development of other easy-threshing varieties, but it is not particularly gluten-rich. Neither is gluten required in the preparation of many flat breads, including stars of the modern globalized fast food menu, such as pizza and Indian breads. Cracked wheat is an acquired taste because of its strong, distinctive flavor—but a taste worth acquiring; bulgur wheat grains, in the form of couscous, are a staple of Middle Eastern cultures and trendy restaurants alike. I like wheat grains boiled and dressed with garlic and olive oil (though, in obedience to a law of Spanish culture, I must—irrationally, perhaps—have bread to eat with them).

Some people, I am told, even claim to like the instantly soggy wheat-based break-fast cereals which aggressive marketing has promoted way beyond their merits (above, p. 44). Still, all these dishes and others like them are the historic by-prod-ucts of the triumph of bread. Without bread, wheat would be just another grain among many rivals.

This only deepens the mystery. For what is so special about bread? In terms of nutrition, digestibility, durability, ease of transport or storage, versatility and appeal for texture or flavor, the balance of advantages and disadvantages, com-pared with other potentially equivalent foods, seems nicely poised. Yet the trouble, time and technical expertise which have to be invested in successful baking are enormous. Professional bakers seem to have emerged early in every bread-eating culture. The many hobbyists who make bread at home, in conditions resembling those of early agrarian society, without exact means of measuring quantities, tem-peratures and timings, know how easily the process can go wrong, and how exact the baker's judgment has to be. No convincing theory of how or why bread making began has ever been proposed. Perhaps that is the key to bread's success: it is one of those "magical" foods, in which human mastery effects an unrecogniz-able change on the ingredients of the recipe. Just as the first farmers made grass edible, so the first bakers transformed tiny grains into a voluminous food. I should like this to be true; but it is obviously an unverifiable speculation. This vital episode in food history is likely to remain forever obscure.

SUPER TUBERS, ROOTS THAT RULE

Beyond the realm of bread, before wheat was elevated to its present global king-ship, roots and tubers, rather than grasses, provided the basic staples of many of the world's farming cultures and some of the world's most conspicuous civiliza-tions. Some of them may have a history of cultivation at least as long as those of edible grasses. Taro, perhaps, came first; but it is impossible to assign a date to its domestication, since—unlike grains—this corm has no indigestible parts and the leaves, though of treelike proportions in some varieties, degrade to nothingness. Still, in default of conclusive evidence, the balance of probabilities favors the sus-picion that some roots, at least, were cultivated before grains, simply because some of them are so easy to replant. Taro reproduces asexually, which made it simple for early cultivators to develop varieties by selection. Because it is a kind of super-food—with an enormous yield for little effort, a huge repertoire of technically undemanding cooking methods and a high starch content accessible to every human digestive system from early infancy to strenuous old age—it seems a likely candidate for the place of honor due to the world's first farmed plant.

Taro showed some historic adaptability: some varieties are suitable for swamp-lands and dry hills. When agriculture began in New Guinea, in the wake of the great climatic changes that split "Greater Australia" and opened a strait between New Guinea and Australia ten thousand years ago, it was probably based on native varieties of taro, planted in swampy hollows in the western highlands. In the Kuk swamp, drains, ditches and mounds for taro growing were formed fully nine thousand years ago. By about six or seven thousand years ago, taro was cultivated in widely separated regions around the Indian Ocean and western Pacific. The heartlands of taro eating remain, however, where they have always been, where those oceans meet, in Southeast Asia, especially in New Guinea and the Philippines, and in two areas where it was a latecomer: the Pacific islands that received the plant with the eastward spread of settlers bearing the Lapita culture system during a period of uncertain date (probably complete by the mid-second millennium B.C.), and Japan, where, presumably, it was a late implant from China or Korea, but where it remains a ritual food of the annual autumn moon-viewing feast.

Taro could never rival the great grains or superior tubers: unlike potatoes, wheat, rice and maize, it cannot function as the chief or sole constituent of a society's common diet; it is useful only as a supplementary food—a filler that ekes out varied meals. Typically, it contains 30 percent starch, 3 percent sugar and a little more than 1 percent protein, with traces of calcium and phosphorus. It does not keep well and therefore fails to meet the requirements of long durability, for store-housing and redistributing, which seem to have been characteristic of the staple foods of the most successful early agrarian societies. The taste for taro seems, moreover, hard to acquire: most varieties are insipid, with a character reminiscent of potatoes for texture and yams for such taste as there is. Hawaiians make a taro paste known as poi, from the pink-fleshed variety, reputedly "royal"—the nearest thing Hawaiians had in their imperial age to a courtly dish. To make poi, one steams the corms and crushes them to dough, which is left to ferment for a few days. It is the pride of what might be called the national cuisine of the islands, but it has not caught on anywhere else.

Though historically important, taro has dwindled in significance and no longer makes a statistically impressive contribution to the nourishment of the world. Yams, cassava (to a modest extent), sweet potatoes and—above all—potatoes, by contrast, have histories of remarkable growth. As far as we can reconstruct it in the present state of knowledge, the history of yams begins with the gathering of wild varieties in Southeast Asia, verifiable from remains in sites in Thailand at least nine thousand years old. At present there is, as far as I know, no evidence of where and when yams were first cultivated, though a good case has been made for their role in the independent development of indigenous West African agriculture around the fifth millennium B.C. According to this reconstruction, which is the work of D. G. Coursey, domestication was the outcome of progressive sacralization: the plants were first worshipped, then enclosed, then nurtured, then replanted in spaces which served both as shrines and nurseries. Their appearance in almost all the islands of the eastern Pacific at dates in the second millennium B.C. is compatible with the theory that they were domesticated in Southeast Asia or New Guinea and spread from there. Like taro, yams may have been part of the nursery of the earliest agriculture of New Guinea.

What yams and taro were to Southeast Asia and the Pacific, cassava, sweet potatoes and potatoes were to parts of the tropical Americas. Of these, cassava—though, as we shall see below (p. 178), it played some part in the worldwide "ecological exchanges" of modern history—has found least acceptance outside its native area, which is in the tropical lowlands of South America and the Caribbean region. Like taro, cassava is a big plant with potentially huge edible roots; so part of what it lacks in appeal by way of nutrition and flavor, it makes up in yield. It defies droughts, while relishing humid environments. Like other root crops, it cannot be devoured by locusts and is good at eluding most tropical predators. It became the staple of choice of early tropical forest cultivators in parts of the New World where maize could not be successfully introduced; but the triumph of maize helped to limit its area of influence.

Most roots and tubers, indeed, seem incapable of challenging the world's favorite grains as staple foods; the exception is the potato, which now ranks fourth by weight consumed among the world's foodstuffs, behind wheat, rice and maize—but with a significant share of the market and a remarkable record of cross-cultural appeal. Its ascent to this eminence is surely one of the most remarkable stories in the world, since, to an objective scrutineer, it must seem incredible that it should ever have been domesticated in the first place—let alone taken up beyond the peculiar environment, in the high Andes, where it first grew wild. Some wild varieties are carnivorous; all are more or less poisonous. The idea of selecting them for eating by man may have arisen by way of an analogy with sweet potatoes, which were almost certainly cultivated first. Sweet potato tubers of a kind very similar to modern cultivated varieties were eaten in the central coastal region of what is now Peru at sites dated to around 8,000 B.C. If these were indeed produced by agriculture, the sweet potato would have to be counted as the New World's earliest farmed food crop—perhaps the earliest anywhere. As with maize, the wild ancestor of the farmed plant has disappeared. The domesticated potato may have developed in the course of an effort to find a plant with some of the advantages of the sweet potato, but exploitable at higher altitudes. The earliest known experiments took place in central Peru or the environs of Lake Titicaca about seven thousand years ago. Once tried with success, the potato gave mountain dwellers parity of power with peoples of valleys and plains.

Thirty thousand tons of potatoes were produced annually at the high-Andean imperial city of Tiahuanaco before its collapse over a thousand years ago. One hundred fifty cultivated varieties were known in the Andes by the time of the Spanish invasion. The relative distribution of maize and potatoes at that time showed how the political ecology of the region worked. Maize was a sacred crop, sedulously cultivated, by disproportionately painstaking means, in priestly gardens, at altitudes where it could never be viable, where the aridity was deadly and the frost destructive, so that small amounts were available for religious rites. European observers noticed nothing of the kind in connection with the potato, which was the workaday basis of the universal diet. "Half the Indians," it was said, "had nothing else to eat." This is believable: two peculiar features gave the potato the unique power of the potato to sustain civilization in the Andes: tolerance of extreme altitudes, for some varieties can grow at thirteen thousand feet; and unrivaled nutritional merit. The potato, if eaten in sufficient quantities, provides all the nutrients the human body needs.

Yet, as we shall see when we turn to trace the global migrations of the potato (below, p. 179), at every stage of its progress the tuber has suffered contempt. In the eighteenth century Count Rumford had to disguise potatoes to get workhouse inmates to accept them, while Parmentier had to trick peasants into growing them by pretending that their cultivation was a state secret. One of the reasons for this resistance, which may also help to explain the failure of taro and cassava to find worldwide acceptance, may be the fact that taro, cassava and potatoes all have the same mysterious property: unprocessed, they are poisonous—or, at least, wild potato varieties are poisonous and even cultivated varieties of taro and cassava contain toxic crystals which can only be eliminated by careful techniques. To rid cassava, for instance, of its prussic acid content, you have to peel it, grate it, squeeze it, sieve it and then boil the pulp or toast the flour. "The juice of it," reported a French observer of Native American customs in the early eighteenth century, "so dangerous, so deadly, becomes, after boiling well, a sweet, honeyed licquor, very good to drink." The discovery that these naturally toxic plants could be worth cultivating and transforming into food is another of the miracles of "primitive" agronomy, and another of the unsolved mysteries of the early history of farming.

Food and Rank

—

Inequality and
the Rise of Haute Cuisine

Where is the food-hall, foyer of feasts?
Where the pleasures of the place?
The goblet's glint, the gleaming guests?
The palgraves' grandeur, great ones' grace?

—THE WANDERER, 93–95

I sit at my table en grand seigneur,
And when I have done, throw a crust to the poor;
Not only the pleasure itself of good living,
But also the pleasure of now and then giving:
So pleasant it is to have money, heigh-ho!

—ARTHUR HUGH CLOUGH, SPECTATOR AB EXTRA

THE SUCCESS OF EXCESS

Food became a social differentiator—a signifier of class, a measure of rank—at a remote, undocumented moment when some people started to command more food resources than others. It happened early. There was never a golden age of equality in the history of humankind. Inequality is implicit in evolution by natural selection. Wherever hominid remains survive in sufficient quantities and in states of preservation good enough to permit conclusions to be drawn, there are differences in nutrition levels among members of what seem to be the same communities. Paleolithic burials show, in many cases, correlations between levels of nutrition and signs of honor. In the earliest human class systems we know about, food played a differentiating role.

At that stage, as far as we know, it was quantity that mattered, rather than the dishes selected or the way they were prepared. No doubt cooking increased the prejudice in favor of big meals: an insidious, or, at least, equivocal effect of cooking is that it makes eating pleasurable. It becomes a temptation to gluttony; a primrose road to obesity, and therefore a fount of social inequality. Differences followed, of course, in the way food was dressed and served. These, in as far as they matched gradations of rank, were not among the causes of inequality, but its results, whereas differences in the amount of food available to people of differing status were discernible at the very inception of inequality and can be numbered, if not among its causes, at least among its defining characteristics.

Certainty is impossible, given the imperfect state of most of the early evidence, but socially differentiating cuisines probably occurred relatively late in history and, until remarkably recently, were found only in some parts of the world. Quantity mattered more than quality. The gigantic appetite has normally commanded prestige in almost every society, partly as a sign of prowess and partly, perhaps, as an indulgence accessible only to wealth. Except where it is commonplace, as in the modern West, fat is admirable and greatness goes with greatness of girth. Gluttony may be a sin but it is no crime: on the contrary, up to a point it can be socially functional. Big appetites stimulate production and generate surplus—leftovers on which lesser eaters can feed. So, in normal circumstances, as long as the food supply is unthreatened, eating a lot is an act of heroism and justice, similar in effect to other such acts, such as fighting off enemies and propitiating the gods: it is usual to find the same sort of people engaged in all three tasks. Legendary feats of digestion were chronicled in antiquity, like heroes' tallies of battle victims, wanderers' odysseys or tyrants' laws. Every day, Maximinus the Thracian drank an amphora of wine and ate forty or sixty pounds of meat. Clodius Albinus was celebrated because he could eat five hundred figs, a basket of peaches, ten melons, twenty pounds of grapes, one hundred garden warblers and four hundred oysters at a sitting. Guido of Spoleto was refused the French throne because he was a frugal eater. Charlemagne could not manage dietary temperance and refused his physicians' advice to mitigate his digestive problems by eating boiled instead of roasted food: this was the gustatory equivalent of Roland's refusal to summon reinforcements in battle—recklessness hallowed by risk. To comply would have been an act of self-derogation.

Abundant food is part of the panoply of every earthly paradise, and of some heavenly ones, too, like the reward of Muslim martyrs or the feasting halls of the Viking Valhalla. Big meals were a feature of the good life in the land of the Sirens, according to a fragment of Epicharmus:

"In the morning, just at dawn, we used to barbecue plump little anchovies, some baked pork, and octopus and drink down some sweet wine with them."

"Oh you poor fellows."

"Hardly a bite, you see."

"What a shame!"

"Then all we would have was one fat red mullet and a couple of bonitos split down the middle and wood pigeons to match and scorpion-fish."

Conspicuous consumption works as a generator of prestige, in part simply because it is conspicuous, but also because it is useful. The rich man's table is part of the machinery of wealth distribution. His demand attracts supply. His waste feeds the poor. Food sharing is a fundamental form of gift exchange, cement of societies; chains of food distribution are social shackles. They create relationships of dependence, suppress revolutions and keep client classes in their place. The story is told of how Consuelo Vanderbilt, when she became chatelaine of Blenheim Palace, reformed the method by which leftovers were distributed among the poor neighbors of the estate: the broken meats were still slopped into jerry cans and wheeled out to the beneficiaries, but Consuelo was fastidious enough to insist that, for the first time in the history of the house, the courses be separated— meat from fish, sweets from savories, and so on. Consuelo's generosity belongs in a long tradition of noblesse oblige, scattered with crumbs from the rich man's table, haunted by the ghosts of guests from the highways and byways.

This tradition goes back to the redistributive palace storehouses operated by the elites of early agrarian societies: the labyrinth of Knossos contained no minotaurs but it was filled with oil jars and bins of grain. Egypt was a food engine and the pharaonic economy was dedicated to a cult of the abundance of the everyday: not individual abundance, for most people lived on bread and beer in amounts only modestly above subsistence level, but a surplus garnered and guarded against hard times, at the disposal of the state and the priests. In an environment of scorching aridity, periodically doused by promiscuous floods, defiance of nature meant not only refashioning the landscape and punching pyramids into the sky: above all, it was a matter of stockpiling against disaster, to make mankind indestructible, even by the invisible forces that controlled the floods. The temple built to house the body of Rameses II had storehouses big enough to feed twenty thousand people for a year. The taxation yields painted proudly on the walls of a vizier's tomb are an illustrated menu for the feeding of an empire: sacks of barley, piles of cakes and nuts, hundreds of head of livestock. The state was a stockpiler it seems, not for the permanent purposes of redistribution—the market took care of that—but for famine relief. When "the starvation-year" was over, according to an old tradition collected in a late text—of about the late second century B.C.—people's "borrowing from their granaries will have departed."

The royal banquets of Mesopotamia originally functioned as means of distributing food according to a hierarchy of privilege determined by the kings. Like everything else in the Assyrian world, they became inflated to gigantic proportions when an imperial system replaced the city-states. When Ashurnishabal (883–59 B.C.) completed the palace of Kalhu, he had 69,574 guests at a banquet that lasted ten days. One thousand fat oxen, 14,000 sheep, 1,000 lambs, hundreds of deer, 20,000 pigeons, 10,000 fish, 10,000 desert rats and 10,000 eggs were served. In the *Edda*, the heroes Loki and Logi engaged in an eating contest: the latter won by eating "all the meat and bones and the platter itself." This triumph of heroic eating was not considered selfish. In a more equivocal instance, Nero's banquets, according to his enemies, lasted from noon till midnight. Rules composed two thousand years ago in India specified rice, pulses, salt, butter and ghee for everyone; but menials should have only a sixth of a gentleman's allowance of rice and only half his mede of ghee. Some differentiation on grounds of quality was also made: laborers, who needed plenty of nutrition, got the rice husks and slaves the broken bits. Although the excluded may evince resentment, rulers' feasts bind political alliances and create affinities, retinues, patronage networks and household aristocracies. The "baronial" banqueting halls of the medieval West were designed for meals of allegiance, at which lordly largesse was cooked and served in stunning quantities. At the enthronement of an archbishop of York in 1466, the bill covered 300 quarters of wheat, 300 tuns of ale and 1,000 of wine, 104 oxen, 6 wild bulls, 1,000 sheep, 304 calves, 304 swine, 400 swans, 2,000 geese, 1,000 capons, 2,000 pigs, 400 plovers, 100 dozen quail, 200 dozen female sandpipers, 104 peacocks, 4,000 mallards and teals, 204 cranes, 204 kid, 2,000 chickens, 4,000 pigeons, 4,000 crays, 204 bitterns, 400 heron, 200 pheasants, 5,000 partridge, 400 woodcock, 100 curlew, 1,000 egrets, more than 500 deer, 4,000 cold venison pasties, 2,000 hot custards, 608 pikes and bream, 12 porpoises and seals and unspecified amounts of spices, sugared delicacies, wafers and cakes.

It is striking how the sheer quantity of food served—and sometimes eaten—persists as an index of status. Reverence for excess remains widespread in the world outside the West. Modern Trobriand islanders relish the prospect of a feast so big that "we shall eat until we vomit." A South African saying is, "We shall eat until we cannot stand." The aesthetics of obesity are widely prized. Among the Banyankole of East Africa a girl prepares for marriage at about eight years old by staying indoors and drinking milk for a year until corpulence reduces her walk to a waddle. Habits of atavistic overeating recur in high-status individuals, even in societies which have abundant other ways of honoring rank, and in cases where the eaters in question can have had no doubt of their entitlement. This is particularly remarkable in the history of early-modern Europe, where table manners were becoming a cult and where selfish overindulgence was coming to be seen as repellent. Montaigne reproached himself for greed so urgent that it made him bite fingers and tongue and spare no time at table for talk. Louis XIV incapacitated himself with food at his own wedding feast. Doctor Johnson ate with such concentration that the veins on his forehead stood out and he broke out in sweat. Brillat-Savarin, for all his attention to quality in foodstuffs, admired gargantuan appetites. He wrote with awestruck reverence of the priest of Bregnier, who, without hurry or fuss, ate a meal of soup, boiled beef, a leg of mutton à la royale "down to the ivory, a capon down to the bone," and the "copious salad . . . down to the bottom of the dish" before finishing off with a quarter of a large white cheese with a bottle of wine and a jug of water. This gourmet justified gourmandism on the grounds that it showed "implicit obedience to the commands of the Creator, who, when he ordered us to eat in order to live, gave us the inducement of appetite, the encouragement of savor, and the reward of pleasure." Brillat-Savarin's representative menus for different income groups are calibrated by quantity as well as finesse of preparation and conclude with a meal for the wealthy: a seven-pound fowl, stuffed with Perigord truffles until it is made spherical; a huge Strasbourg pâté de fois gras in the shape of a bastion, a big Rhine carp à la Chambard, richly adorned and garnished, truffled quails à la moelle, served on basil-flavored buttered toast, a stuffed and larded pike baked in creamy crayfish sauce secundum artem, a well-hung roast pheasant, larded en troupet, served on toast dressed à la Sainte Alliance; a hundred early asparagus, five or six threads in diameter, with osmazone sauce; two dozen ortolans à la provençal.

A. J. Liebling, sportswriter and Paris correspondent for *The New Yorker*, described the apotheosis of this tradition in dozens of magazine stories. His exemplar was Yves Mirande, theatrical impresario and the last representative of the "heroic age" of eating before the First World War, who

> would dazzle his juniors, French and American, by dispatching a lunch of raw Bayonne ham and fresh figs, a hot sausage in crust, spindles of filleted pike in a rich rose sauce Nantua, a leg of lamb larded with anchovies, artichokes on a pedestal of foie gras, and four or five kinds of cheese, with a good bottle of Bordeaux and one of champagne, after which he would call for the Armagnac and remind Madame to have ready for dinner the larks and ortolans she had promised him, with a few langoustes and a turbot—and, of course, a fine civet made

from the marcassin, or young wild boar, that the lover of the leading lady in his current production had sent up from his estate in the Sologne. "And while I think of it," I once heard him say, "we haven't had any woodcock for days, or truffles baked in the ashes."

A well-laden board was a sign of status throughout the nineteenth and early twentieth centuries in the West and the growing opportunities for diversity at table tended to multiply the numbers of dishes. Yet an equivocal attitude is detectable in the satirical tone of some descriptions. The domestic regime of Trollope's Archdeacon Grantly demonstrated not only his wealth but also his worldliness.

> The silver forks were so heavy as to be disagreeable to the hand, and the bread-basket was of a weight really formidable to any but robust persons. The tea consumed was the very best, the coffee the very blackest, the cream the very thickest; there was dry toast and buttered toast, muffins and crumpets; hot bread and cold bread, white bread and brown bread, home-made bread and bakers' bread, wheaten bread and oaten bread, and if there be other breads than these, they were there; there were eggs in napkins and crispy bits of bacon under silver covers; and there were little fishes in a little box, and devilled kidneys frizzling on a hot-water dish; which, by-the-by, were placed closely contiguous to the plate of the worthy archdeacon himself. Over and above this, on a snow-white napkin, spread upon the sideboard, was a huge ham and a huge sirloin; the latter having laden the dinner table on the previous evening. Such was the ordinary fare at Plumstead Episcopi. And yet I never found the rectory a pleasant house. The fact that man shall not live by bread alone seemed to be somewhat forgotten.

Upper-class indulgence grew increasingly comic. This dialogue from Somerset Maugham's *Lady Frederick* is typical of a tradition in which the meal gets funnier as the menu gets longer.

> FOULDES: Thompson, did I eat any dinner at all?
> THOMPSON [STOLIDLY]: Soup, sir.
> FOULDES: I remember looking at it.
> THOMPSON: Fish, sir.
> FOULDES: I trifled with a fried sole.
> THOMPSON: Vol-au-vent Rossini, sir.
> FOULDES: It has left absolutely no impression upon me.

THOMPSON: Tournedos à la Splendide.

FOULDES: They were distinctly tough, Thompson. You must lodge a complaint in the proper quarter.

THOMPSON: Roast pheasant, sir.

FOULDES: Yes, yes, now you mention it, I do remember the pheasant.

THOMPSON: Pêches Melba, sir.

FOULDES: They were too cold, Thompson. They were distinctly too cold.

LADY MERESTON: My dear Paradine, I think you dined uncommonly well.

FOULDES: I have reached an age when love, ambition and wealth pale into insignificance beside a really well-grilled steak. That'll do, Thompson.

Today, the cult of abundance abides in America, where it thrives on "the embarrassment of riches"—an example of splurge and overspill in a culture always struggling to escape from a past dominated by the Puritan gospel of thrift. It may have started in colonial times. It was well established in the mid-nineteenth century, when "every day at every meal you see people order three or four times as much . . . as they could possibly eat, and, picking at and spoiling one dish after another, send the bulk away uneaten." A hotel in New York listed 145 items on its dinner menu in 1867. The longest menu in the history of restaurant going has to be that of the Airport Diner in Newark, New Jersey, which daily listed over 50 appetizers, 40 soups, 300 sandwiches, 200 salads, 400 main courses, 80 different vegetables and 200 desserts. Over 100 items at dinner and 75 at breakfast were not unusual. But overindulgence was too cheap and easy to obtain and austerity, like every kind of rarity, was by then becoming the creed of arbiters of taste. Sarah Hale advised postbellum hostesses to "provide enough, and beware of the common practice of having too much." The abundance of America is best evoked by the legendary eating habits of Duke Ellington, the jazz wizard. He was, perhaps, outside fiction, the world's last real heroic eater. He liked "to eat till it hurts."

In Taunton, Mass, you can get the best chicken stew in the United States. For chow mein with pigeon's blood I go to Johnny Cann's Cathay House in San Francisco. I get my crab cakes at Bolton's—that's in San Francisco too. I know a place in Chicago where you can get the best barbecued ribs west of Cleveland and the best shrimp creole outside New Orleans. There's a wonderful place in Memphis too for barbecued ribs. I get my Chinook salmon in Portland Oregon. In Toronto I get duck orange, and the best fried chicken in the world is in Louisville, Kentucky. I get myself half a dozen chickens and a gallon jar of potato salad so I can feed the seagulls. You know, the guys who reach over your shoulder. There's a place in Chicago, the Southway Hotel, that's got the best cinnamon rolls and the best filet mignon in the world. Then there's Ivy Anderson's chicken shack in Los Angeles, where they have hot biscuits with honey and very fine chicken liver omelettes. In New Orleans there's gumbo filé. I like it so well that I always take a pail of it out with me when I leave. In New York I send over to the Turf Restaurant at Forty-ninth and Broadway a couple of times a week to get their broiled lamb chops. I prefer to eat them in the dressing-room where I have plenty of room and can really let myself go. In Washington at Harrison's they have devilled crab and Virginia ham. They're terrific things.

He conceded a place of honor to crêpes Suzette and octopus soup in Paris, mutton in London, smorgasbord in Sweden and an hors d'oeuvre trolley in The Hague—"eighty-five different kinds, and it takes a long time to eat some of each." But, like Daniel Hines, Duke remained faithful to the excellence and excess of his homeland.

There's a place on West Forty-ninth Street in New York that has wonderful curried food and wonderful chutney. At old Orchard Beach, Maine, I got the reputation of eating more hot dogs than any man in America. A Mrs. Wagner there makes a toasted bun that's the best of its kind in America. She has a toasted bun, then a slice of onion, then a hamburger, then a tomato, then melted cheese, then another hamburger, then a slice of onion, more cheese, more tomato, and then the other side of the bun. Her hot dogs have two dogs to a bun. I ate thirty-two one night. She has very fine baked beans. When I eat with Mrs. Wagner, I begin with ham and eggs for an appetizer, then the baked beans, then fried chicken, then a steak—her steaks are two inches thick—and then a dessert of applesauce, ice cream, chocolate cake and custard, mixed with rich, yellow country cream. I like veal with an egg on it. . . . Durbin-Park's in Boston has very fine roast beef. I get the best baked ham, cabbage and corn bread at a little place near Biloxi. St. Petersburg, Florida, has the best fried fish. It's just a little shack, but they can sure fry fish. I really hurt myself when I go there.

Just as individuals, for most of history, gained prestige in proportion to their food consumption, so modern America owes part of its world-beating renown to its image as a land of plenty.

THE RISE OF GASTRONOMY

Stupefying quantity is an important historic feature of elite food styles: eating for greed or waste is a commonplace form of aristocratic display; heroic eating is model behavior. Yet mere quantity did not remain the only criterion of a prestigious diet. Taste as well as waste has an ennobling effect. Selection for quality also seems to be programmed into evolution. Compared with other primates of similar size, the human diet is high in nutrient quality per unit of weight. Diversity, as well as quality, typifies high-status diets and may also be a craving sanctioned by evolution, the ideal of an omnivorous species. As the incomparable food journalist Jeffrey Steingarten said, "Lions will starve in a salad bar, as will cows in a steak house—but not us." Diversity in diet is a function of distance: it attains impressive proportions when the products of different climates and eco-niches are united on the same table. For most of history, long-range trade has been a small-scale, hazardous, costly adventure; so diversity of diet has been a privilege of wealth or a reward of rank.

Paradoxically, quantity, in some cultures, is not enough. It has to be combined with other forms of profligacy, as in the potlatch of the American Northwest, where surplus feast food is flung into the sea as a gesture of conspicuous consumption; or in the fashionable banquets of Renaissance Rome, when gold vessels were flung, with fake ostentation, into the Tiber (where concealed nets ensured ease of retrieval); or in the meals Lady Mary Wortley Montagu ate in the harem of the Topkapi Saray, where fifty dishes of meat were served, one at a time. The tables were laid with tiffany silk, of which the napkins, too, were made; the knives were gold and their hafts set with diamonds. Alternatively, the same effect can be contrived, with greater economy, by variety and refinement.

The apotheosis of prestige cuisine is, perhaps, kaiseki ryori, the courtly food of imperial Japanese tradition, in which tiny slivers and cubes and shoots and buds—a single small egg, a trio of beans, "a curl of carrot, a fried gingko nut"— become individual dishes, selected and presented for aesthetic pleasure, as much for the eye as the palate and for the mind rather than the stomach: "fourteen courses of airy-fairy fantasy," as the distinguished American food critic M. F. K. Fisher puts it. The effect of a meal in this tradition can be as sensual as a gross blowout, if more subtle. A great chef such as Shizuo Tsuji, renowned for the school of cookery he runs today in Osaka, can select fish for the table by texture "like the bloom of youth on a young girl." In default of a "suitably artistic" platter, he advocates a piece of fragrant wood or "a flat stone, with a few leaves at one side." The leaves, will, of course, symbolize the season, like the mood of a haiku.

Gustatory delicacy and understatement, restraint of appetite, refinement in food—these have been indices of rank in Japan at least since the late tenth century, when Sei Shonagon, the famous diarist, affected revulsion at the way workmen guzzle their rice. The dishes which pleased her best were duck eggs—the only food she mentions repeatedly—and "shaved ice flavoured with liana syrup on a silver bowl." So the aesthetic behind kaiseki ryori goes back to the Heian period. Dietary austerity, of course, is most conspicuous when honored in the breach—for instance, by a fictional monk of the thirteenth century, who would have been worthy of a place in the *Canterbury Tales*, and who listed with affected distaste the dishes his patroness might be expected to provide "until my brief existence draws to its close": aromatic pears, branches of nuts and acorns, sweet seafoods, rice cakes and rice paste, prize turnips, "those splendid dried melons from below Komatsu," pine seeds, dried shrimp and mandarin oranges. "If, however, you cannot supply all this, give me some simple things such as dried beans."

The modern repertoire of kaiseki dishes—in which the main ingredient is often disguised and sometimes crafted from tofu or red bean paste to resemble something else—seems to date only from the period of Zen influence on aristocratic lifestyles, from the fourteenth to the eighteenth centuries. Thereafter, almost all visitors attested that frugality was genuinely embraced as a virtue, even by diners who could afford to eat copiously. "The rich, as well as the poor," observed a Russian captive who made extensive observations of eating habits in the early years of the nineteenth century, "spend but little in eating and drinking." Queen Victoria's envoy, Sir Rutherford Alcock, attributed to aristocratic abstinence the extraordinary abundance of unkilled game. "Think of that, ye epicures," he taunted his fellow Europeans,

> and instead of a shooting or a fishing season in Norway with its hackneyed fjelds [sic] and fiords, come to Japan to catch salmon, hunt the deer, the boar and the bear and, if you like it, shoot the pheasant, snipe, teal, and wild-fowl without stint. It is rather far off—some sixty odd days—but then think of the game and the novelty—to say nothing of the chance of being becarved by the two-sworded samurai in pursuit of *their* game.

Visitors who arrived in this spirit could be deceived by generous hospitality. An insensitive American tourist in 1921 got the impression that, for quantity, a Japanese meal was "simply stupendous." Having eaten his way through pickled vegetables, terrapin soup with quails' eggs and onions, baked fish with sea urchin paste, sushimi, fried prawns and eels, steamed cakes of duck, fish and vegetables, and

roast duck, he was surprised to be offered a "second table" of vegetables, fish consommé, grilled eels with rice, and fruits. "I am told," he concluded, that indigestion
is a prevalent ailment of the Japanese. . . . The toiling coolie is the only man in
Japan who might reasonably be expected to digest an elaborate Japanese meal, and
he, of course, never gets one. This observation was made where the visitor's
uncharacteristically big feast was consumed: in a club for foreigners.

Today, a myth of a golden age, when all Japanese took aesthetic and ascetic
pleasure in their food, stirs dismay at the encroachments of inelegant eating.
M. F. K. Fisher imagines "a porter or streetcar vendor," at a street stand, ignorant
of the symbolism of "the significant tangle of the *udon* in their clear broth, the
cloud-form of steam that rises" to heaven, pushing the noodles into his mouth and
slurping his soup before hurrying back to work: this seems directly related to Sei
Shonagon's revulsion of the "truly strange" way in which the lower orders gobbled
their rice and "dived into" their soup bowls; but the kaiseki ryori tradition would
be meaningless without its opposite. In reality, it is probably stronger than ever
today, because rich bourgeois are reviving it and encouraging restaurateurs to
recapture its spirit.

Like kaiseki ryori, all the earliest recorded courtly cuisines emphasized
painstaking preparation. Surviving Mesopotamian recipes advise browning meat
or birds before boiling in water with thickenings of blood, and flavorings of garlic,
onion, leek, turnip and dressings of cheese or butter; or braising is recommended
in fat and water. From ancient Egypt no direct evidence survives but medical treatises sometimes echo courtly recipes, such as the minced pigeon cooked with liver,
fennel, chicory and iris recommended by a physician from Krokodilopolis on the
grounds that the broth was thought to be good for stomachache. Dishes to cele-
brate the completion of the harvest and tempt the souls of the dead to earth were
listed with obvious yearning by a Chinese poet of the second or third century B.C.:
"the cunning cook slices pigeon and yellow heron and black crane with peppered
herbs into millet pies." He concocts badger stew, fresh turtle, sweet chicken cooked
in cheese, pickled suckling pigs and the flesh of newborn puppies floating in liver
sauce, with radish salad and Indian spices, roast daw, steamed widgeon, grilled
quail, boiled perch and sparrow broth "in each preserved the separate flavor that
is most its own." Since feasts for the dead had to be of unblemished food, this suggests that elaborate preparation, in the writer's opinion, left ingredients uncom-
promised and even, perhaps, enhanced in purity. Around the turn of the second
and third centuries A.D., Athenaeus of Naucratis combined all the elements of
emerging haute cuisine into his sketch of the most luxurious meal he could imagine: copious amounts, distinctive dishes, exquisite service, impressive variety and

inventive cookery. In the banqueting room he envisaged, on well-rubbed tables, under hanging lamps which "shone on festive crowns," "well stuffed conger," was served, in a glistening dish "to delight a god" with snowy-topped loaves. Course by course, there followed soused ray, shark, stingray and squid and sepia-coloured polyps with soft tentacles; then a fish "as large as the table, exhaling spirals of steam"; then breaded squid and toasted prawns. "The navel of the feast" was a sweet course, intruded at this point: "flower-leaved" cakes, spiced sweetmeats and puff pastries. Next came tuna, sliced "from the meatiest part of the belly." The courses paraded so fast that "I almost," said the poet whose account of the banquet Athenaeus quotes, "missed out on the hot tripe." A home-bred pig provided chitterlings, chine and rump with hot dumplings; then came a milk-fed kid's head—boiled whole—and more pork delicacies: boiled pettitoes, skin-white ribs, snouts, heads, feet and a tenderloin spiced with the rare African relish, silphium; then roast lamb "and the tenderest morsel of underdone entrails" of lambs and kids, "such as the gods love"; then jugged hare, young cockerels, partridges and ringdoves, before a dessert of yellow honey, clotted cream and cheese.

In some cultures, fastidiousness vies with excess in the world of noble values and obligations. Some elites—or, sometimes, conflicting factions within high-consuming elites—have tried to challenge the heroic ideal of eating with a subtler ethos, advocating an alternative approach, which condemns unrestraint as barbarous and exalts the nobility of austerity and simplicity. Confucian foodways represent a gentlemanly ideal. According to the sayings attributed to the sage, austerity is not breached by food which is perfectly fresh, expertly cooked and finely presented. On the contrary, it would be bestial to compromise standards in any of these respects. But meat should be eaten sparingly—not so much as to be detectable on one's breath; robust seasonings, such as ginger, should be applied with prudence; and wine must not be taken indecorously. Mencius denounced the self-indulgence of the rich in the presence of needy poverty. He recommended "the reduction of the heart's desires" as the best means to true happiness. A small appetite is a sign of Buddhahood. The Quran says, "The greater part of celestial and terrestrial pleasures consists of the consumption of desirable dishes and drinks," but in Arab court cuisines, the simplicity of the desert opposes the luxury of the town in ever creative tension. Brahmins are supposed to affect indifference to food, like Professor Godbole in *A Passage to India*, who encountered it "as if by accident." Pythagoras enjoined abstinence. Moderation was a stoic virtue. According to Epictetus, eating, like copulation, "should be done in passing." In the circle of Christ, five barley loaves and two small fishes were as good as a feast. Few, if any, of these sages seem to have had much immediate impact on upper-class eating; but abstinence gradually established itself as evidence of refinement in all the societies touched by their influence.

The effect, in part, was to nourish another paradox typical of the history of high-status food. Lavish entitlement becomes a sign of true aristocracy only when it is voluntarily renounced. The true leader shares his people's hardships. Augustus Caesar was supposed to be an archetype of frugality. His successors showed their inferiority in proportion to the amount by which they exceeded his diet. He "preferred the food of the common people"—coarse bread, hand-pressed cheese, figs from the second crop. He snacked in the saddle rather than respect time-wasting mealtimes. He claimed to fast "more rigorously than a Jew on his Sabbath" and reputedly used cucumber and sour apples as a digestive instead of wine. Genghis Khan never allowed the cultures of his conquests to seduce him from the "harsh life of the north." Bonnie Prince Charlie was loved by his men because "he could win a battle in four minutes and eat his dinner in five." It is impossible to know whether Napoleon's preference for fried potatoes and onions was a real demonstration of taste or an affectation contrived to signify his self-perception as the embodiment of popular sovereignty.

There are three ways of reconciling the ideals of austerity and excess. The first is by selecting choice or rare or frankly bizarre foods, conspicuous enough in themselves to count as ennobling in small quantities. The second is by elaborate preparation of unostentatious amounts. Both these methods encourage what is now called foodism—connoisseurship, which can, in the words of Juvenal, "pinpoint a sea-urchin at a glance," and which makes eating esoteric. The last method is by developing peculiar rules of etiquette, which can be practiced only by select initiates: this liberates the eaters from eating particular sorts of food, served in large quantities or prepared by special means. What matters, instead, is how it is eaten.

The first method was notoriously exemplified by the third-century Roman emperor Heliogabulus. He was the personification of overindulgence but he was driven neither by gourmandizing—though he is often accused of it—nor by his undeniable passion for luxury. His real obsession was novelty. He sought unprecedented sensations. He wanted to live in a world where strangeness was normal. His appetite was for culinary surrealism. He made conspicuous consumption an art. He fed goose livers to his dogs. His human guests were offered peas laced with gold and lentils with onyx, beans dressed with amber and fish scattered with pearls. He is supposed to have created a dish of six hundred ostrich heads. At table, he favored stage management above savor and comedy over cuisine, ordering fish in blue sauce to resemble the sea. His only rival among Roman emperors in this respect was Vitellius, who designed a "Shield of Minerva," represented in a platter of livers of sea bass, lamprey and milt with pheasant and peacock brains and flamingos' tongues. Of course, reports about these meals should be taken with a pinch of salt. Baroque banquets may have made Romans vomit: the descriptions we have of them usually come from stoically minded critics, who certainly wanted to induce nausea in their readers.

Eclat can be achieved by the spectacle of unseasonal dishes—another feature of high-status food which suggests heroism by defiance of nature. "Do not marvel," wrote a great seventeenth-century cook disingenuously, "if I sometimes order things, for example asparagus, artichokes or peas . . . in January or February and others that seem at first to be out of season." The household chef of the Gonzaga of Ferrara, Bartolomeo Stefani, was writing precisely in order to *épater les bourgeois* who were the customers for his cookbook: he prided himself on dishes that demanded "a good purse and good horses." At a banquet he served to Queen Christina of Sweden in November, the first course was of strawberries with white wine. This was a surprise with a certain sprezzatura. Before the Renaissance cult of restraint reached the kitchen, surprises could be unabashedly splendid. At the wedding feast of the Duke of Mantua in 1581 there were venison pasties in the shape of gilded lions, pies in the form of upright black eagles, pasties of pheasant "which seemed alive." Peacocks were adorned with their tails and embellished with ribbons "which were arranged erect, as in life, with a perfume emanating from the kindled wadding in their beaks and an amorous epigram placed between their legs." Marzipan statues represented Hercules and a unicorn.

Even this was a faint echo of one of the most bravura banquets in Western history, more than a century earlier, in Lille, on February 17, 1454, when Philip the Good of Burgundy took the "Vow of the Pheasant," exacting a crusading oath from the banqueters, rather as modern fund-raisers extort subventions at charity dinners. According to a participant, "there was a chapel on the table, with a choir in it, a pasty full of flute-players, and a turret from which came the sound of an organ and other music." The duke was served by a pantomime horse and elephant, ridden by trumpeters. "Next came a white stag ridden by a young boy who sang marvelously, while the stag accompanied him with the tenor part, and next an elephant . . . carrying a castle in which sat Holy Church, who made piteous complaint on behalf of Christians persecuted by the Turks." The tradition of banqueting-as-showmanship continues. Financier James Buchanan, the "Diamond Jim" Brady (famous for his ability to consume four dozen oysters as first course before dinner), was a guest at the legendary "Horseback Dinner," hosted at

Louis Sherry's New York restaurant, which featured riders and their horses who were lifted to the third-floor ballroom via the elevators.

The taste for bizarre foodstuffs, tabletop spectacle and table-side cabaret was merely gross. Liking for surprise foods—"blackbird" pies in the Middle Ages, modern bachelor night cakes which burst with dancing girls, pollo sorpresa and bombe surprise—illustrates the theater of cookery, but it surely has an intellectual side, too: a surprise is a puzzle and disguised foods are the fodder of intellectual games. In societies where education is an elite privilege, this makes them part of the high-class menu. In old Kyoto, it was the custom for banqueters to vie in attempts to guess what they had eaten, rather like the custom of guessing the name and vintage of the wine being consumed at certain tables today. Dorothy L. Sayers made the latter the key to a mystery story. Her secret agent, Lord Peter Wimsey, proved his identity in competition with his impostors by his unerring nose, palate and oenological knowledge.

Still, as a means of contriving exclusiveness without excess, tabletop theater has its drawbacks. Because it is ostentatious it can never seem austere. A better method is, perhaps, to emphasize cuisine over quantity—to try to create dishes which cost time to prepare and suggest aristocratic otium. As with all the other ways in which food is adapted as a social differentiator, this is represented by its apologists as a stage in the civilizing tradition. As the Chevalier Jaucourt said in his entry on cooking in that Enlightenment bible, the *Encyclopédie*, "The art of the chefs consists almost exclusively of the seasoning of dishes: it is common to all civilized nations. . . . Most seasonings are injurious to health. . . . And yet it must be granted that by and large only savages can be satisfied with the pure products of nature, eaten without seasoning and as nature provides them."

Alongside seasoning, the essence and evidence of elaborate preparation lies in the saucing. This can also be a means of disguise and mummery. The sauce is supposed in modern cookery to enhance or elicit the flavor beneath it; but it is still a mask, which coats what it complements. The "plain cooking school" derides sauces as a way of concealing poor ingredients. In reality, sauces are most likely to adorn the most select foods because they are a feature of courtly cuisines. They are expensive because they generally require that voluminous ingredients be reduced. They are labor-intensive because they involve combinations of ingredients. They are often impressionistically magical because their chemistry effects surprising transformations on their ingredients—like mayonnaise and aioli, in which, respectively, egg yolks or garlic are emulsified by olive oil; or curry, which makes buffalo fat uncloying; or Thai nam pla, which turns rotten fish into an indispensable flavoring. And they belong in a world of specialized expertise because, especially in the more ambitious reaches of sauce making, they require practice and informed judgment if they are to be successful. Sauces generate a learned tradition of cooking because the recipes are complex and hard to remember: they therefore have to be written down and become a privilege of the literate. Reputedly, the oldest recipe in the world is for a sauce: a marinade said, in texts of the late second millennium B.C., to have come from the Chou court: slices of raw carp are steeped in radish, ginger, chives, basil, pepper and knot grass.

The results of socially differentiated cuisine included the rise of a culinary profession of high status, a litany of techniques and a code of kitchen practice. Livy dated the decline of Rome from the moment when banquets became elaborate. "And it was then that the cook, who had formerly had the status of the lowest kind of slave, first acquired prestige, and what had once been servitude came to be thought of as an art." Cooks became artists or "performers," according to a fragment of Alexis. Though few cookbooks of real antiquity survive, the world they might have documented can be glimpsed in satires, like the cook's dialogue captured by the ear or imagination of Antiphanes:

> But no, the bit of bluefish to simmer in brine as before, I tell you.
> *And the bit of bass?*
> Bake whole.
> *The dogfish?*
> Boil in hypotrimma.
> *The piece of eel?*
> Salt, oregano, water.
> *The conger?*
> Same.
> *The skate?*
> Green.
> *There's a slice of* tuna.
> You bake it.
> *The kid?*
> Roast.
> *The other?*
> The reverse.
> *The spleen?*
> Stuffed.
> *The intestine?*
> You've got me there.

The art of Apicius—the Roman cook so esteemed that his name was appropri-
ated for numerous recipe collections, like Escoffier's or Fannie Farmer's today—
was largely consecrated to creating sauces, over 200 of the 470 recipes in the
earliest surviving text which bears his name. If Heliogabulus disliked a sauce, he
made his chef eat nothing else until the recipe was improved. At the courts of
sybaritic Muslim rulers in medieval Spain, recipe research was a serious scientific
vocation. The same scholars who worked on horticulture, agronomy and irrigation
techniques devised aromatic vinegars, potent garnishes and methods for improving foie gras. The cult of the sauce has remained an elite rite wherever it is known,
a lashing of aristocratic propriety. According to Brillat-Savarin, the Prince de
Soubise is supposed to have had a single ham dressed with sauce made from the
concentrated juices of forty-nine others. His steward presented the prince with a
bill for fifty hams. "Bertrand, have you gone mad?"

"No, your Highness; only one ham will appear on the table; but I shall need
all the rest for my brown sauce, my stock, my garnishings, my . . ."

"Bertrand, you're a thief and I shan't pass that item."

"But, your Highness," answered the artist, hardly able to contain his anger,
"you don't know our resources! You have only to say the word, and I'll take those
fifty hams you object to and put them onto a crystal phial no bigger than my
thumb."

Soubise is himself immortalized in Sauce Soubise—a béchamel with onions.
The recipe represents a tenacious concept among inventors of sauces: that you
create them by adding ingredients to a few basic "mother" types—hollandaise,
velouté, béchamel, espagnole. This doctrine—which is really rather misleading
since most savory sauces are reductions made from the juices exuded by whatever
is cooking—was devised by Antoine Carême—a pastry cook by training and
talent—whose vocation as chef to the most pretentious of clients was sustained
successively in the households of Talleyrand, Tsar Alexander I, the British Prince
Regent and James de Rothschild.

Part of the function of a sauce is to make food, in one sense, less foodlike: to
replace nutritional value with aesthetic appeal, to remove food from the state of
nature and smother it in art. Like the invention of cooking, it is a human act of
self-differentiation from nature, a repudiation of savagery, a further step in the civilizing process. Manners are similar—the sauces of gesture. Table manners are our
acts of complicity in the cook's attempt to civilize us, signs of our renunciation of
the savage within us. Just as the most soigné techniques of preparation character-
ize the most courtly cuisines, so etiquette grows ever more elaborate as we ascend
to the top table. Since cooking turned eating into a socially constructive act, food

has become surrounded with rites of politesse. Etiquette is always in evolution because part of the purpose of manners is to keep outsiders excluded and the code has to change whenever interlopers crack it. Different cultures honor different practices and a lot of modern humor has been inspired by the spectacle of diners trapped by contradictions between cultures: the unwary Asian, for instance, is a robust belcher who delicately refrains from blowing his nose; the Western guest who refuses the dish of honor at an Arab banquet; the ignoramus in Japan who tastes pickles before finishing his soup. A much told anecdote in Madrid society is of the dinner party at the Chinese embassy, where King Simeon of Bulgaria accepted three helpings of rice: in traditional Chinese etiquette, a guest is supposed to flatter his host by affecting satisfaction with the fancy dishes which precede the rice. When Jeffrey Steingarten was in Japan he delayed too long before raising the lid of his soup bowl; the moist heat of the soup sealed the lid and he was compelled to forsake the delicate program enjoined by etiquette—transferring lid to table and bowl from hand to hand according to the approved ritual. Instead, he had to wrench the lid, spill the soup, wreck the artistry of the dinner table and revert to the defensive role of dumb barbarian.

The serious barriers of etiquette—those which are actually enforced—exist not between classes but between cultures. In 1106, the disciplina clericalis of Petrus Alfonsi—a former rabbi of Toledo, converted to Christianity—specified a set of table manners that can still guide a modern dinner guest on a pilgrimage of social ascent. He justified them, however, not on grounds of courtesy to others, or of customary inertia, or of obligation to God, but because they served practical self-interest. In any company, he began, eat as if in the presence of a king. Wash your hands in advance. Gobble no bread before other dishes appear on the table "lest men call you impatient." Do not take big bites or dribble food from the corners of your mouth: otherwise you will be thought gluttonous. Chew each mouthful thoroughly: this will help to save you from choking. For the same reason, do not talk when there is food in your mouth. Do not drink on an empty stomach unless you want a reputation for drunkenness. Do not help yourself to food from your neighbor's plate: this might excite indignation. Eat a lot: if a friend, your host will be gratified; if he is an enemy, you will pile coals on his resentment. Within two or three hundred years in the West, codes of manners became more important as social differentiators at table than the food or even the cuisine. Hartmann von Aue, German translator of Chretien de Troyes, "I prefer to pass over what they ate, because they paid more attention to noble behavior than to much eating." One of our leading historians of food calls this, with a little exaggeration, the "birth of good manners, of a ritual conviviality, founded upon elegance." Where the correct etiquette was observed the food became irrelevant—at least, it could become irrelevant in a satirical imagination. Lewis Carroll's lampoon had Alice offer a slice off the joint to the Red Queen, who refused with every appearance of shock. "It isn't etiquette to cut anyone you've been introduced to." Pudding arrived. "Pudding-Alice, Alice-Pudding," interjected the Queen. "Remove the pudding."

THE EMBOURGEOISEMENT OF COURTLY COOKING

One reason for the importance of etiquette was the impossibility of preserving hieratic or esoteric foodways. "Secret" recipes are legendary but they usually get divulged. The most ethereal sauces trickle down from kingly tables to become bourgeois treats. Like other forms of technology, cuisine is easily imitated and transferred.

Indeed, courtly eating styles in the West have always been imitated from other cultures. In classical antiquity, upper-class foodways were denounced by Horace as "Persian" and by a Greek proverb as "Sicilian." When what Gibbon called "the triumph of barbarism and religion" interrupted the continuity of Western civilization, memories of Greek and Roman cuisine grew dim. Western courts looked to Islam for culinary inspiration. This is odd, on the face of it. Christendom and Islam were rival civilizations, formally at war, locked in mutual hatred. Crusading propaganda depicted Muslims as demons. In Islam, Christians were seen as vice personified. Yet at a high level of culture the world of Islam commanded admiration and imitation. In the tenth century, when Gerbert of Aurillac—an emperor's tutor and a future pope—wanted to learn mathematics, he went to Muslim Spain. The same route was followed by would-be practitioners of magic, seekers of the latest medical wisdom and collectors of ancient texts. Thanks to scholars working in Syriac and Arabic since the fall of the Roman Empire, a formidable corpus of manuscripts unknown in the West, including fundamental texts of Aristotle and Ptolemy, was preserved in libraries in lands under Muslim rule.

As general Islamic superiority in science and medicine was then beyond cavil, so, too, the specific advantage in what might be classed as "food sciences," such as agriculture and practical gardening. For cooking is a kind of alchemy, which transmutes base ingredients into luxuries. And the medicine of the period was, in great measure, a science of diet. Specific prophylactics were few but nourishment was known to conduce to health; the distinction between medicine and good food was inexact and the medicinal properties of foodstuffs were diligently monitored, recorded and reflected in kitchen practice. Science, magic and cookery blended into one another with no formally distinguished limits. The *Picatrix*, a twelfth-century book of magic, associates flavors (like other sensual associations) with the planets: pepper and ginger for Mars, camphor and rose for the moon. Bad tastes attract Saturn, bitter Jupiter, sweet Venus. This context of scientific admiration, which made Christian cooks wish to imitate their Muslim counterparts, was reinforced by the enviable image of luxury and ostentation evinced by Muslim courts. In Sicily in the mid-thirteenth century, Frederick II incurred opprobrium from Christian apologists for his fondness for Muslim savants and sybarites. Frederick, grandson of Barbarossa and Holy Roman Emperor, was a fanatical amateur scientist, who starved criminals to death in order to observe the physiological effects; he combined science with self-indulgence and enjoyed "Moorish" arts and manners—lounging on thick carpets, dressing in flowing garments. In the next century Peter the Cruel of Castile affected the status of a sultan and surrounded himself with Moorish decorations in his palaces in Tordesillas and Seville. These royal Islamophiles were extreme but not altogether unrepresentative cases of elite values in high-medieval Christendom: there was a strong tendency to cannibalize Muslim wisdom and defer to Muslim taste.

The culinary arts of Muslim courts became the fodder of Western recipe books when these began to appear on a significant scale in the thirteenth century. The West absorbed influences in three main areas: the aesthetics of the table, an accent on certain traditional exotic ingredients and a bias toward rich, sweet flavors. The aesthetics of food in Muslim courts resembled the aesthetics of the sacred arts in the West—a bias toward goldsmithy and jewelwork, which it was the aim of the best cooks to echo. They used saffron for gilding, sugar like diamonds and meat sliced alternately in white and dark "like gold and silver coin," according to the tenth-century text known as The Baghdad Cook. They made dishes to imitate carnelians and pearls. Just as sacred spaces and altars were heavily censed in Christendom, so royal banqueting halls and tables in Islam were perfumed with heavy aromas. Sweet flavors and scented ingredients were the most esteemed. Milk of almonds, ground almonds, rose water and extracts of other perfumed flowers, sugar and all the spices of the East—to which the Islamic world had privileged access by comparison with Christendom—became essential ingredients.

Almonds appear in sauces for chicken, rabbit, pork, pigeons and all the sweet Egyptian stews described by Abd al-Latif al-Baghdadi in the early thirteenth century. Fowl, he recommended, should be boiled in rose water on a bed of crushed hazelnuts or pistachios, with purslane seeds, poppy seeds or rose hips, cooked until they coagulated, and then enlivened at the last minute with precious spices, since to cook these for long would diminish their flavor. A characteristic banquet dish should include three roasted lambs, stuffed with chopped meats fried in sesame oil, with crushed pistachios, pepper, ginger, cloves, mastic, coriander, cardamom and other spices, sprinkled with musk-infused rose water; the spaces between and around the lambs on their dish should be filled with fifty fowls and fifty small birds, which in their turn were best stuffed with eggs or meat and fried with grape or lemon juice. The whole should then be enveloped with pastry, liberally sprinkled with rose water, and baked—presumably in an oven of remarkable size—to "rose red." Aristocratic tables in the West retained some tastes inherited from antiquity and, of course, many local and regional traditions, but the effect of Muslim magnetism is evident in the balance of influences suggested, for instance, by a menu from Richard II's England. Pig's umbles, boiled in stock with leeks, onions, blood, vinegar, pepper and cloves, was a dish which would have done justice to a Roman table. But the rest of the meal was fit for a sultan: small birds boiled in almond paste with cinnamon and cloves, and rose-scented rice boiled soft in almond milk, mixed with chicken's brawn, cinnamon, cloves, mace and scented with sandalwood. Dishes prominent in late-medieval Western cookery books regularly betray Muslim influence by these unmistakable signs, or by the inclusion of telltale ingredients, such as pomegranate seeds, raisin paste or sumac berries sweetened with almonds.

The movement known as the Renaissance transformed courtly cookery, as it transformed other arts. In the kitchen, reversion to ancient texts and Greco-Roman sources of inspiration demanded the abjuration of Arab influence. When Renaissance cooks tried to revive habits of antiquity they discarded the old palette of the culinary artist, with its gold hues, fragrant odors and sweet savors. The result, according to the outstanding historian of the process, T. Sarah Peterson, was "a shock" which has reverberated through Western food ever since. It used to be generally assumed among food historians that a new "salt-acid" repertoire of flavors, derived from ancient Rome, came to dominate Western cookery. This seems to be exaggerated. Roman food's reputation for saltiness derives from the ubiquity in Roman recipes of the fish sauce called garum or liquamen—made from red mullet, sprats, anchovies and mackerel mixed with entrails of other large fish, salted, exposed to the sun, concentrated, sieved and stored. The best quality liquamen, however, was not excessively salty: it was used, for instance, to freshen over-salty sea urchins; and when it became too salty with age, cooks were advised to refresh it with honey or grape must. Most of the new recipes of the Renaissance were not particularly salty, though they certainly represented a revulsion against the cloying sweetness favored in the Middle Ages. I suspect that this has little to do with Roman inspiration and more to do with the fact—to which we shall return in the next chapter—that sugar, formerly an exotic luxury, became a plentiful, everyday product in the same period. The real era of classical revivalism in food was in the eighteenth century, when the hero of a picaresque novel entertained guests at a reconstructed Roman dinner so accurate that it made them all sick. Later in the same century, Abbé Barthélémy devoted a chapter of *Voyage du jeune Anacharsis en Grece* to a meticulous description of an Athenian meal; Carême organized Roman meals under Napoleon; Parmentier was hailed "the Homer, Virgil and Cicero of the potato."

Meanwhile, there were certainly other Renaissance effects. Among the most beneficial, though not the most far-reaching, were a new prominence given to dairy products and vegetables and the rediscovery of fungi as food. (They were not universally welcomed: Henri II's physician, Buyerin, called them "phlegmy excretions" and reminded readers that mushrooms had massacred banqueters in antiquity and that Agrippina had murdered Claudius with poisoned morels. He admitted, however, that the "rage of the gullet" could not be assuaged without them.) Other vegetables with a certain viscosity of texture received new acclaim. Asparagus and artichoke bottoms were a Renaissance rediscovery, inspired by Pliny's gibes against "cultivated thistles." A surfeit of them made Catherine de Medici ill. The most important effect of the new cookery, however, was that by renouncing the exoticism of "Moorish" food, and reverting to a more familiar Western shopping basket, it made the cuisine of kings and aristocrats more accessible than ever to eaters in the middle ranks of Western society. The embourgeoisement of haute cuisine had begun. The seventeenth century was a critical period, in which the noblest recipes came to be communicated to a wider public than ever before. The point of diffusion was France.

Henri IV, the king who famously aimed to put "a chicken in the pot" of every peasant in his kingdom, was supposed to have simple, rustic tastes. He liked garlic and nursery food but acknowledged the need for sumptuous banquets as an aid to diplomacy and a lubricant of policy. His heir, Louis XIII, was brought up on a diet of intimidating scale and dazzling variety, recorded in the notebooks of his personal physician. Giblets figured prominently, as did asparagus; but every kind of meat and vegetable also appeared on his table, together with twenty-two kinds of fish, without counting the shellfish, and twenty-eight fruits. But in maturity he lost interest in overeating in consequence of poor health. It was therefore left to Louis XIV to introduce enlightened gluttony to the French court, for he had—as a courtier observed—"a most complaisant digestion, which enabled him to recuperate his strength whenever he so required." His sister-in-law often saw him "eat four bowls of different soups, a whole pheasant, a partridge, a big plateful of salad, sliced mutton in its juice with garlic, two big lumps of ham, a plateful of pastries and fruits and preserves." His meals were usually taken in private but sometimes turned into public performances, rites of majesty conducted before an audience of three hundred members of the royal household and a limitless public, confined behind barriers.

Paradoxically, courtly cuisine spread through society, becoming first a standard of aspiration, then—surprisingly quickly—the norm for every bourgeois family at its best. Louis XIV's kitchen kept no secrets: they were diffused by cookbooks, beginning with *Le Cuisinier françois* by François Pierre La Varenne, cook to a noble household, in 1651. By 1691, when François Massialot published a work whose title summed up the process of social diffusion—*Cuisinier royal et bourgeois*—100,000 copies of such works were in print.

CROSS-CLASS TRANSFERS

The *Gesta Romanorum*—a collection of anecdotes apparently intended as a trove for sermon writers—has a story of Caesar's demand for a boar's heart "because the emperor loved the heart best of any beast, and more than all the beast." But when the cook dressed it and saw how good and fat it was he ate it himself and said to his servants, "Say to the emperor that the hog had no heart." Who knows what moral medieval homilists drew from this? For us, its message is clear: it is hard for elites to monopolize select foods. It is almost equally hard for the underprivileged to claim their stake to their own dishes without exciting elite envy. Appropriations by the aspiring downgrade the creations of high cookery. *Nostalgie de la boue* and affectations of populism spread recipes up the social scale. Goldilocks is always transgressing class boundaries and stealing other people's porridge.

Of course, particular dishes, peculiar ingredients, certain culinary techniques and, indeed, entire menus have their own class profiles. Sometimes these are rooted in dietary restrictions typical of caste systems, like those in India, where foods are ranked in order of pollutant effect, or among Cushitic linguistic groups in East Africa who—if they have proper pride—still refuse to eat fish. More commonly, class differentiation starts with the crudities of basic economics. People eat the best food they can afford: the preferred food of the rich therefore becomes a signifier of social aspirations, pretensions or affectations, like those of the poor knight in Lazarillo de Tormes who went about with a toothpick in his mouth to suggest that he had been eating meat. Some foods become badges of honorable poverty: the fare of hermits or scholars. In Greece and Rome, the okralike mallow, asphodel and fenugreek, with its currylike aroma, were poor men's foods: according to Lucan, if you were served last in a wealthy household, nothing but mallow would be left. Galen told an anecdote of "a young medical student in Alexandria," who lived for four years on meals dressed with nothing else, except lupins (which are poisonous in their raw state). "He ate them with garum, of course" or with oil or vinegar. "He was healthy all through these years and his physical state was no worse at the end than at the beginning."

More commonly, the food of the poor is imposed by the rich. It is easy, amid the intricacies of class-differentiated menus, to forget the grim fact that for most of history "class-based nutritional inequalities were literally a matter of life and death." One of the "social measures" for which Peter III of Aragon was renowned was that sour wine, stale bread, rotten fruit and acidified cheese be put aside for alms. According to an old Romagnol harvesters' song, "The master gets the grain, the peasant gets the straw." Baldassare Pisanelli, a late-sixteenth-century physician, assured readers that "the leek is the worst food, the poorest and most detestable that can be used . . . it is the food of rustic folk," who should shun the food of their betters for their own good. "The only harm there is in the pheasant is that it causes asthma in rustic folk. The latter should abstain from eating them and leave them for noble and refined people." Courtly cuisines often have hallmark ingredients, which are forbidden to outsiders, such as swans in England and honey wine in Ethiopia. Gradually, however, in almost all known cases, social differentiation becomes a matter not only of what foods are eaten but also of how they are prepared. Messibugo, the arbiter elegantiarum of mid-sixteenth-century Tuscany, distinguished recipes suitable for "great princes" from those for "ordinary use": though the ingredients were essentially the same, on special occasions, the amount of spicing went up. The poor of industrializing Paris in the nineteenth century were advised to buy fat blended from the leftover butter, drippings, pork fat and poultry fat from bourgeois tables. Not much else was likely to be left over. In *La France gourmande* of 1906, Fulbert Dumontelli recommended scrap meats combined in croquettes— "it perfumes the whole house"—and garnished with slices of truffle cooked in champagne.

Limits between eating styles at different levels of society can, in exceptional circumstances, remain unchanged for eons, trapped in continuities which no amount of contact or exchange can unprise. In Emilia, according to the leading authority on the culinary history of the region,

> the "fat" cuisine acclaimed in the language of gastronomic tourism is not a dietary reality but a cliché, a convention bordering on mystification, a gastronomic myth, a topos, a commonplace only approximately related to the truth. The "historic" Emilian diet is quite different: it bears a strong peasant stamp—simple, crude, rooted in barbarian traditions.

Peasants ate more or less the same meals in the early twentieth century as when Gregory the Great ruled Rome. A typical Lombard-period family meal in winter comprised a loaf of bread, a pot of minestra and a thick foccaccia made of beans and millet, spread with animal fats or oil. A prodigious amount of wine would accompany it—as much wine, cup for cup, as soup. A modern menu in the same season would be little changed: the minestra would have pasta as well as beans, cooked in water with lard or onions for flavor and herring or bacon and ground chestnuts spread on polenta. "The elegant food many people associate with Bologna . . . has never belonged to the majority of the city's population. Bechamel sauce, for example, which is cited ad nauseam as a typical feature of the 'delicate,' 'smooth' and 'harmonious' Bolognese style of cooking, has never been known to the ordinary people of the city," who might, however, add cream to minestra. "Their diet, like their character, is sober and frugal, solid, essential, without too many subtleties and refinements." Minestra is known in the region as "the fodder of man."

This situation is now over, of course. But even while it prevailed it was not typical of the way foodstuffs changed their social profiles. Foods shift places in the hierarchy of social acceptability with bewildering ease and rapidity. Sometimes, the shift is induced by changes in availability: factory farming in the twentieth century stripped chicken of all rarity value in the Western world. Oysters and cod, on the other hand, leapt up the social scale as their breeding grounds shrank. Sometimes, the mere mechanisms of fashion are responsible: celebrity endorsement, novelty value, the oscillations of chic. Even slow changes—or those discernible to us only over long periods—surprise us by their scale. Educated palates in ancient Rome craved viscous textures: the prestige of pigs' glands and jowls, gelatinous feet, liver engorged by hypertrophy, fungi, tongues, head cheese, brains, sweetbreads, testicles, udders, wombs, marrow: the prestige of these foods is incontestably confirmed not only by the frequency with which they appear in surviving recipes but also by the fact that almost all of them became subjects of sumptuary laws. Foie gras was already a delicacy in the time of Homer, to judge from Penelope's pride in the "twenty geese I have at home, eating wheat soaked in water." For an elite experience, Roman eaters had to burrow deep in offal. This preference was never fully revived when the Renaissance restored Roman cuisine, and offal has remained, until recently, poor people's food. In modern Emilia and Romagna, according to reports in the 1960s, "there is a sharp decline in the consumption of offal or 'trimmings' like tripe, tongue, sweetbreads and filoni (spinal cords); the grilled treccine (plaits) of lambs' guts and the omelettes of lamb bottoni (testicles)—traditionally eaten on Easter Eve in Romagna—have become almost clandestine delights." Now, however, chefs bent on retrieving traditional cuisines are renewing the chic of tongues and testicles, brains and head cheese, tripes and trotters. Foie gras and calves liver were formerly exceptional—licensed lusciousness which was admitted at refined tables because it was always expensive to produce. Other organ meats remained cheap as long as they were undemanded by the wealthy; now they have caught up in cost with the rest of the edible animal parts.

Brown and white bread have swapped social profiles in a way that would surely bewilder an anthropologist from another planet. White bread has enjoyed, for most of history, universal esteem because it seems to embody refinement: compared with its brown and black cousins, it is the product of a longer process, a more intense use of labor, a greater degree of waste and a demand for subtler flavor. It often involves superior—that is, costlier—grains. In the eleventh century, Gregory, Bishop of Langres, did penance by eating barley bread. According to a sermon of Humbert of Romans, a postulant at the altar when asked "What do you seek?" replied "White bread and often!" In France, until the last generation, to eat pain de seigle was to lose caste. In Britain, the superiority of white bread was an unquestioned assumption until industrial baking made it universally available. The upper classes then discovered the virtues of bread the workers would no longer eat. Coarse texture was redefined as "fiber" and to eat it became a sign of discrimination. Royal tables in India of two thousand years ago were furnished with the choicest rice—the most highly polished grains selected.

Oysters are commonly regarded as a food which has ascended the social scale in the modern West; but their history is more complex. The oyster was a sublime delicacy in antiquity and Middle Ages. Pliny rated it "the most delicate morsel of the sea." It was boiled in spiced almond milk and wine in fifteenth-century England. In sixteenth-century Italy it was baked in pastry in elaborate savory custards. It was stuffed in soles in seventeenth-century France. It was proletarian food, on which Tiny Tim could dine with freedom, only during a brief era of abundance in the nineteenth century. While oysters have risen socially, chicken has fallen. It is hard now to recapture the longing evinced in a son's reproach to his honest peasant father in a thirteenth-century tale by Werner der Gartenaere, "Father, I eat polenta but I want what they call roast chicken." Today, it seems, we have to recontrive socially distinctive forms of chicken by privileging rare breeds, insisting on poulet de bresse, or inflating the prices of the products of free range or organic farming. Similarly, something like a socially differentiated range of pasta has been created by artificially adjusted pricing. Yet even pasta, which we think of as universally accessible nourishment, was once a luxury item. In 1600 in Rome, vermicelli cost three times as much as bread; even in 1700 the price of pasta was still double that of bread. Seventeenth-century Romans affectedly denigrated pasta as a foreign,

Neapolitan invention: the real motive for eating bread instead may have been rational economy rather than patriotic preference. The descent of pasta to the rank of a universal food occurred in eighteenth-century Naples as the result of a technological innovation—the kneading machine and mechanical press.

There was a time when caviar was popular. Pierre Bellon reported it as a commonplace foodstuff in Constantinople soon after the Latin conquest. Throughout the Levant, it was said, "there is no one who does not eat it except Jews, who avoid it because the sturgeon has no scales." The increasing cheapness and popularity of salmon today represents a regression to former habits: by local statute, apprentices in Gloucester in 1787 could not be forced "to dine off salmon oftener than twice a week." Meanwhile, in France, the potato registered a slow but relentless social ascent from a stomach filler for the poor to a garnish of universal esteem. In 1749, "Les gens d'un certain ordre mettait au-dessous d'eux d'en voir paraitre sur leur table"; by 1789 "ce poison commence a se glisser jusque chez les personnes aisées." The same tuber followed a quite different trajectory in Cordoba, Argentina, where it began as an innovation favored by the rich, as garnish for meat or as an entrée, stuffed or boiled; it then spread down through the ranks of society. In the early nineteenth century it cost as much as meat. By 1913 potatoes cost twelve cents a kilo, while beef was at fifty-five or sixty cents. Food always feeds class differences, but how, and with what dishes and ingredients, from time to time and place to place, seems impossible to predict.

COURTS WITHOUT CUISINE?

Courtly cuisine is the high point of socially differentiated eating and in much of the world kingly kitchens have set the standards of high-class cooking. Indeed, in most of Eurasia and North Africa, the evidence is overwhelming: the development of peculiar cooking techniques and eating habits was a feature of court life in every instance we know about. In some parts, at least, of the Americas, similar generalizations can be supported by documents.

When Bernal Díaz reported his part in the conquest of Mexico, for instance, he was anxious for his readers to know the greatness of Montezuma. In part, this was for the usual conquistadors' reasons: to enforce or inflate their own achievements in subjugating impressive empires. He had an additional, personal reason. He was sensitive about the modesty of his origins—his greatest boast was that his father had been a town councilor. He was a minor figure among Cortés's men, and is virtually unmentioned in the early annals of the conquest, except those he wrote himself. He was therefore inordinately proud of his claim that Montezuma had hailed him as a gentleman: from a truly majestic sovereign, this would be almost equivalent to an accolade. So he took every opportunity to write up the magnificence of Montezuma's person and the luxury of his court. Nevertheless, Díaz's description of Montezuma rings true. It accords with other accounts of Aztec palace life and the prodigal ethic of conspicuous consumption which dazzles readers of Aztec tribute lists.

The chieftain ate behind a painted screen in a hall illuminated by scented torches of smokeless wood, at a table laid with white cloths and napkins. Three hundred dishes, kept warm by burners, contained thirty different preparations, including chicken, turkey, small songbirds, doves, ducks both wild and domestic, rabbits and hare, game birds which Díaz calls pheasants, partridges and quails, "and many kinds of birds and things they grow in this country that are so numerous that I would not have time to name them all." Díaz "heard say that they used to prepare the flesh of boys of tender age for him" but witnessed no such thing. After Montezuma had washed his hands, tortillas were served and bitter chocolate in a gold cup. Fruits from all over the empire were also offered but with a proper sense of abstinence the chief tasted little of any of them. The large snakes which were featured at other lords' feasts seem not to have featured on Montezuma's menu. Of course, Montezuma's meals were not merely a display of indulgence, wealth or power, but part of a system of lordly giving and redistribution of resources. When he had finished eating, a thousand dishes of the same food were distributed among his entourage. The ingredients came from the stupendous weight of tribute delivered to the major cities of the Aztecs' predatory empire, every day, on the backs of carriers. At the palace of Montezuma's ally, the chief of Texcoco, enough tribute was delivered daily to feed over two thousand people with maize, beans, tortillas, cacao, salt, chilies, tomatoes and squashes.

As in Europe and the great civilizations of Asia and North America, the courtly model was imitated by the aristocrats and plutocrats of the Aztec world. According to the Franciscan compiler of Aztec memories, Bernardino de Sahagún, "When one of the merchants made a fortune and thought himself rich he laid on a feast or banquet for all the principal merchants and lords, for he held it a mean thing to die without undertaking something splendid and costly to add luster to his name and to give thanks to the gods who had given him his wealth and gratification to his relatives and friends." Offerings of flowers, songs, incense and dances accompanied the feasts. Guests arrived at midnight for banquets which might last three days. The menu customarily opened with hallucinogenic mushrooms, served with honey, which induced visions "and even provoked lust." The meat of about a hundred chickens and between twenty and forty dogs might be needed for a typical entertainment, with corresponding quantities of chili and salt, maize and beans, tomatoes and cacao. At the end, washing bowls, cacao and smoking tubes would circulate, and flower gifts and hundreds of blankets would be distributed to departing guests.

The regions conventionally credited with "great civilizations" in Mesoamerica and the Andes had similar traditions. Where there is little evidence about courtly cuisines, chieftainly eating styles can be inferred, at least, from the existence of privileged foodstuffs—the marlins shown in depictions of rulers' hunting parties among the Moche, for instance, or the sea fish borne inland across the mountains by runners for the Incas' table at Cuzco. In parts of the Americas there were surely societies where the differentiation of cuisine was arrested by poverty or by the limitations of an unvaried environment. Yet even in places where people at all social levels ate the same kinds of food, evidence of courtly cuisines in the making can be glimpsed in such practices as selecting relatively rare or well-esteemed foodstuffs for chiefs' entertainments and for the reception of ambassadors or leaders from outside. A chieftainly feast was offered, for instance, to William Bartram at Talahasochte, Florida, in the 1770s. Bear's ribs were served, together with "venison, varieties of fish, roasted turkeys (what they call the white man's dish), hot corn cakes, and a very agreeable cooling sort of jelly, what they call conte and what they prepare from the root of the China brier."

The question of how widespread is the development of courtly cuisine raises further questions in turn: are cultures which do not have it simply cases of arrested development? Is there a universal model of civilization, of which the progressive sophistication of cooking is an index? Jack Goody, one of our most sensitive and unprejudiced anthropologists, has sought courtly cuisine in sub-Saharan Africa without finding it. It is, he says, almost unknown: "only in Europe and Asia did we find the development of an haute cuisine that was clearly class-based and marked off those continents from Africa south of the Sahara." Among the evidence he has gathered from West Africa are cases of how privileged access to food affects the courtly way of life. Tribute means that chiefs have been able to maintain large households—Chief Gandaa of Biriku, for instance, whose funeral Goody attended, had thirty-three wives and more than two hundred children. But, like other chiefs in the region, he "lived just like everyone else, but with more of everything." No separate style is apparent, though chiefs normally have to eat out of public gaze. Among the traditional Yoruba, it was a customary obligation for a king to eat his predecessor's heart and other special ritual foods were prescribed; but this hardly seems to have the makings, or to constitute the potential ingredients, of a courtly cuisine. In Gonja, in northern Ghana, feasts of yam or cassava with fish or meat relish are laid on under the chief's auspices at *rites de passage* and, though food tributes have been small during the recorded past, chiefs have had a historic responsibility for entertaining strangers. Among the LoDagaa heads of household are in charge of daily distributions of grain. The food of their region is porridge and soup of ground nuts or leaves.

Yet where large states and wealthy courts have emerged in black Africa, professional cooks have always seized the chance to develop their art. The most spectacular case is that of Ethiopia, where the imperial kitchen has played an exemplary role similar to that of courtly cuisines in Eurasia and North Africa. When Laurens van der Post was entertained at the court of Haile Selassie, the banquet was preceded by fireworks so fierce that they shattered the palace windows. Every pair of guests was served by a footman in green velvet, gold brocade and satin breeches. Two parallel meals were served simultaneously: at every course, guests could select from a choice of French dishes and wines or Ethiopian cooking and the buckthorn-flavored mead known as tedj. Van der Post's meal—he naturally disdained the French offerings in favor of the native ones—combined both kinds of Ethiopian stew: red wat, which is flavored with red pepper, and green alicha, which normally uses ginger but which, on the occasion in question, was seasoned, with uncharacteristic restraint, with "all the spices of Ethiopia." Since elaborate combinations of spices are considered essential even in modest Ethiopian homes, this suggests an explosive concentration of savors. It would certainly have included the ubiquitous Ethiopian cardamom, which hardly resembles real cardamom and has the scent of camphor. Other peculiarly Ethiopian flavors would have been imparted by the regional variety of black cumin, which tastes like an acrid onion, and carom, which resembles caraway.

Ethiopia, of course, is always Africa's exception: exceptional for the antiquity, longevity and tenacity of its literate traditions, its spectacular monumental culture, its Christianity. It is, indeed, the home of a civilization, distinctive by any standard of comparison, with no close analogs since the fall of ancient Nubia and Sabaea. So perhaps we should not evince surprise at its peculiar cuisine and the unusual courtly pedigree of its elite foods. Yet it does seem to demand special commendation for heroism in this respect because—normally—socially differentiated menus and recipes are impossible, or very hard to contrive, in lands as isolated as Ethiopia is by its highland elevation. Variety is essential for differentiation, except by mere quantity of food. Rarity and expense, which are the usual indicators of elite ingredients, are conferred, most readily, by strangeness and distance, and are therefore supplied by commerce. The story of courtly cuisines leads on, across seas and cultural frontiers, to the subject of the next chapter: the revolution of long-range trade.

SIX

The Edible Horizon

—

Food and the Long-Range Exchange of Culture

And still she slept an azure-lidded sleep
In blanchéd linen, smooth and lavendered,
While he from forth the closet brought a heap
Of candied apple, quince and plum and gourd
With jellies soother than the creamy curd
Manna and dates in argosy transferred
From Fes, and spicéd dainties, every one,
From silken Samarkand to cedared Lebanon.

—KEATS, THE EVE OF ST. AGNES

"Avez-vous any potted lobster?" "Non," said the garçon, "potage aux vermicelle, au riz, à la julienne, consommé et potage aux choux." "Old shoe! Who the devil do you think eats old shoes here? have you any mock-turtle or gravy soup?" "Non, monsieur," said the garçon, with a shrug of the shoulders. "Then avez-vous any roast beef?" "Non, monsieur; nous avons bœuf au naturel—bœuf à la sauce piquante— bœuf cornichons—bœuf à la mode—bœuf aux choux—bœuf à la sauce tomate— biftek aux pommes de terre." "Hold hard," said Jorrocks, "I've often heard that you can dress an egg a thousand ways and I want to hear no more about it."

—R. S. SURTEES, JORROCK'S JAUNTS AND JOLLITIES

THE HORIZON AT ARM'S LENGTH:
OBSTACLES TO CROSS-CULTURAL EATING

I am rarely allowed to cook at home because my wife says I make too much mess. When allowed, though I try to build up a huge repertoire, I always seem to revert to flavors in which I have a high emotional investment. Garlic intrudes;

olive oil is almost inescapable. Personal experience and anecdotal evidence suggest that this habit of reversion to a trough of one's own is typical. Even with the world's markets at their command, most people restrict their usual menus and demand the same dishes over and over again. In the prosperous West, this is particularly true of breakfast, a meal which seems to be enhanced, for most of the people who eat it, by the comfort of predictability: cereal every day; in some cases, the same cereal every day. Those who favor eggs will often choose to have them cooked in the same way every day. Even the partisans of fried eggs divide into those who like them viscous—"easy" in American restaurant lingo—and those who like them congealed. There are unremittingly ichthyophagous breakfasters; others who will have bacon every day but never sausages and vice versa. The kind of fruit preserved or the density with which its peel is shredded or the proportions in which it is combined with sugar become matters of inflexible dogma and unvarying practice.

When tasters are tempted to experiment, the palate often rejects unfamiliar flavors. The processed food industry makes "reliability" and "consistency" of flavor a major criterion for its products, so that every batch of food or drink which bears a particular brand always tastes the same and the customer is never surprised. Particular novelties can conquer markets with astonishing rapidity: "a swift-changing market in food—where pizza has swept its manufacturers into a multi-million dollar market, where kiwi fruit from the Antipodes has become a fashionable accompaniment for fish, and where frozen yoghurt competes with ice cream" puzzled Mary Douglas, without shaking "the sturdiness of belief in consumer conservatism."

Eaters' bias in favor of the familiar affects entire cultures. "Organ meats" repel the American detective hero of *Masquerade*, a clever story by Walter Satterthwaite. When a case takes him to Paris, he is tricked into eating andouillettes, which he finds delicious until he learns that they are pigs' entrails stuffed with tripe and chitterlings. His vexation with foreign food begins with ruptured taboos—the consumption of the unwholesome rejects of his home culture; but it extends to any cooking which seems elaborate or, as he thinks, evasive. Haute cuisine is an un-American activity. To mask food with the maquillage of the great tradition of the chefs seems an act of dissimulation. To expend care, time and money on it offends his all-American puritanism; to invest emotion in it seems unmanly. He yearns for a steak grilled simply, without sauces, and scorns the superfluity of the pâté de foie and madeira sauce in tournedos Rossini. But he is condemned to unremitting gastronomy, guided between restaurants by a murderer who meticulously discusses every menu with the waiter, recipe by recipe, and who deflects an interview with a policeman into a debate about the merits of rival recipes for coq au vin. The hero's American identity is threatened with submersion under the motley and masquerade of sauces and sausage skins.

Satterthwaite's satire is particularly clever because it locks into a long tradition of gastronomic hostility to French food in *le monde anglo-saxon*, where plain is preferred to fancy and the fastidious are not fussy. These pairings were already apparent in the late seventeenth century, when French cookery writing was only just beginning to set standards for fashion in eating. Samuel Johnson described the famous libertine John Wilmot, Earl of Rochester, thus: "in a course of drunken gaiety and gross sensuality, with intervals of study perhaps yet more criminal, with an avowed contempt of decency and order, a total disregard to every moral, and a resolute denial of every religious observation, he lived worthless and useless, and blazed out his youth and health in lavish voluptuousness." Rochester, who might be presumed to know something about pleasure, promised,

> *Our own plain fare, and the best terse the Bull*
> *Affords, I'll give you and your bellies full,*
> *As for French kickshaws, sillery and champagne*
> *Ragouts and fricassees, in troth w'have none.*
> *Here's a good dinner towards, thought I, when straight,*
> *Up comes a piece of beef, full horseman's weight.*

According to one of the popularizers of culinary antiquarianism in late eighteenth-century England (above p. 122), French cookery was all very well in France but the pretense of "disguising meat" was superfluous in England. "It is, here, the art of spoiling good meat. . . . In the South of France . . . it is the art of making bad meat eatable." By the time of that pronouncement, the French Revolution had started and the chaos of the state seemed to complement the indiscipline of the kitchen. Over the next few years, the roast beef of old England became, in Gillray's cartoons, an emblem of solidity, unyielding to Napoleon's *batterie de cuisine*. In the famous opening passage of Sir Walter Scott's *Ivanhoe*, the transformation of "old Alderman Ox" into "Monsieur de Veau" was cited as evidence of the corrupting effects of a former "French" invasion.

Despite the indebtedness of American independence to French help, the patriotism of plain cooking was one feature of Englishness that survived on the far side of the Atlantic. If anything, it grew during the nineteenth century, along with "Know-Nothing" resentment of immigrants who did not conform to the Anglo-Saxon Protestant pattern. To forsake one's home cuisine in favor of plain American food became a badge of the "assimilation" which qualified immigrants for citizenship. In 1929 dining car franchisees on the Santa Fe Railroad's crack *California Limited* line found, when framing their menus, that "Small Tenderloin, mushrooms" hugely outsold "Filet Mignon, champignons." The dishes were identical. Duncan Hines, who can claim an important place in the history of food as the originator of restaurant guides, shared the Anglo-American heritage of prejudice against French methods. *Adventures in Good Eating*, which he began to compile in 1936, had a title that promised more than his singularly unadventurous tastes could deliver. He aimed to inform the long-range motorist—the sort trapped twenty-four hours from Tulsa with no place to eat. He liked homey roadside eateries that served "simple fare" and his most important criterion was cleanliness. "I steer clear," he announced proudly, "of dishes disguised with French names that don't mean a thing in a Midwestern hotel." He never went abroad until he was nearly seventy: his motive was a gastronomic fact-finding tour in Europe, where he professed to like English food best on the grounds that it most resembled that of America. In 1961, John F. Kennedy appointed a French chef to run the White House kitchen. As if to make up for this, his wife had to sacrifice the Parisian fashion houses she had formerly patronized and entrust her wardrobe, formerly the responsibility of Hubert Givenchy, to American designers like Oleg Cassini and Donald Brooks (though she continued to wear line-for-line copies from the French house Chez Ninon). The devoted American gourmet A. J. Liebling regaled readers of *The New Yorker* with self-parodic stories of his love for French food. His columns were calculated to evoke the same sort of combination of sensuality and revulsion played on in the popular vampire movies of the time. His experiences in 1926–27 threaded stupefyingly rich and costly meals between low-life encounters, in his penurious pension, with all the denizens of the Parisian demimonde: matelots, apaches, whores, pimps and lice. His descriptions of meals were triumphs of black humor. Truite au bleu was "simply done to death in hot water, like a Roman emperor in his bath" with "enough melted butter to thrombose a regiment." A snail was forced back into his shell after cooking with "not even a sentimental justification for his reincarnation." Alternatively, the same dish was served in crocks called "pots de chambre." Liebling's father, on a visit to Paris, opted for "Plain food, no *schmier*."

In France—until recently, when the game changed and America's new ethos of pluralism opened her mouths to the tastes of the world—American rejection of French food seemed so perplexing that it demanded sociological investigation: this was the revenge of a culture wounded in its pride by barbarians' failure to recognize its superiority. English indifference to French food was easily dismissed as the contrivance of a rival notorious for hypocrisy: one could understand it without quite believing it. America, however, had nothing to fear in France and everything to admire. It was as if Rome had rejected Greece. Roland Barthes declared that the differences that made French and American menus incommensurable could be defined as sweet versus unsweet. This had long been a vulgar opinion in France. It was and is quite unconvincing. No one can generalize about the French palate without taking into account the taste for sweet aperitifs, for sauternes with foie gras, for patisserie, for meat sauces made intense with reductions of strong dessert wines.

In reality, the historic chasm between French and Anglo-American tastes is only an extreme example of a common fact. Food—at least as much as language and religion, perhaps more so—is cultural litmus. It identifies and, therefore, necessarily, differentiates. Fellow members of cultural communities recognize each other by what they eat and scan the menu to spot the excluded. Although food fads are commonplace and advertisers can whip up a craze, food culture is conservative. The obstacles to cross-cultural eating start a long way back in history, and deep in individual psychology. Personal taste is hard to modify. Babies suckled on the sweetness of mother's milk retain a sweet tooth for life unless weaned toward new flavors as well as new textures. Children are tenaciously resistant to experiments in eating. Cheap tourism shrinks from gastronomic horizons. People recur to familiar flavors. Households with limited budgets refrain from experiment to limit waste. Wives are exasperated by the cry of the spouse in the song: "Gimme a plate of the bangers 'n' mash me mother used t'make!"

Contempt for foreign food and foodways was well established in antiquity. According to Herodotus, in Egyptian temples the heads of sacrificed animals were cut off, cursed and sold to Greeks, if any Greeks were available. Otherwise, the heads were thrown in the river. Egyptians, countered Galen, ate "grubs and hedgehogs." The Greeks' food prohibitions were part of their common culture, which distinguished them from other peoples. Dolphins they held sacred. They were "doubtful of turtle and tortoise, seldom ate dog and very seldom horse." Many of the Greeks' neighbors found their eating habits showed irreverence before heaven: their gods had to be content with the discards of sacrifice—"the tail-end and the gall-bladder, the bits you can't eat." Within the Greek world, similar prejudice was evinced between different cities and colonies. The polarity represented by French and American cuisine today echoes antiquity's between the indulgence of Syracuse and the indifference of Athens. The Syracusan gourmet Lynceus disliked Attic dinners.

They have a sort of foreign unpleasantness about them. They serve you a big dish with five little dishes on it: one with garlic, one with two sea urchins, one with a sweet bird-pastry, one with ten shellfish, one with a bit of sturgeon. While I eat this, he's finished that; while he's still on that, I've finished this. I want some of this and some of that, my dear fellow.

Archestratus could detect a foreigner by his attitude to aperitifs. "As you imbibe," he advised,

chew on some such dessert as this: tripe or boiled sow's womb marinated in cumin and sharp vinegar and silphium, and the tender tribe of birds, such as are in season. But have nothing to do with those Syracusans who simply drink, like frogs, without eating anything.

This was self-mockery: he was Syracusan, too.

Migrants resist the food of host communities: when Japanese workers were introduced to Fiji in the last century to compensate for the thousands of natives killed by measles, they found themselves in a land of abundance where the indigenous diet was so rich that deficiency diseases were unknown. Yet they eschewed local products and tried to subsist on white rice: as a result, most of them died of beriberi and the rest had to be repatriated. During the Korean War American POWs died of malnutrition because they refused to eat rations which, though perfectly nutritious, seemed to them repulsive. The mutual farewell of Spaniards during the colonization of an alien hemisphere in the sixteenth century was, "God keep you from losing sight of bread." A Mayan highland chief, refusing Spanish sweetmeats, protested, "I am an Indian and so is my wife, and our food is beans and chile, and when I want a turkey I have that too. I do not eat sugar, nor is candied lemon peel food for Indians nor did our ancestors know such a thing." These polarities lend piquancy to a story which Nicolás de Mastrillo, future Jesuit Provincial of Peru, told in a letter home during his days as a missionary rookie at the Andamaca station in the high Andes. In company with an older priest, he set off on his first mission, a journey of many days through mountains and jungle, in search of unevangelized Indians. When he encountered them, their friendliness and generosity delighted him, as they all sat down together to a banquet under the trees. But then a moment of danger arose, when one of the Indians—who believed the Jesuits and secular Spaniards belonged to different races, so different were their codes and manners—suddenly changed the mood. "I believe," he said, "that these men are not true Fathers, but Spaniards in disguise." The tension lasted for a moment, while Mastrillo's life flashed past him. Then, "No," the Indian declared, with a relaxed tone. "They must be Fathers, for they are eating our food."

A sort of natural multiplication of these effects makes cultures collectively hostile to new culinary influences. Whatever is foreign becomes the butt of excluding prejudices. "National" cuisines are never originally national. They begin as regional cooking habits with ingredients limited by the natural environment. They are open to local exchanges of influence and modification by such new products as can be accommodated in a regional tradition, whether in preserved form or because of natural longevity or traveling properties. When a cooking style acquires a national label, it undergoes a kind of fossilization: its purity has to be protected from alien influence. This is why so much of the literature of food describes revulsion of foreign dishes, or else a fascination with them which readers are invited to classify as morbid.

Traditional cuisines are always definable in terms of a few staples and seasonings which are readily available in the places concerned: these seep into collective tastes and inform palates which remain saturated in memories of them and, commonly, become indifferent or intolerant toward other flavors. Even methods of preparation can become cultural characteristics or badges of identity within regions where the same foods are available throughout. The chickpea is an indispensable product on most shores of the Mediterranean. At one end of that sea, however, people know them as garbanzos, stew them with flavorings, seasonings and sources of animal fat and blood and eat the pale globes hot, when they are tender enough to crush with the tongue against the roof of the mouth. At the other end, or the farther shore, they like to simmer the chickpeas to a pulp and serve them as humus, a cold puree mixed with oil and flavorings which commonly include lemon. An ingredient which, at the western end of the sea, has never escaped from the cooking pots of peasants has been blended and bludgeoned to refinement in the east. Neither way of dressing this pulse has ever appealed in the other's traditional lands.

Food is not easily communicable between cultures. Yet today, we not only eat high cuisines which call themselves "fusion" and "international." We also feed in a globalized world where dishes and ingredients are swapped with enthusiasm from one side of the world to the other. "McDonaldization" is mirrored, if not matched, by world conquests which start in Italy (pizza, pasta), Mexico (tacos and "wraps"), China (wontons and spring rolls, for instance), India (curries and poppadoms) and even New Zealand (kiwis and pavlova, the invention of which, though disputed by Australia, is unquestionably a New Zealander's honor). When I visited Madison, Wisconsin, I was taken to Turkish and Afghan restaurants. I knew of no typical Wisconsin dishes except cheese and fudge: even so, it was surprising to find no place that claimed to offer a regional menu, and to realize that my hosts esteemed only the extremely exotic. It is tempting to represent this as the culmination of a progressive story of horizons widened by improving communications. That would be false—or, at least, oversimplifying to the point of distortion. There is no more intriguing problem in the history of food than that of how cultural barriers to the transmission of foods and foodways have been traversed or broken.

THE BREAKERS OF BARRIERS: THE EFFECT OF EMPIRE

There are forces capable of penetrating cultural barriers and internationalizing food. These include war. Armies are great vectors of cultural influence, and modern warfare, which mobilizes great masses of ordinary people and shunts them around the globe, has had paradoxical effects on international understanding. It is hard to keep servicemen, gastronomically speaking, "down on the farm now that they've seen Paree." Taste for Indian food in Britain, or Indonesian in the Netherlands, might have been confined to immigrants and members of the former administrative elite if returning servicemen had not spread familiarity with it to other people of their class. Kushuri—a popular Cairo street food of rice and lentils with onion and spices—is presumably Indian kitchri, and was brought to Egypt by British forces. "Colonial circulation" is an older phenomenon in food history than hamburgers and fried chicken. Departing conquerors leave behind them an originally foreign conception of what constitutes properly soldierly food. Roast chicken with bread sauce and roast beef with Yorkshire pudding still appear on Pakistani mess menus.

Hunger, of course, or some analogous emergency such as war can dispose people to accept food which in other circumstances they might reject as foreign. In the sixteenth century, sweet potatoes became acceptable in China and Japan after introduction in times of famine. Taste for spam, introduced as American food aid, outlasted the Second World War in Britain. Today, the surpluses that developed countries dole out to the famine-stricken Third World are drawn from wheat "mountains" and dairy "lakes": they convert lactose-hostile cultures to milk products and gruel eaters to bread. Similarly, economic self-interest can persuade people to change diet in the case of exceptionally exploitable foodstuffs. In the late eighteenth century in New Zealand the Maoris refocused their food production on pork and potatoes—foodstuffs previously unknown to them— to sell to European naval and whaling ships. Tourism in the twentieth century is often credited with effecting mass changes of taste. There is also an unaided power of culture which is capable of transmitting taste: what might be called cultural magnetism, in cases where communities ape the foodways of cultures of superior prestige.

Even in history as complacent as that of Western Europe, this effect has often been observed. Evidence of the most striking instance accumulated in the high Middle Ages, when influences from Islam infused West European tastes in food. As we have seen (above, p. 119), this was a genuine case of imitation as a form of flattery: the tribute of an inferior to a superior civilization. It was not "acculturation": on the contrary, parts of Europe which were closest to Islam in the Middle Ages, or reconquered from it, tended to react against it and reject its food. The cookery of most of Spain is dependent upon olive oil, but not because of the medieval Muslim presence. For centuries, the preferred medium of Christian cooks was lard: indeed, it was the defining ingredient of Christian cookery, because Muslims and Jews were forbidden to eat it. The late-fifteenth-century chronicler Andrés Bernáldez was only a parish priest in a peripheral province but, perhaps because of the very modesty of his circumstances, he was a faithful spokesman of his times—the times of the expulsion of the Jews and the final conquest of Spain's last Muslim kingdom. His long catalogue of Jewish and Muslim vices culminates, as if it were worse than their alleged offenses against humanity, morality, decency, honor and truth, in a denunciation of "their disgusting stews, which they make with olive oil." In any case, Christian food was the food of the parts of Spain the Muslims neglected and did not bother to conquer or tenaciously to defend—the forests and mountains and cold plateaus and zones of Atlantic climate, where olives would not grow but where pigs could be reared in great numbers. The present role of the olive in Spain only began after the Jews and Muslims had been expelled, dispersed or converted and the great expansion of the olive industry in the seventeenth century was uninhibited by confessional hatred. Many traditional dishes still use no olive oil. The classic, slow-cooked pot dishes of chickpeas and beans—the cocidos and fabadas—are bound together with silky pork fat.

Cases of influence exerted by way of sincere imitation can be surprising because they sometimes reverse the flow of the cultural mainstream. It would be no surprise, for instance, to find Iranian cooking imitated in India because of the high status of Persian learning from what we think of as the Middle Ages onward; Persian was the court language of the Mughal Empire. Yet, in cooking, the preponderant influence has been exerted in the opposite direction and Iranian cuisine has borrowed from India a reliance on rice—despite the fact that the varieties Iranians eat are not suited to the climate. In Iran, expensive varieties are preferred—evidence of the high status rice conferred on those who ate it when it was first introduced. When grown in the country, these decline in productivity over time and seed has to be imported from India. Cooking methods are elaborate, as befits what began as a courtly foodstuff. After two hours' soaking and boiling to an al dente consistency, the rice is "steamed" in fat for half an hour under a raffia lid. Then the flavorings are added: roast mutton, sour cherries, herbs, dill, saffron or turmeric, to cite only a few ingredients mentioned in Safavid period recipe books.

No source of influence in cookery—perhaps, in the exchange of culture generally—has exceeded imperialism. Empires can sometimes be powerful enough to enforce a metropolitan taste on a peripheral area, and they usually promote human migration and colonization. These in their turn transmit eating habits alongside other aspects of culture, or reeducate the palates of expatriates who become vectors of new tastes when they return home. The tides of empire run in two directions: first, the flow outward from an imperial center creates metropolitan diversity and "frontier" cultures—cuisines of miscegenation—at the edges of empires. Then the ebb of imperial retreat carries home colonists with exotically acclimatized palates and releases the forces of "countercolonization," dappling the former imperial heartlands with enclaves of sometime subject peoples, who carry their cuisines with them. In consequence, there are three types of imperial cuisine: the high cuisines of the nodal points of empire, which sweep ingredients, styles and dishes from all over the regions of conquest into the central menu; the colonial cookery which juxtaposes the food of elite colonists from the "mother country" with the "subaltern" styles of their local cooks and concubines; and the countercolonial effect, whereby the imperial people are introduced to the food of their subject races and former victims when the latter start migrating toward the center.

Of the first type, Turkish cuisine is the outstanding example. Though gourmets and food historians are now rediscovering the delights of regional and preimperial Turkish foods, the menu which has made Turkish food famous and established it as one of the world's great cuisines was concocted in Ottoman Constantinople among a court aristocracy and, above all, in the sultans' kitchens at the Topkapi palace. Today, the palace is palpable evidence of what the empire was like in the era of its greatness, from the sixteenth to the eighteenth centuries. The throne room is a pavilion and many apartments are scattered through the grounds, like the tents of a nomad's camp—reminders of an imperial lifestyle which never definitively forsook the memory of the ruling dynasty's steppeland origins. The imperial stool is capacious enough for a sultan of morbid corpulence—for the memories of nomadism were sustained through centuries of sedentary overfeeding. In the warren of the harem, with its lavish alleys and secretive culs-de-sac, one can sense the arcane methods by which the empire was ruled:

here pillow talk was of politics, and women and eunuchs conspired to secure the succession for a potential patron from among the sultan's brood. The harem could accommodate two thousand women, the stables four thousand horses.

The scale of everything in the palace attests to the size of the empire and the reach of Ottoman rule but the statistics of the kitchen management beggar all others. In the sixteenth century, the kitchens were equipped to serve five thousand diners daily and ten thousand on holidays. The head cook had a corps of fifty sous-chefs, the chief confectioner thirty assistants and the chief taster a hundred subordinates. These figures grew as the empire got bigger, the dishes grew more refined, the range of culinary influences expanded and the work became more specialized. By the mid-eighteenth century there was a dedicated kitchen for each of six kinds of halva, each with its own chef and a hundred assistants. The number of staff rose to 1,370. Wood for the kitchens was carried in daily by a hundred carts. Daily deliveries were taken of dates, plums and prunes from Egypt, honey from Romania or—for the sultan's own table—from Candia, oil from Coron and Medon and butter from the Black Sea, packed in ox hides. In the early seventeenth century the daily intake of meat comprised two hundred head of young mutton and one hundred lambs or kids in season, 330 brace of fowl and four calves for the eunuchs' anemic meal.

The cookery of the Topkapi was genuinely at once both imperial and metropolitan—a sort of fusion food—because it combined ingredients from all over the empire in new dishes. I see what is now called "Tex-Mex" food as a typical frontier cuisine. The hybrid name suggests colonial miscegenation and the heartlands of Southwestern cooking are all lands which the United States effectively wrested from Mexico during America's great nineteenth-century expansion. The fulfillment of "manifest destiny" was an imperial enterprise like other white empires of the time. The fact that America's was an empire contiguous with the existing territory of the state does not make it any less of an empire than the far-flung dominions of West European countries. Britain, France and Germany had to acquire their empires by long-range maritime outreach because there was no room to expand in their own hinterlands (though France had tried it under Napoleon and Germany would try it again under Hitler). America's effort had a close contemporary parallel in Russian imperialism, which, over a rather longer period, built up a similar land empire at neighbor's expense. The role played by territories seized, in America's case, from Canada and Mexico, was played in Russia's case by conquests from Finland, Poland, the Ottoman Empire and Muslim Central Asia; the Russian equivalent of America's Indians were the indigenous nations of Siberia and the Russian tundra and taiga, whom Russians called "small peoples of the north." Both empires grew in similar ways—by marginalizing, exterminating or acculturating the victim-peoples. When Russia and America became Cold War enemies and rivals in the twentieth century, Americans adopted a censorious attitude to Russian imperialism, forgetting or ignoring how similar the two countries' nineteenth-century trajectories had been.

Imperial worms always turn and some of the peoples America conquered in those days have begun to take suitable revenge. "Hispanics" recolonize the wrested lands and—indeed—spread beyond them to constitute a big countercolonial presence in much of the United States. Meanwhile, the food of the Southwest had been re-Mexicanized, as the defining ingredients of Mexican cuisine stake out ever more of the culinary territory. Chili is the hot brand of this cuisine, corn and black beans its solid symbols; limes provide its lashings; filmy expanses of cheese form its flag. Chili—con carne, which, in its common form, consists of whole black beans slow-cooked in water with plenty of chili powder, cumin, which perhaps represents the Spanish contribution to the evolution of this cuisine, and ground meat—could fairly be called its signature dish. It is also the official State Dish of Texas, where purists do not use beans.

The chilies come in many fresh varieties, from the fairly mild anchos to the stingingly hot habaneros and scotch bonnets. They get their kick from a pungent alkaloid called capsaicin: according to the rate at which this substance disperses in a mixture of alcohol, sugar and water, the varieties are ranked in America on a scale calibrated in "Scoville units." The relatively unaggressive cayennes rate up to four thousand units, the mind-blowing habaneros can attain 300,000 units. However, in making chili con carne, powders are used, frequently in a combination which, like "curry," is not a unique spice, but rather a mélange. The origins of the dish are much disputed: with varying degrees of plausibility, they have been assigned to vaquero cooks of the mid-nineteenth century, Mexican "chili queens"—street vendors of San Antonio—and promotionally minded Dallas restaurateurs. Whatever its origins, however, it clearly uses part of the repertoire of ingredients which predated the American annexation of the Southwest and which, since then, have gradually conquered the conquerors. Taco Bell has mass-marketed Mexican snacks all over the American heartland. In a popular science fiction film, this was portrayed as the restaurant chain that would take over the planet.

Tex-Mex food has overleapt its historic frontiers—which may account for its adulteration by metropolitan tastes. A frontier cuisine that demonstrates real harmony between indigenous and metropolitan ingredients is that of the Philippines. By the time the Spaniards began their long, slow, painful colonization of the archipelago in 1572, they had learned a thing or two about colonialism. Deliberate missionary policy ensured that one element of the indigenous cultures—the local languages—would be inviolate. Of the other two great features of culture—religion and food—the first would be transformed completely by a spiritual conquest which was remarkably successful in most of the islands, while the second would end up as a hybrid. The hybrid is exceptionally complex because Chinese colonization, which—despite periodic crises in community relations, punctuated by massacres, expulsions and bans on Chinese immigration—was absolutely vital to the islands' economy in colonial times, has contributed as much as that of the Spaniards, while the Malay foundations of the cuisine have never been compromised by the changes wrought by settlers from outside. Fluffy rice, often flavored with banana leaves, is the basis of almost every dish, but bread is usually served alongside it in perpetuation of the Spanish legacy. Some Filipino bread is flavored with coconut, which, in one form or another, features in most meals and supplies the universal cooking oil. The Spanish presence is detectable in three conspicuous areas: first, the lexicon of the kitchen—prawns are called gambas, for instance, and the aromatic stews are adobos (or, by Malay corruption, adobong), while sweet pancakes are known as turrón (a name which in the Spanish of Spain signifies almond-based candy). Some of the popular dishes in the repertoire are lightly adapted from Spanish models, such as paella, or suckling pig, roasted in the Spanish manner and called lechón, and caldereta, made with kid. Finally, a sweet course ends Filipino meals and the items in it are all of Spanish origin, including crème caramel—"flan," the only Spanish dessert to have won a place in the global repertoire—with confections of egg yolks and sugar and marzipan cakes.

Frontier cuisines arise not only because of exchanges of migrants between center and periphery, but also because of the way empires shuffle populations around to meet the needs of imperial politics and economics. The name of Cajun cooking derives from that of the "Acadians" deported from Canada in the eighteenth century: but its spicy flavors, typical of other Caribbean cuisines, suggest a long period of acclimatization in the Acadians' new environment. The best traditional cooking in South Africa is that of the Cape Malays, shipped in by the Dutch in the seventeenth and eighteenth centuries to provide specialized labor which could not be recruited locally. Their Ramadan feasts display influences garnered from the breadth of the Indian Ocean, and the influence of the food the white master class brought from Holland. In Buriyanis, layers of boiled rice alternate with hardboiled eggs and lamb, cooked in onions, ginger, fennel, garlic, cumin and tomatoes, sealed and simmered for hours. Ingelegde vis is fried, snook, pickled in curried vinegar. Smoorvis is salted snook braised to a pulp with onions, chilies and peppers. In bobotie, curried minced meat is baked and covered with a crust of beaten eggs. Sosaties are brochettes of meat in piquant marinade. Pumpkin, slowly cooked in oil with chilies, is the classic bredie.

The slave foods of the Americas have a similar character. Some of the characteristic ingredients made the transatlantic journey with the slaves and in the many colonies where slaves were given plots of ground to grow food for their own subsistence, and where they maintained households of their own with individual kitchens, they naturally cultivated tastes of home. Mainstays of the black menu were transplanted from Africa: yams, okra, plantains and watermelons, which became symbols of blackness in a satirical tradition. Other items have a less certain provenance. Collard greens—a kind of mild kale, which in the black tradition of the American Deep South is cooked with pork fat—is not an indigenous New World variety, but its route to America is undocumented. The black-eyed "pea" or cowpea, without which no Southern menu could be called complete, was probably introduced alongside the slaves, though there is no clear evidence that this was a food in parts of Africa which supplied plantation labor. The pigeon pea, known as the no-eye, was certainly brought from Africa to feed slaves, but has not established a place in the repertoire to rival the black-eyed. In any event, most of the menu now called "soul food" was created in the new American environment, much of it borrowed from the Native Americans. Hominy grits bear a certain resemblance to the fine-ground millet porridge widely eaten in West Africa, but in America it is made with maize. Corn bread was a hybrid which owed nothing to Africa—made of native meal, laboriously raised in the white men's manner by the addition of lime to make up for the lack of gluten. Molasses, the ingredient which, together with the suppurating fat, makes the food of the South, both black and white, characteristically cloying and comforting, was a New World intrusion, but probably had no background in the native cuisines of Africa until white traders introduced it. The greens and black-eyed in slaves' stewpots were flavored with cuts of pork the whites disdained—cheeks, feet, chitterlings.

When the tides of empire ebb, returnees travel with them, taking—typically—tropical tastes to Europe. Countercolonization follows up with cooks and restaurateurs who supply those tastes and help to spread them to classes of patrons with no colonial experience. England, France and the Netherlands became, in the postcolonial era, springboards for the worldwide projection of Indian, Vietnamese and Maghribi and Indonesian food respectively. Migrants, as we have seen, tend to resist the food of host communities, but can be forced to adapt. One way migrants survive is by copying the eating habits they encounter, or accepting food offerings in the manner commemorated, for instance, in the American Thanksgiving menu.

Darwin's informant Sir Andrew Smith saw Bechuanas in Southern Africa, who, driven from their homes by Zulus, "looked like walking skeletons." They learned what was edible from observing baboons and monkeys. A few years later, white men forced by shipwreck to live in the Arctic came to appreciate seal as "not fishy but sealy.... With patience and a good deal of sauce piquante" it could even seem "very excellent." As well as a survival strategy, habituation to an unfamiliar cuisine can work, in imperial contexts, as a method of control: of showing solidarity with natives and exploiting their expertise. Consider, for example, the Dutch.

Dutch cooking has a woeful reputation—not least with the Dutch. This is unfair and unfortunate, as it may inhibit gourmets from experiencing the pleasures of a well-structured herring or the freshness of native North Sea shrimps, or the friendly feeling induced by a well-prepared boerenkool of soft green cabbage blended with potato and flavored with well-seasoned meat. On the other hand, Dutch modesty about the national cuisine has made them exceptionally responsive to the food of other cultures. Indonesian rijstafel has some claim to be considered the Dutch national dish—its rival, hùtspot, a sort of puree made of scraps of root vegetables in commemoration of the ill-nourished defenders of Leiden during the siege of 1574—has only sentiment to commend it. The rijstafel is as far removed from hutspot as can be imagined: exotic, rather than domestic; celebratory, rather than commemorative; lavish, rather than austere; variegated, rather than limited. Such memories as it evokes are of plenty and privilege, of days when Dutch colonialists shared the feasts of rajahs. When we eat it we reenter the world of Colonel Verbrugge (the "good" character in the great anti-imperial novel of 1860, *Max Havelaar, Or, the Coffee Auctions of the Dutch Trading Company*—see page 182, who tried to make his spurs jingle on the clay floor of his dining room while entertaining the Regent of Lebak to an abundance of dishes.

Whereas the hutspot evokes the time when the Dutch were struggling for their own independence, the rijstafel belongs to the period when they deprived others of theirs. It is hard to do well, because it involves so many dishes, each of which demands many ingredients. Around the central bowl of rice, upward of a dozen different dishes are served at once, kept hot on small braziers or spirit lamps. Sambal goreng is obligatory—chili, numerous spices, onions and garlic are fried to make a base in which meat or fish is bathed: it is particularly good with squid. Other sambals, usually based on mixtures of chilies, perhaps with citrus zest or shrimp paste, usually appear. Rendang is the essential curried dish in a rijstafel: in Dutch restaurants it is usually made with beef, though the classic version demands water buffalo meat, which is marinated in coconut milk with the native spices of Sumatra—turmeric, ginger, gingery galingale, garlic and salam leaf (which resembles bay leaf in looks and curry leaf in flavor), as well as the chili introduced in colonial times. It is then simmered in its marinade until almost dry.

Before French colonization, Vietnamese food, despite long permeation by Chinese influence, had no great international esteem. The first meal Thomas Bowyer reported on his pioneering journey there in 1695 was of boiled snake and black rice. The Vietnamese cookery which reached France in the postcolonial era was already influenced by French gastronomy. Baguettes and crêpes remain part of the repertoire. Essentially, it is a typical Southeast Asian cuisine, based on a kind of fish sauce even stronger than that of Thailand and alive with the flavors of tamarind and lemongrass. But soigné preparation gives it an edge. The cuisine has obvious potential for the fast food industry, for its highlights include "finger foods": little parcels of savory stuffings coddled in lettuce leaves and spring rolls wrapped in translucent rice noodles; but the Vietnamese tend to share French solemnity about food and to believe that it must be prepared with care and enjoyed at leisure.

Gordon West's expedition "by bus to the Sahara" in the 1920s involved a lot of meals in which—as it were—the colonial moment of Moroccan cuisine seemed captured. He encountered two coexisting cooking and eating styles, French and native, which were only just beginning to exchange influences. He began his odyssey in kabob bars in Tangier, eating crisply grilled bits of liver and meatballs sandwiched in flatbread, followed by mint tea. In Meknes he dined on crème St. Germain, omelette aux fines herbes and a fowl roasted quickly for crispness. By contrast, in Fez, an eminent caid fed his guest from his own hand, in the traditional manner, with bits of chicken made meltingly friable through long, slow cooking; wild ducks followed, stuffed with rice and herbs and accompanied by a salad of radishes, orange and raisins. Then came "a great roast of mutton." All the meats were cooked to the point of collapse, where knives and forks are superfluous. The diners shredded them with their fingers and fed one another with the tastiest morsels. Couscous with almonds, green beans and raisins taxed West's dexterity. Little balls of it had to be rolled against the palm of the hand for ease of eating. The end of the meal—a course of sweetmeats—was signified by the polite belching of the guests.

When West's bus descended from the Atlas, at the edge of the desert, in the old Berber fortress city of Ksar es-Souk, the local hotelier in his mud bungalow proudly served

Consommé

Filet de Truite Sidi Ali

Poulet de Grain en Cocotte
Haricots Verts
Cotelettes de Veau Zerhoun
Pommes Mignonettes
Caramel Ziz. Fruits Variés

M. Berujon, whose cooking attracted "all the custom of the camp"—even humble Legionnaires, spending a week's pay on a meal—evidently gave his dinners a calculatedly exotic zing. Unfortunately, the meaning of the Arab names he threaded through the menu is unrecorded. Presumably, they indicate the beginnings of gradual assimilation of local flavors to the saucing and seasoning of French food. Trout "Sidi Ali" must surely have owed something to the sweet almonds of the country, perhaps with the addition of raisins. In the name of veal "Zerhoun" my imagination detects a garnish which might include red pepper and barley sprouts. To West's teeth and palate, the contrast of textures marked the difference between the food of the colonials and the natives, more even than the contrasts of flavor. "The further south we travel, the tougher becomes the meat." Poor grazing and the need, in the Saharan climate, to eat slaughtered meat quickly, without hanging, makes it essential to imitate the natives but the French "obstinately" preserve "their national methods of preparation."

The last great category of expatriate cuisines is that of exiles. Outside lands contiguous with China, emigration has never been promoted by the Chinese state. The spread of Chinese cooking around the world has therefore been colonial but not imperial, carried by peaceful migrants in self-imposed "economic exile." At least, this is true of most recent Chinese migration, though that of the last century was genuinely imperial in another sense, as European governments shunted the conscripted labor of coolies and laundrymen around their own empires. It has produced hybrids of its own, of which the most notorious is "chop suey"—a mixture, say, of bamboo shoots, bean sprouts, water chestnuts and other vegetables with slivers of meat or chicken: an invention of pioneer Chinese restaurateurs in nineteenth-century North America. Most of the Vietnamese who have carried their cuisine to the West since the 1950s have been political refugees. So were the victims of the Russian Revolution who made Russian food fashionable in Paris after the First World War. The opportunity for this Russian invasion of the capital of haute cuisine arose from the long-standing reputation of Russian tables for great luxury. In the second and third quarters of the nineteenth century, a style of service attributed to Russian origins, and called *service à la russe*, became fashionable in Western Europe: first in France, from where it seems to have spread to neighboring countries. Instead of varied courses of dishes being placed on the table for guests to help themselves in the manner then traditional, each dish would be handed around separately by a servant. This allowed for the doubling of meal-time spectacle: the festive board, vacated by food, could now house more magnificent tableware and flowers. The multiplication of footmen was itself a display of wealth. The balletics and discretion of service was a new form of theater, under the patronage of the wealthy, with its own specialized training. "Franco-Russian" cuisine had already become an acknowledged subset in the chefs' repertoire before the Revolution, thanks to the exchange of cooks, maîtres d'hôtel and diners across old Europe. Still, when George Orwell, playing at being "down and out in Paris," worked in the kitchen of a Russian restaurant in the 1920s, he joined other staff in watching anxiously for their first French client and hoping against hope that the establishment would acquire a reputation among the natives.

TRADE, THE WAITER: SALT AND SPICES

As a means of the interpenetration of widely separated cuisines, the only activity to rival imperialism and colonization is trade. Trade hovers and shimmers like a waiter at the table of world food, carrying surprising dishes to unsuspecting diners, or shuffling seating for unexpected guests. Global circulation of ingredients by way of trade is assisted by what I call the "stranger effect"—the tendency many peoples have to revere the exotic. Ingredients brought from afar at trouble and cost, or exchanged as gifts with alien plenipotentiaries, derive prestige from their journey out of all proportion to their intrinsic value or their practical merits as foodstuffs. They are received as flavors of the divine horizon, or treasured as mirabilia or prized, initially, for their exclusivity. This is similar to the added interest which travelers acquire as they go, according to how far they journey: pilgrims gain sanctity, leaders charisma, warriors fearsomeness and ambassadors attention if they come from afar. Unfamiliarity forestalls contempt. Sometimes the stranger effect is strong enough to overcome the ingrained hostility that most cultures have for foreign food.

Indeed, one measure of a great cuisine is the diversity of the provenance of its ingredients. This was a fact already appreciated in antiquity. "Tell me now, muses," commanded Hermippus, "how many good things Dionysus has brought here to men in his black ship since he has plied the wine-dark sea." From Cyrene, came silphium (a curious flavoring, to which we shall return in the next chapter); from the Hellespont, mackerel and all sorts of salt fish; from Thessaly, wheat meal and ox ribs. "The Syracusans send pigs and cheese . . . Rhodes raisins and dreamy figs." Pears and fat apples came from Euboea. "The Paphlagonians send the chestnuts and glossy almonds which are the ornaments of the feast." Phoenicia provided dates and wheat for baking. The same values, in the context of the increasingly generous range of trade, were evinced by Brillat-Savarin, for whom of the

> various components of a connoisseur's dinner, the principal parts are of French origin, such as the meat, fowl and fruit; some are imitated from the English, such as beefsteak, Welsh rarebit, punch, etc., some come from Germany, such as the sauerkraut, Hamburg smoked beef, Black Forest fillets; some from Spain, such as the olla podrida, garbanzos, malaga raisins, Xerica pepper-cured ham, and dessert wines; some from Italy, such as the macaroni, Parmesan cheese, Bologna sausages, polenta, ices, and liqueurs; some from Russia, such as the dried meat, smoked eels and caviare; some from Holland, such as the salt cod, cheeses, pickled herring, curaçao and anisette; some from Asia, such as the Indian rice, sago, curry, soy, Shiraz wine, and coffee; some from Africa, such as the Cape wines; and lastly, some from America, such as the potatoes, pineapples, chocolate, vanilla, sugar, etc.; all of which provides sufficient proof of the statement . . . that a meal such as may be had in Paris is a cosmopolitan whole, in which every part of the world is represented by its products.

This should give pause to those who think of "international" cuisine as "new."

For most of history, however, long-range trade in food has been limited to luxury items. Every society grows its own staples, unless and until they can be imported cheaply. A common motive for the expansion of empires is the program of diversifying diet by imposing ecological collaboration on regions specializing in different foodstuffs. Andean imperialism, from the age of Tiahuanaco, to that of the Incas and Spaniards, has always been based on enforced exchanges of food and, when necessary, labor between producers at different altitudes or among the different microclimates which are characteristic of terrains of mountains and valleys. For much of Chinese history, the empires that have united the contrasting environments of northern and southern China have been bound by the supply of southern rice for northern consumption. The Roman world worked because provinces specialized in the supply of basic products to the rest—Egypt, Sicily and the North African littoral were the "granaries" of the empire, Betica its olive grove. In the Aztec Empire, shifts of tribute between ecologically specialized zones supported the hegemony of a few communities in and around Lake Texcoco. Over seven thousand feet above sea level, where local agriculture was confined to garden mounds dredged and piled from the lake bottom, the lakebound environment was incapable of feeding the huge population—variously estimated but probably at least eighty thousand people—concentrated in the capital at Tenochtitlán. The city's tribute rolls show 240,000 bushels a year of maize, beans and amaranth levied from subject communities. The cacao needed for the elite drink, essential for every ceremonial occasion, would not grow in the region at all and had to be brought in vast quantities by bearers from the "hot lands" of the far south.

Sometimes, however, even basic essentials have to be brought from afar and cannot easily be forced into an imperial system. The foodstuff of which this is normally true is salt. It is essential to sustain life. Most metabolisms seem to crave it in quantities far above what is strictly necessary. Its role as a preserving agent, which kills bacteria and suppresses decay, makes it essential in seasonal food management strategies. Where there are no mines or salt pans, it has to be extracted from seawater by evaporation or coaxed from plants such as coltsfoot or samphire, which absorb salt from the earth. But some peoples cannot obtain adequate supplies locally; all demographically buoyant communities have to import it as soon as their population exceeds a certain threshold. So salt is one of the world's oldest items of bulk trade. Some of its historic effects are well known. Every student knows the role of salt taxes in the making of medieval monarchies, the triggering of the French Revolution. Anyone familiar with the life of Gandhi knows the impact of salt upon the rise of the Congress Party in India. These episodes seem of slight significance, however, compared to the way the existence of two great salt-deficient markets of the past warped world history into new directions: the West African market in the late Middle Ages and the huge food-salting industry of Northern Europe—especially of the Netherlands—in the seventeenth century. The first of these sustained the medieval gold trade, the second profoundly influenced the course of early long-range imperialism.

Salt was the chief commodity that kept the trans-Saharan gold trade going in the bullion-starved Western world of the late Middle Ages. When Ibn Battuta, the widest-ranging pilgrim of the Middle Ages, crossed the Sahara in 1352, he accompanied a salt caravan from the mining center of Taghaza. The scenes he described can still be witnessed today because the densely populated Niger valley still relies on salt imported across the desert by traditional means. Taghaza, to Ibn Battuta's sophisticated Maghribi mind, was

a village with no attractions. A strange thing about it is that its houses and mosque are built of blocks of salt and roofed with camel skins. There are no trees, only sand in which is a salt mine. They dig the ground and thick slabs are found in it, lying on each other as if they had been cut and stacked under the ground. A camel carries two slabs.

The only people living there, the traveler reported, are the slaves of the chief of the dominant tribe, who dug for the salt and lived on camel meat, supplemented by dates brought to them from Da'ra and Sijilmasa, and a kind of millet,

> which is imported from the country of the Blacks. The Blacks come from their country to Taghaza and take away the salt. A load of it is sold at Walata for eight to ten miqtals, and in the city of Mali for twenty to thirty, sometimes forty. The Blacks trade with salt as others with gold and silver; they cut it in pieces and buy and sell with these. For all its squalor qintars of gold dust are traded there.

Much of the gold generated by this trade ended up in Christendom, which had little gold of its own. Bullion deficiency in Western Europe was one of the great motors of change in the late medieval world, stimulating the voyages of exploration which eventually led European mariners across the Atlantic and around Africa. An even more urgent shortage, in Northern Europe, was that of salt— especially when the population began to rise in the sixteenth century and the food industry struggled to keep up. In the early seventeenth century, while well-known nutmeg wars were fought between Dutch and English merchants in Amboina for access to relatively rare and luxurious commodities, a less glamorous but more intense drama unfolded in the west: the Netherlanders' efforts to secure their salt supply. The so-called United Provinces of the Netherlands constituted a new country: a republic that began to coalesce in the 1570s, formed by an uneasy alliance of particularists to fight free of the centralizing control of the sovereign they shared at the time: as the result of dynastic strategy and accident, Philip II also happened to be king of Spain and, therefore, to command resources from outside the Netherlands. These threatened the local power of the aristocracy and towns and of the new clerical elite which had arisen in parts of the region as a result of the success of the Reformation. The main industry in the Netherlands as a whole (if one can speak of such an internally divided area as a whole) was cloth making. In the provinces most resolved to fight for independence; however, food processing was of greatest importance: above all, herring salting and the making of salted butter and cheese.

Poland, France and parts of the Baltic had extensive salt deposits, on which the Dutch industries had traditionally drawn, but these were getting expensive and supply was unreliable in time of war. The most coveted supplies were controlled by the Spanish monarchy, in Portugal and the Caribbean, where salt said to be particularly suited to herring was produced. It was also cheap. Dependence on Spanish salt was one reason why the Dutch made peace with Spain in 1609. It was want of salt that caused some Dutchmen to imperil that peace by trying to seize Caribbean salt for themselves. While the peace lasted, the salt trade with Portugal rivaled the traditional Dutch North Sea and Baltic trades. Andres Lopes Pinto of Lisbon freighted two hundred Dutch ships to carry Portuguese salt between 1615 and 1618. The quest for salt was a principal reason for the establishment of the Dutch West India Company in 1621, when the peace with Spain finally broke down, and the company's claim to a salt monopoly was one of the main causes of the ensuing dissension in the republic. In January 1622, twenty-seven ships from Hoorn and Enkhuizen—two of the most prominent herring industry centers—landed a large force at the rich Venezuelan salt pans of Punta de Araya, with the aim of seizing them and turning them into a Dutch imperial outpost; but like subsequent expeditions, they were bloodily beaten back.

In the late 1620s, the beleaguered Dutch food industry was saved by the exploitation of new salt pans at Tortuga, where Spanish rule had never been firmly established. In 1632, however, the Spaniards flooded the pans and over the following few years seized or destroyed all the Dutch garrisons in salt-producing areas of the Caribbean. The Dutch herring fleet was nearly wrecked by the ensuing crisis. The catch reported in the town of Schiedam fell by a third in the 1620s, and another third in the 1630s. The value of herring exports collapsed despite higher prices. Dutch customers for salt had to rely on licenses granted from Spain, where—fortunately for the Dutch—the costs of the war were also grievously felt and where the monarchy was obliged to get money from every possible source. It was beginning to look as though the Dutch would have to abandon the war when, in 1640, they were rescued by a new crisis within the Spanish monarchy: the revolt of the Portuguese, who elected a king from their own aristocracy and abjured allegiance to the king of Spain. By allying with the Portuguese rebels, the Dutch were able to recover control of trade in Portuguese salt, which they had been in danger of losing altogether to German competitors. In return, they supplied arms and provisions to the rebel armies in a system of exchange masterminded by David Curiel, a Jewish agent for Portugal in Amsterdam. By 1648, hostilities with Spain were over: the Dutch position was recognized in Madrid as unassailable. But salt did not cease to determine the pattern of diplomacy: the Dutch remained interested in getting a share of Caribbean salt and the long, slow, ultimately successful effort to effect a rapprochement between Spain and Holland, between 1648 and 1677, would have been unthinkable without this inducement.

By comparison with the high-bulk, high-value, vital trade in salt, a luxury commerce such as that in spices ought to be less important. But pepper, which accounted for about 70 percent of the world's spice trade in the sixteenth and seventeenth centuries, was close to being a vital product, for the menus of the world's elites demanded it. The other main constituents of the trade—cinnamon, mace and nutmeg—were exchanged in relatively small quantities but commanded such high profit margins for the merchants who shipped them that they acquired a disproportionate importance in the marketplace. Salt cannot be said to have changed cooking cultures: its effect is to enhance flavor, not subvert the integrity of traditional cuisines; spices, however, contributed to the creation of new food cultures in the areas that received them by way of trade. Moreover, the history of the spice trade relates fundamentally to the biggest problem in global history: that of the nature and shift of the balance of wealth and power between the West and the Orient—the rival civilizations at opposite ends of Eurasia.

The earliest documented episodes precede that period by thousands of years. Cinnamon and its inferior cousin, cassia, were among the products shipped to Mesopotamia along the Persian Gulf from the Arab kingdoms of Dilmun and Magan, the exact whereabouts of which are still not known but which probably corresponded to Bahrain and perhaps Yemen. Similar exchanges belong to the context of ancient Egyptian trade with the mysterious land of Punt—an exchange of staples for luxury aromatics and flavorings. We do not know where Punt was, but the route involved a long voyage down the Red Sea. Any Red Sea voyage under sail tends to be long and hazardous because of the torturous sailing conditions; to judge from the plain and obvious meaning of the most detailed text— wall paintings in a temple endowed by Queen Hatshepsut, probably in the thirteenth century B.C.—Punt was a tropical or semitropical destination, near the sea, and had a recognizably African culture. Although scholars have never been able to agree on a single place of origin for all the products of Punt, Somalia makes a close match and allowance must be made for changes in the range of available biota over nearly three and a half millennia. We think of Somalia today as one of the most blighted and underprivileged places in the world. To the ancient Egyptians, it was a magnet for adventure and a spring of riches. The products were small objects of desire; but the Egyptians had to send five ships to get them because the products offered in return were of small unit value and great bulk. Whereas Punt specialized in precious luxuries, Egypt was a mighty food producer, with an economy single-mindedly geared to massive, intensive agriculture. The mission to Punt was more than a cultural encounter: it was a meeting of contrasting ecologies and an occasion of exchange between them.

Unless the Egyptian text is self-serving hyperbole—as it may well be—the people of Punt were duly astonished at the explorers' arrival. "How have you reached this land unknown to the men of Egypt?" they are made to ask, with hands uplifted in surprise. "Have you descended hither by the paths of the sky or"—they added, as if it were equally improbable—"have you sailed the sea?" Columbus claimed that the islanders who greeted him at the end of his first transatlantic crossing used similar words, with a similar gesture. It later became a topos of travel literature, designed to show explorers' hosts as technically inferior and easily gulled. The Egyptian artists caricatured the people of Punt with other signs of savagery and simplicity: they made the king grotesquely obese, the aquiline courtiers were given pendulous lips. The exchange of gifts was said to be very much in favor of the sagacious Egyptians, who were reckoning the goods at their own valuations: from the point of view of the negotiators from Punt, the transaction may have been perfectly satisfactory. In any case, the treasures of Punt were of a different order of splendor from anything the Egyptians had to offer in return. Punt possessed "all marvels," while Egypt offered "all good things." Punt's principal products were the incense trees that yielded myrrh for rites of worship and death; these are clearly depicted in the wall paintings in Hatshepsut's temple. The gold of Punt was measured out with bull-shaped weights, and the live incense trees were potted and carried aboard the Egyptian vessels. The Egyptians paid for them with "bread, beer, wine, meat, fruits." There was, however, no clear line between sacrifice and cookery or between aromatics and spices at the Egyptian court: pharaonic food was divine.

The Arabian and African spice trades of the Sumerians and Egyptians ultimately reached Greece and Rome. Yemen was regarded as a land "where men burn cassia and cinnamon for their everyday needs." The earliest surviving report of a Greek explorer of the Arabian seas raved about the fragrance exuded by the coast of southwest Arabia:

> It is not the sort of pleasure that is derived from spices that have been stored and become stale nor that produced by a plant separated from the stem which bore and nourished it, but that of one blooming at its divine peak and giving off from its own natural sources a wondrous scent so that many come to forget human blessings and think that they have tasted ambrosia, seeking a name for the experience that matches its extraordinary character.

The obviously romantic and mythical elements in this sort of rhapsodizing do not suggest firsthand acquaintance; and it may be that some of the spices handled by Arab middlemen—the Sabaeans, Gerrhaeans and Minaeans of Greek texts—deluded their customers about the provenance of their wares. The plant we now call cinnamon, for instance, is not known to have grown in Arabia. As ancient gazetteers "of the Erythraean Sea" extended their range to embrace much of the western Indian Ocean, the name came to be reserved for a product Arabs imported from India and Ceylon.

These broadened contacts are reflected in the exoticism of Roman recipes. Of the sixty condiments recommended in the recipes of Apicius, only ten came from outside the empire. But some of them—especially Indian ginger, cardamom and pepper, which were heavily used in the Apician tradition—represented the remotest reaches of the spice trade. One of Pliny's objections to spice-rich food was that it enriched the Indian economy and impoverished the Roman. "They arrive with gold and depart with pepper," as a Tamil poet put it. The mystery of the spice market was deepened, and the value of its products increased, by the fact that production was a highly specialized and regional business. Cassia, perhaps, was available from native sources in Arabia in antiquity, but in the Middle Ages true cinnamon became a Ceylonese near monopoly. For pepper, merchants went to the Malabar coast of India. Nutmeg, mace and cloves were produced in only a few places in the Indian Ocean and what is now Indonesia—above all, in the twin "Spice Islands" of Ternate and Tidore. The vast bulk of the products of all these lands was exported to China, where the market was biggest and the economy richest. Marco Polo reckoned one thousand pounds of pepper a day entered Hangchow in his time. But if the European market was of small importance to the producers, it mattered greatly to the Western merchants who tried to take part in it.

The idea that the demand for spices was the result of the need to disguise tainted meat and fish is one of the great myths of the history of food. It is an offshoot of the myth of the progress—the assumption that people in earlier times were less competent, or less intelligent, or less capable of providing for their needs than we are today. It is more likely that fresh foods in the Middle Ages were fresher than today, because locally produced, and that preserved foods were just as well preserved in their different ways—by salting, pickling, desiccating and conserving—than ours are in the age of canning, refrigeration and freeze-drying (a technique which, by the way, was known in antiquity and developed to a high degree by Andean potato growers in what we think of as the Middle Ages). Both fresh and preserved foods were probably healthier in those days because they were not grown with chemical fertilizers. In any event, the role of spices in cooking was determined by taste and culture. Spice-rich cuisine was expensive and, therefore, socially differentiating (see above, p. 120). For those who could afford it, this made it an ineluctable luxury. It was liked because it was a defining characteristic of the era's model haute cuisine, imitated from the Arabs (above, p. 119).

The nature of the European love of spices—rhapsodical, romantic, enlivened by imagination—is captured by the story told by Joinville, Louis IX's biographer, of the fishermen of the Nile, whose nets filled with ginger, rhubarb and cinnamon dropped from the trees of the earthly paradise. In the most successful recipe book of the era, the Menagier de Paris advised cooks to add spices to their dishes at the last possible moment so that none of the flavor was impaired by heat. The profits that beckoned anyone ingenious or determined enough to buy spices at or near source inspired heroic efforts by medieval merchants to penetrate the Indian Ocean. The routes all involved hazardous encounters with potentially hostile Muslim middlemen: you might try to cross Turkey or Syria to the Persian Gulf or, more usually, attempt to get a passport from authorities in Egypt to ascend the Nile and transfer, via desert caravan, to the Red Sea at Massaweh or Zeila. Not surprisingly, few of these attempts succeeded and the merchants who did manage to effect them successfully became part of the existing trading networks of the Indian Ocean. Before the 1490s, no one in the Middle Ages succeeded in opening direct access from the European market to the Eastern sources of supply.

The great change which converted the world of the traditional Eastern spice monopolies into a new world—a global system in which Western powers controlled the trade and, to a great extent, the production of spices—happened in three stages: first, the westward transfer of the world's main centers of sugar production, which started in the late Middle Ages; then, in the sixteenth and seventeenth centuries, the development of new trade routes to which Western merchants had privileged access; finally, from the seventeenth century onward, the progressive takeover of control of production by Western powers, deploying violent methods.

The switch started with sugar, because, uniquely among the exotic condiments favored by palates in Latin Christendom, this sweetener could be grown in the Mediterranean with relative ease. Sugar is not normally classified as a spice today; it is, at best, an anomalous spice, since it has little fragrance; but, in antiquity and the Middle Ages, it was an exotic condiment which could only be obtained at great cost by way of trade. It proved, however, technically possible for merchants to exploit sugar in a new way, eluding the expensive end-purchaser role to which they were accustomed in the Oriental spice trade by growing it themselves. This was the basis of the Venetian experiments in sugar production in the Kingdom of Jerusalem in the twelfth century and of the Venetian Cornaro family's vast sugar operation in fourteenth-century Cyprus. The first Genoese-owned sugar estates on a commercially influential scale seem to have been in Sicily, from where, in the fifteenth century, the crop was taken first to the Algarve, then to the newly colonized archipelagos of the eastern Atlantic, where (in Madeira, the western Canaries, the Cape Verde Islands and those of the Gulf of Guinea) it became the basis of the islands' economy by the end of the fifteenth century.

Sugar was the only Atlantic product which could compete as a high-value condiment with the spices of the East. The Atlantic centers of production formed together a sort of rival spicerie—sugar islands of the West, rivaling the spice islands of the East. Cane sugar replaced honey as the Western world's sweetener. It may have been one of those cases where demand follows supply, for in the last quarter of the fifteenth century, when Atlantic sugar production "took off" with the development of new sugar lands in the Canaries, sugar confections were still luxuries, featuring prominently, for instance, in the household accounts of Isabella the Catholic as Christmas gifts for the royal children. But, as with tea and coffee in the eighteenth century and chocolate in the nineteenth, popular taste quickly responded to increased supply. By the time Piero de Cosimo painted his imaginative reconstruction of *The Discovery of Honey* in 1500, apiculture was, in a sense, already a thing of the past, a primitivist image, which could be used to typify a remote age. A few years later, the first sugar mill on Hispaniola opened and the slow transfer of the industry to the Americas began. In 1560 Henry II's physician reported that "sugar is used in place of honey. . . . There is hardly anything today prepared for the stomach without sugar. Sugar is added in bakery and mixed into wines. Water with sugar improves in taste and healthiness. Meat is sprinkled with sugar, as are fish and eggs. We make no more use of salt than we do of sugar."

By then Vasco da Gama had opened a new route to the spice trade of the Indian Ocean, around the Cape of Good Hope, in 1497. The voyage has acquired legendary status in Western memory, though most of the contemporary sources have perished and those that survive convey an unglamorous, strenuous story, dogged by failure. The Cape route was occasionally broached as a possible target for explorers during the Middle Ages. Generally, however, it was dismissed as impracticable and those foolhardy enough to try it had disappeared—such as the famous Vivaldi brothers, who had launched an attempt from Genoa in 1291, and the searchers who had followed in their wake. According to the geography of Ptolemy, which became popular, especially in Portugal, in the fifteenth century, it was an impossibility, as the Indian Ocean was deemed to be landlocked. It is quite misleading—though depressingly common—to suppose that the voyage to the Cape of Bartolomeu Dias in 1487–88 inspired the breakthrough. On the contrary, though Dias did find that the coast began to trend northward beyond the Cape he had, if anything, contributed to the dampening of expectations. He had found a Cape of Storms and an entrance to the Indian Ocean guarded by ferocious currents.

This helps to explain the consequences that have baffled most inquirers: the fact that no known voyages followed up Dias's efforts for nine years.

Between 1488 and 1497, however, we do know of three or four positive developments. First, the pace of investment in Atlantic exploration quickened owing to the increase of returns on capital during the previous decade: this was the result of the growth of the sugar industry, the opening of new trading posts in Africa, with a resulting improvement in trade in such valuable commodities as gold and slaves, and an upturn in the long stagnant North Atlantic trades in such products as seal skins, whale blubber and walrus ivory. In consequence, Italian bankers in Lisbon became interested in new maritime ventures. Secondly, the first two voyages of Columbus had increased the pace of competition between Spain and Portugal for the rewards of oceanic expansion. Though few experts believed that Columbus had reached Asia, the possibility that he might yet do so could not be ruled out. On his third voyage, Columbus carried letters of commendation with which to greet Vasco should they meet in the East. Thirdly, the balance of factions at the Portuguese court changed with the accession of Manuel the Fortunate in 1495. The new king had always favored the idea of developing Portugal's long-range trade, rather than expending energy on crusading in North Africa. Finally, an intelligence-gathering expedition to India, Arabia and Ethiopia, dispatched from Portugal in 1490, had returned with a report. We do not know what the report said, but it seems likely that it established the fact that the Indian Ocean was not landlocked.

Vasco da Gama was a minor nobleman of some maritime experience but little personal prestige. His choice to command the expedition of 1497 shows that its prospects were not highly rated. Once he got to sea he made almost every possible error. The plan was to sail way out into the Atlantic to catch the westerlies of the far south. But Vasco turned east too early and instead of rounding the Cape, and avoiding the storms and currents discovered by Dias, he came up on the west coast of Africa by mistake. He was then condemned to a torturous struggle against the currents to get into the Indian Ocean. He was able to cross to India with local guidance but once he reached Calicut he alienated the authorities by his undiplomatic arrogance and mean gifts. By mistaking Hinduism for a form of Christianity, he seriously deluded the Portuguese who came after him. And when it was time to return home, he rejected expert advice about the timing of the monsoon and undertook a terrible, three-month voyage against the wind, at almost the worst season of the year, to get back to Africa. By the time his voyage was over, he had lost half his men and one of his ships.

Nevertheless, by demonstrating the viability of direct trade with Indian pepper producers, he inaugurated a new age in the history of the Atlantic. Instead of a barrier to communication with the rest of the world, the ocean now became a highway. The effects on Portugal and, in the long run, on Western Europe generally, were profound. To the civilizations of maritime Asia, however, the arrival of the Portuguese was of little significance. They became one more community of intrusive traders, among hundreds of others. Their imperial adventures were tolerable: confined to a few coastal outputs and to what scholars now call a "shadow empire" of individuals who took service with indigenous kings or blended into the commercial networks of native states, beyond the reach of Portuguese rule. The Portuguese benefited the existing economy by adding shipping, by supplementing the existing intra-Asian trade and, from the producers' point of view, by adding to competition. They did not deflect or "siphon" existing trade from traditional routes. On the contrary, under the stimulus of improved communications, the total volume of the spice trade continued to grow and the amount handled along the traditional routes via Central Asia or the Persian Gulf or Red Sea was higher in the sixteenth century than ever before. When it faltered, it was because of political instability in Central Asia, which interrupted the peaceful conditions on which caravans relied, rather than because of Portuguese competition. The Portuguese handled 10 percent of the output of Malabar pepper in a good year. This was enough to supply Western Europe demand but left the old trade to the Middle East untouched. The myth that the opening of the Cape route "diverted" the spice trade of the East still appears in popular histories and textbooks; but scholarship has exploded it.

Spices would never make a major difference to the world balance of trade and power until Europeans succeeded in controlling supply as well as securing trade. The revolution in spice production was gradual, but it had specific critical moments. In the early seventeenth century Portuguese practice on Ceylon, the island which produced most of the world's cinnamon, demonstrated the possibilities. By heavily garrisoning the perimeter of the island and imposing production quotas and monopoly terms, Portugal was able to regulate supply to the point of virtual control. But this was a highly exceptional operation: generally, the Portuguese relied on local collaborators to supply their needs and kept costs down by accepting the constraints of the existing markets and submitting to the conditions imposed by native rulers.

When the Dutch broke into the Indian Ocean circle in the early seventeenth century, it looked as if their operation would merely be a more efficient version of what the Portuguese had already done. They cut costs by making as few stops en route as possible. In the second decade of the century they developed a new, fast, efficient route across the Indian Ocean, with the roaring forties and the Australia

Current—a great, sweeping arc, relying, for the outward voyage, on fixed winds and bypassing the monsoons with their slow seasonal rhythms and long turn-around times spent waiting for the wind. From 1619 the Dutch station at Batavia became the gateway to the new route.

Pricing was the essence of the competitive edge the Dutch achieved: their strategy was to drive down costs and maximize profits. Paradoxically, this committed them to escalatingly expensive political and military interventions in the market. The fate of Bantam, the Dutch residency in Java, demonstrated the trajectory that became typical. It boomed with the increased demand for pepper in China and Europe. Land was converted to pepper production until the island became a net importer of food. When the Dutch arrived they found a trade already established on a vast scale. Sancho Moluco, the leading native trader, could supply two hundred tons of pepper at a time. Islanders dealt on a vast scale with Chinese and Gujerati merchants. The Dutch could not handle, at most, more than about a quarter of the island's production, but they could not remain indifferent to the power of their competitors in the marketplace, nor the freedom producers enjoyed to adjust the market to suit themselves. After a series of disputes the founder and governor of Batavia, Jan Pieterszoon Coen, decided to destroy Bantam's trade. The war waged intermittently but ruthlessly for most of the 1620s. Over that period, the island's production fell by more than two thirds. Ironically, Lim Lakko, the sultan's Chinese adviser who had organized the cartel that provoked the Dutch, was obliged to move to Batavia, "utterly down and out," to found a new fortune trading with Taiwan. Bantam switched to making sugar for the Chinese market. When pepper production revived for English customers in the 1670s, the Dutch moved in again in force and imposed a humiliating treaty on the sultan at gunpoint in 1684.

Meanwhile, an even more dramatic case of production wrested by force occurred further east. Makassar was a small sultanate on Sulawesi. In the first half of the seventeenth century her economy boomed with the work of refugees from Dutch aggression elsewhere. Malays filled her ships' crews. Moluccans brought savoir faire in spices. Expelled from their principal emporium at Melaka, the Portuguese introduced their long-range contacts. It became their "second and better Melaka" and, in the opinion of a Dominican who visited in 1658, it was "one of the greatest emporia of Asia." The Kunstkammer of the ruler included a library of Spanish books, a globe and a striking clock. The mastermind of the sultanate's foreign and commercial policies was Francisco Vieira, the Portuguese factotum, a model of happy deracination, who moved through the East with ease on his luxuriously appointed yacht. Like other trading communities of maritime Asia, the

Makassarese were not particularly interested in the European market: it was too small and distant to be worth their while. For European traders in the East, however, their own rivalries were all-important. By the mid-seventeenth century, the Dutch had already invested so much in the forcible elimination or restriction of Portuguese (and, to a lesser extent, English) rivals, that they could not tolerate a native state which effectively acted as a surrogate and refuge for continued Portuguese profiteering.

"Do you believe," the sultan asked them, "that God has reserved for your trade alone islands which lie so distant from your homeland?" The first war they provoked against Makassar, from 1652 to 1656, left the sultanate with "no powder left, no munitions, nor anyone who could supply them." The most heavily gunned fleet in the history of the Indian Ocean assembled in Batavia to finish the sultanate off. The Dutch renewed the war in 1659. On June 12, 1660—an almost forgotten date, but one which deserves to be remembered as a turning point in world history— Makassar fell when a Dutch landing party seized the fortress. The sultanate was reduced to subservience. The Dutch had now completed their ring of force around the spice islands. They could control supply at the source of production as well as the first level of distribution. According to their reading of the fluctuations of the market, they devastated lands, burned plantations, uprooted crops and destroyed competitors' ships. Plantings of clove, nutmeg and mace rapidly fell to a quarter of their former levels. In "depopulated lands and empty seas," Southeast Asia's "age of commerce" came to an end as indigenous cultivators "retreated from the world economy." Previously, the new routes tacked to world trade by European interlopers in the East had supplemented the traditional system and expanded its total volume, without modifying its essential character or shifting its main axis. Now a valuable slice of the gorgeous East really was held in fee and the economy of part of the Orient was impoverished for the benefit of the stockholders of the Dutch East India Company. This was a reversal of the eons-old balance of trade, which had enriched the East at Western expense. The results can still be seen on the Heerengeracht of Amsterdam, the avenue of merchant palaces lining a canal, where the spice-rich elite concealed what Simon Schama famously termed their "embarrassment of riches"—luxurious living behind unpretentious facades.

While it slipped into European control, the production of Oriental luxuries for the food trade remained regionally specialized. There were still "spice islands" and "pepper coasts." Ceylon still specialized in cinnamon, Amboina in nutmeg, Ternate and Tidore in cloves and mace, Malabar in pepper. The expectation started by Columbus, that the New World would yield new, undiscovered spiceries, had proved disappointing. Gonzalo Pizarro lost an army seeking a "land of cinnamon" in Peru. Chilies were more piquant than Oriental black pepper and ginger but could only supplement them—extending the culinary repertoire without replacing traditional dishes. In West Africa, Portuguese venturers had discovered "malaguetta pepper" in the fifteenth century, but this had never succeeded in the European market. So although the distribution of the profits changed in the seventeenth century, and the routes multiplied, the general direction of the spice trade remained much the same as ever.

Now, however, all that was about to change. The next great revolution in the history of food was the process we have come to know as the "Columbian Exchange": an ecological turnaround in world history, as a result of the enormous extension of global shipping routes in the early-modern period. This made it possible to transplant crops to new climates, by a mixture of adaptation and accident, in the worldwide reshuffle of biota which is the subject of the next chapter.

Challenging Evolution

—

Food and Ecological Exchange

Alas! What various tastes in food
Divide the human brotherhood!

—HILAIRE BELLOC, ON FOOD

THE VOYAGE OF THE BOUNTY

Its size makes it look efficient. The mature fruit of the breadfruit tree is as big as a man's head or a large melon. It resembles a well-buffeted pineapple, with higgledy-piggledy spikes. Conspicuous, ample, adaptable, the breadfruit appears, on superficial examination, to be a nutritionist's dream, perhaps even a wonder food. Inside the skin of one variety, which captured the esteem of Europe in the eighteenth century, lurk large seeds, resembling chestnuts. They are good boiled and sweetened or fried. They can also be ground to flour. The flesh slices well, yields to the palate and has a flavor reminiscent of other tropical fruit. Perhaps because it can be eaten satisfactorily at different stages of ripeness, its enthusiasts contradict one another when they describe its consistency: "between yeast dumplings and batter pudding" to one set of teeth, or to another "as soft and creamy as an avocado, or runny as ripe camembert." When he was in the Moluccas, working toward the theory of evolution by natural selection, Alfred Russel Wallace found that "with meat and gravy it is a vegetable superior to any I know, either in temperate or tropical countries. With sugar, milk, butter or treacle, it is a delicious pudding, having a slight and delicate but characteristic flavour, which, like that of good bread and potatoes, one never gets tired of." Apart from the fairly thin skin, there is no waste.

The breadfruit was an eye-catching part of the abundance that made the South Sea islands wonderful to eighteenth-century European sailors: places of restoration where the long-felt wants of seaboard life were supplied. Along with the sexual license of Tahitian life, on an island where "the only god is love," ample fresh food helped to make the South Seas seem "certainly the paradise of the world," according to Captain Bligh. In the lingo of modern economists, this was a world of "subsistence affluence," where there was little specialization in food production and limited trade in food products, but where, in normal times, abundance was spectacular. In most islands, yams, taro and plantains contributed most to the basic diet but, when in season, breadfruit was the making of every feast— the starchy complement to the festive meats: pigs, turtles, dogs, chicken, fish and some prestigious larvae, such as the grubs of the longhorn beetle, which infests coconuts. The most widely favored method of preparation was to bake the breadfruit whole in hot embers or in pits with hot stones. It could be also encountered in fish stews, cooked in liquids extracted from coconut. Because it is a seasonal product, and—unlike taro—cannot be left for long before harvesting, it was also prepared for drying, fermenting and smoking. It helped to communicate an illusion of nutritional richness and became a fixture in Europeans' mental picture of the South Sea island Eden in the eighteenth century.

The "inestimable benefit" of "a new fruit, a new farinaceous plant" was among the prizes that lured La Pérouse to his death in the South Pacific in 1788. The same search inspired the voyage that ended with the mutiny on the *Bounty*. Bligh's mission was to pluck a bit of the paradise of the South Pacific and transfer it to the slave hell of the Caribbean. On Jamaica, Bryan Edwards, the planter and projector who was always on the lookout for ways of improving the slave economy, believed that breadfruit could energize slaves and turn his island into a hive of industry. In consequence, Bligh was sent to Tahiti in 1787. He brought his single-minded, demonic energy to the task. Most of his men mutinied. The captain and the loyal survivors were cast adrift in mid-ocean and saved, after terrible deprivations, only by Bligh's startling ability as a navigator. Meanwhile, some of the mutineers lived in self-condemned exile with their Tahitian women on an uncharted island. Riven by predictable dissensions, most of them perished in internecine feuding. Others were hunted down and executed by the Royal Navy. After six years' bloodshed and travail, Bligh completed his mission, with an ironic twist: the breadfruit experiment proved disastrous. Breadfruit is not, in fact, particularly useful food. It lacks most nutrients except calcium and vitamin C, which is destroyed by cooking. It does not keep well. The slaves would not eat it.

It has, however, a symbolic value in the history of food. Bligh's saga sums up the tremendous labor of European navigators of the early-modern period in shifting food products around the globe, not just by way of trade but also as samples for planting. What Al Crosby called the "Columbian Exchange" was one of the most impressive "revolutions" or—more exactly—long-term structural shifts in history; it was also one of the biggest modifications ever inflicted by man on the rest of nature. From the time that the continents began to drift apart 200 million years ago to the sixteenth century, evolution followed a broadly divergent course. Developing in isolation, the biota of each continent grew ever more distinctive. When European voyagers traversed the world and linked formerly sundered regions by sea routes, the process went into reverse. Biota were shifted around the globe on a convergent pattern. Now the descendants of merino sheep graze the Southern Hemisphere. There are wallabies in English parkland. The American prairie, which never saw a grain of wheat until the sixteenth century, nor grew it in significant amounts until the nineteenth , has become the wheat bin of the world. Coffee, which originated in Ethiopia, is sought from Java, Jamaica and Brazil. Texas and California produce one of the world's most popular kinds of rice. Chocolate and peanuts, both formerly peculiar to the New World, are among the most important products of West Africa. The staple of the Incas sustains Ireland.

There were, of course, foodstuff migrations throughout history. The diffusion of the great staples of early farming—as recounted in the previous chapter— presupposes ecological as well as cultural transmission. Human agency may have played a part in some accidental transmissions. The plant most prized for flavor in ancient Rome was silphium, a weed never successfully domesticated. It was exported from Cyrene, after introduction from its unique original homeland in nearby Libya, presumably by self-seeding. The natives, and the Greek gourmets for whom they harvested the plant, only nibbled the extremities, but the Romans ate the whole stem and root, sliced and preserved in vinegar. Overcropping to meet Roman demand doomed silphium to extinction. Its spread from Libya was the only recorded transmission of a food plant in antiquity. Others, however, can safely be presumed, including some plants, such as grapes, which advanced with the Roman frontier as far as the climate would allow, while Romans laboriously tried to re-create Mediterranean ecology in distant colonies. Alexanders, balm, balsam, coriander, dill, fennel, garden leek, garlic, hyssop, marjoram, mint, mustard, onion, opium poppy, parsley, rosemary, rue, sage, savory and thyme are all said to be "strong candidates" for Roman introduction to Britain. None of these, however, nor any subsequent transmissions within the Old World or within the New, can compare in importance in world historical terms with the exchanges that began with—or at about the time of—the voyages of Columbus. In part, this is because more recent ecological exchanges have occurred over unprecedented distances on an unprecedented scale. In part, too, it is because of the role of human agency in facilitating and promoting them. Although there is room to debate the exact chronology and means of tradition of many of the plants in question—the sweet potato, for instance, may have crossed the Pacific on driftwoods without human involvement—it remains unquestionable that the great ocean-borne exchange of biota of the last five hundred years constituted the biggest human intervention in environmental history since the beginnings of species domestication.

THE GLOBAL PALETTE

On food, the effects of the exchange were most dramatic in the field of nutrition. The relatively sudden increase in the species available for exploitation in different parts of the world meant that the total nutritional value of the world's food production could leap ahead. Vast, previously unexploited or underexploited lands could be exploited for farming or ranching as suitable crops or livestock became transportable to new environments. The farmed frontier could climb up mountainsides and colonize deserts. Varied diets became accessible to populations previously overreliant on particular staples. Wherever the effects of the ecological exchange were felt, more people could be fed. This is not to say that the exchange of biota "caused" population to increase; but it facilitated it, by making it possible to feed more people. There were countercurrents: among the exchanged biota were not only foodstuffs but also people, who tend to be destructive, and disease-causing microbes, which inflicted terrible losses on populations unused to them. The arrival of Old World diseases, for instance, was the most important single reason for the collapse of the indigenous populations of much of the Americas in the sixteenth and seventeenth centuries. When Italian imperialists took cattle to feed their armies of conquest in Somalia in the 1880s, the rinderpest they brought with them killed millions of ruminants in East Africa and spread across the Zambezi to wipe out 90 percent of the grazing animals of Southern Africa and the people who lived off them. Nevertheless, in most places, to begin with—and, eventually, just about everywhere—the multiplication of foods fed the great demographic upturn of modern history.

There were also obvious political consequences. The people who controlled the routes of transmission could, to some extent, manipulate the consequences, shifting food production and concentrations of labor to wherever suited them. The maritime enterprises of modern times began as desperate efforts at self-elevation by poor, marginal, economically underdeveloped communities on Eurasia's Atlantic rim; but the perspectives opened up by their privileged access to the benefits of long-range ecological exchange helped the Spaniards, Portuguese, English and Dutch to become world-class imperialists—shifting, for instance, sugar production to their American colonies or creating new spiceries under their own control. The power of garnering plants and creatures from a dazzling variety of environments was a boost to Europe's incipient "scientific revolution." Every courtly Wunderkammer became a repository of specimens for scrutiny and experiment. Nothing like this global range of knowledge had ever been available before. Privileged acquaintance with "plant and faunal occurrence and distribution constituted a first step towards an ability to determine the influence of man on the environment." Though, as we shall see, China also benefited enormously from the introduction of New World crops, the worldwide ecological exchange made a major contribution to the long-term shift in the world balance of knowledge and power, as it tilted increasingly toward the West.

The political and demographic revolutions are obviously the most important results but the most vivid evidence of the effects of ecological exchange abide in the taste and colors of what people actually eat. The cooking of Italy is so intensely colored by the tomato that it is hard to imagine what it was like before that fruit arrived. The Italian tricolor represents the colors of the national flag with slices of tomato, mozzarella and avocado. Mozzarella is the cheese of an indigenous variety of water buffalo. Avocados and tomatoes, however, were fruits Italy got from America. The avocado's name derived from the Nahuatl word *ahuacatl,* meaning testicle. Equally indispensable items on the Italian menu—gnocchi and polenta—are made from potatoes and maize respectively. Many ingredients now deeply imbedded in other "national" cuisines of European, African and Asian countries were similarly unknown in their present homelands until the Columbian Exchange. It is difficult to guess what the nutritional histories or menus of Ireland or the North European plain might have been without the potato. Is it possible to reimagine the tastes of India or Thailand or Szechuan without chilies, a source of palatal fire unknown outside the Americas before Columbus? What would the shop windows of European confectioners look like without chocolate? Or is the cuisine of the Malay world imaginable without peanuts for satay? Crème anglaise relies on the taste of the originally American aromatic, vanilla. Liberian foo-foo is made not with native millet but with the cassava which the freed slaves who founded the nation brought with them from America. On English menus, the word "Hawaiian" should be read as a warning that the dish in question, whatever it is, will come garnished with pineapple, but pineapple has a relatively short history in Hawaii: it was one of the more spectacular finds reported by Columbus from the Caribbean during his first transatlantic voyage as the most delicious fruit in the world. Jerusalem artichokes, discovered by Champlain in Canada in 1603, are now prized in France, but neglected in North America. The working-class

English Christmas has come to count on the turkey, which, despite its misleading English name, was once an exclusively New World delicacy. Indeed, at the time of the Spanish conquest of Mexico, eight thousand turkeys were sold every five days in the market of Tepeyácac; one hundred were eaten daily at the court of Texcoco; five hundred daily were fed to Montezuma's zoo. It is "impossible to imagine a Bengali meal without potatoes, tomatoes and chillies": indeed, Bengali consumption of potatoes per head of population is exceeded only by that of the Irish. The provenance of the chilies on which it relies for flavor, and the identity of the carriers who took them from America to India, are encoded in the name Vindaloo, which is universally known as that of strong curry. It was originally a loan term from Portuguese, "Vinho e alhos" (literally, "wine and garlic" and, by extension, meats cooked in such a sauce). By a further quirk of global history, it has been adopted by the English as a sort of national dish and, during the soccer World Cup competition of 1998, was the title of a patriotic supporters' song.

The reverse effects—the new eating habits induced by ecological exchange in the New World and the Southern Hemisphere—have been even more profound, partly because the cultural impact of colonization has been greater (so far) on the New World than the Old, but partly, too, because the peoples of the Americas and the South had fewer edible species at their disposal, especially of fauna, than their counterparts in Eurasia and most of Africa five hundred years ago. Imagine the food of Argentina or the United States without steaks. Or of the Deep South without molasses or yams or pork or collard greens. Or of the Caribbean or the Carolinas without rice. Or the economy of the prairies without wheat. Or of New Zealand and Australia without sheep. Or of Jamaica without bananas. Where would South Africans be without their brij or Australians without their barbie? To make arroz cubano, spread boiled rice and top it with an egg and a banana, both fried in olive oil, and serve with tomato sauce. Eggs and tomatoes were available in the New World before the coming of the Spaniards. Rice, olives and bananas, however, were Old World imports. In Toronto, I had a memorable meal of wild salmon chowder, caribou sausages and bison steak in a restaurant specializing in "First Nations" food. But the soup contained cow's cream, the sausages had peppercorns in them and the steak was well dressed with garlic, which was almost certainly a post-Columbian introduction to the Americas. (In case any readers have been unable to try it, I should say that the meat of the American bison is utterly delicious, with a gamey flavor reminiscent of venison and a consistency similar to free-grazing beef. Not that I care, but it also has less fat and cholesterol than chicken.)

It is tempting to pick out the well-documented, conscious transpositions of biota as the heroic highlights of the story, or focus on the legends of culture heroes who bore the gifts across the oceans. Columbus is fairly credited with a lot of "firsts." From his first ocean crossing, he brought back descriptions and samples, including pineapple and cassava. On his second transatlantic voyage, he took sugar to Hispaniola—but let it grow wild; pigs, sheep, cattle and wheat made their first appearance in the New World on the same occasion. Juan Garrido, a black companion of Cortés, first planted wheat in Mexico. The Franciscan missionary Junipero Serra laid out the first gardens and vineyards in California. The story of Raleigh introducing potatoes to England is false but has an honored place in legend. By inspiring the Suez Canal, Ferdinand de Lesseps made it possible for Red Sea fish to colonize the depleted waters of the Mediterranean (though the difference in salinity between the two seas made the journey impossible until the Aswan dam barred Nile water from the sea: now more than 10 percent of eastern Mediterranean fish are of Red Sea origin).

The real heroes, however, are surely the plants and animals themselves, who survived deadly journeys and achieved leaps of acclimatization, sometimes—in the case of seeds—with little human help, by accident, traveling in the cuffs or pleats of the clothing of unwitting carriers, or in the weft of bales and sacking. In terms of volume and contribution to global nutrition a few instances stand out and demand attention. Out of Eurasia to New Worlds in the Western and Southern Hemispheres went wheat, sugar, rice, bananas and major meat-yielding and dairy livestock. The grape variety *Vitis vinifera* should perhaps be included, because of the importance New World wines made from varieties of it have attained in the world market; but there were grapes of a sort in the pre-Columbian Americas and the natives could have developed wine if they had wanted to. (Perhaps they did: the archaeologist James Wiseman has recently urged colleagues to start looking for evidence.) The correspondingly most important gifts of the New World to the rest were maize, potatoes, sweet potatoes and chocolate. Any review of these goods has to start with wheat, because of the depth of the revolution it effected and the extent of its spread across the world.

THE REVOLUTION OF THE PLAINS

The great natural grasslands of the world lie where the ice age glaciers did not reach, on soils too dry or infertile to bear forests, and in the subtropical niche between equatorial forests and deserts. Three huge areas, all in the Northern Hemisphere, dominate the category and typify the range. The Eurasian steppe curves like a bow from Manchuria to the western shore of the Black Sea, north of the mountains and deserts of Central Asia. The Great North American plain rolls from the Rocky Mountains to the Mississippi valley and the Great Lakes, sloping gently toward the north and east. The North African savanna and Sahel form a strip across the continent between the Sahara and the rain belt.

For most of history, the Eurasian and American environments had much in common: both were more uniform and more tenaciously grassy then their African counterpart, with only patchy intrusions of woodland, except for the tongue of "forest steppe" which laps Central Asia. They had virtually no reliable floodplains, and a relatively limited range of grasses, dominated by types of needlegrass. In Africa, by contrast, the true grasslands of the Sahel blend with savanna to the south, where there is much greater diversity: intermittent tree cover, a more humid climate, plenty of good agricultural soil and a gigantic larder of big game. Even in the most steppelike part of the plain, the native grasses are more varied and more succulent than Eurasia's and America's. The floodplains of the Niger and Senegal Rivers create fields which are fairly good for millet. This was therefore a type of environment where Africans had a historic advantage. By conventional measurements—the extent of farming and sedentary industry, of city life, of monumental architecture, of literate culture—civilizations in grassland Africa achieved more conspicuous modifications of nature than those in other continents.

None of the great grasslands, however, naturally produced much in the way of plants edible to humans. These were environments people exploited vicariously, hunting the creatures that ate the grasses. Although this makes for a satisfactory way of life to those who practice it, the waste of energy is obvious. For maximum efficiency, the best strategy is to grow plants for human food, rather than wait for the ruminants to convert grass into meat. For most of the past, on the Great Plains of North America, three conditions inhibited the introduction of agriculture. There was ample game—giant quadrupeds in Paleolithic times, great herds of bison when the giants became extinct (above, p. 64). The soil, unaffected by the last ice age, was tough and invulnerable to preindustrial tools. And no humanly edible plant was available that would grow in it in sufficient abundance. Even as late as 1827, when James Fenimore Cooper wrote *The Prairie*, it seemed a place without a future, "a vast country, incapable of sustaining a dense population." The habitat lacked the ecological diversity that encouraged civilization in the Sahel; it could and did serve, like the Eurasian steppe, as a highway between the civilizations which flanked it: but, even at the height of their wealth and grandeur, the cities of the North American Southwest, between the Rio Grande and the Colorado, and those of the mound builders of the Mississippi bottom to the east were relatively small-scale adventures which never generated the copious and productive exchanges of culture and technology that rattled back and forth between Old World cultures and made the steppe a vital link.

At the very moment that Cooper described it, the prairie was beginning to experience a slow invasion of white squatters, which would eventually contribute to a new look for the plains as a land of rich farms and cities. Today the Great Plains are the "bread basket of the world" with some of the most productive farming ever devised in the entire history of mankind. They also have a recent history of ranching which is still practiced with prodigious success on the high plains to the west and south of the region. It seems incredible that a land now so thoroughly adapted to human needs should for so long have been the domain of nature, where farming was confined to a few poor and tiny patches and where sparse populations trailed the great American bison. A similar revolution has overtaken the South American grasslands known as the pampa, which were even more wretchedly endowed by nature than the prairie: instead of big meaty bison, their native grazer was the small, skinny guanaco, a kind of wild llama. Now it supports the world's most productive beef industry.

Only invaders from the Old World could effect this magic. The first stage was colonization by European weeds and grasses which made the pampa and prairie able to support sheep, cattle and horses instead of just bison and guanaco. Purslane and Englishman's foot created what Al Crosby called "empires of the dandelion." Weeds made the revolution work. They "healed raw wounds invaders tore in the earth," bound soil together, saved it from desiccation, refilled "vacated eco-niches" and fed imported livestock. The conscious transpositions followed: horses and cattle, first—domesticable quadrupeds of a kind unknown in the New World since the Pleistocene. Then men and wheat: after Juan Garrido's efforts in Mexico, the lower levels of the central valleys proved highly suitable for wheat and although most of the population continued to rely on maize, wheat bread became a badge of urban sophistication. Within a few years of the conquest, the city council of Mexico demanded a supply of "white, clean, well cooked and seasoned bread." The valleys supplied Spanish garrisons all over Central America and the Caribbean.

Not all efforts to introduce wheat in other parts of the Americas were successful, at least at first. The Spanish colonists of Florida in 1565 brought wheat seed, together with vine cuttings, two hundred calves, four hundred pigs, four hundred sheep and unspecified numbers of goats and chickens; in 1573, however, "herbs, fish and other scum and vermin" sustained them when rations were short. Corn bread and fish, foodstuffs copied from the indigenous diet, were their mainstays. Similarly, the first English colonists in Virginia were unable to grow food for themselves and relied on precarious doles from the natives to see them through their "starving time." Investors and imperialists back home blamed colonists' moral deficiencies for these failures; but the problems of the mutual adaptation of Old World agronomy and New World environments were formidable, especially for settlers of exposed seaboards in an era of imperial competition. Colonies sited for defense, behind marshes or swamps, in enervating climates, needed generations of investment and long periods of heartbreakingly high rates of mortality before they could be made viable. At every stage of European colonization of new worlds, the remarkable thing is not the high rate of failure but the perseverance which led to ultimate success.

The Mexican model—exploitation of wheatlands for export and for feeding a few urban centers, with transitional or marginal ranching, perpetuated on unfarmed land—was transferred to the North American plains as soon as the requisite technology became available: powerful steel plows to turn the sod; wheat strains produced by scientific agronomy to flourish in a capricious climate and unglaciated soil. The enterprise had to be underpinned by an industrial infrastructure. Railways transported the grain across what would otherwise be uneconomic distances. "Balloon"-light house frames from precision-milled sticks and cheap nails housed settlers and spread cities in a region bereft of most construction materials. Construction gangs and city dwellers created demand for ranchers' beef. The Spanish army that invaded New Mexico in 1598 came accompanied by thousands of head of cattle, which their masters drove over mountains and deserts—including the terrible sixty-mile waterless stretch known as the March of Death. To Spanish cattlemen, the pampa and prairie were the last frontiers of an enterprise which began in the Middle Ages, when ranching was adopted as a way of exploiting the empty, conquered lands of Extremadura and parts of Andalusia after the Muslim population had fled or been expelled.

Finally, wielders of repeating rifles destroyed the vital links in the earlier ecosystem: the buffalo herds and their human hunters. Myth depicts the plains as an arena of "manifest destiny," where Native Americans were victimized by a white "evil empire." They are better described as a zone of imperial competition where the white men's empire contended with that of the native imperialists, the Sioux; who, by dint of organization and ethos focused on war, almost succeeded in subjugating the other peoples of the prairie. Something similar occurred in the pampa, where the talented war chief of the late eighteenth century, Cangapol "el Bravo" almost succeeded in uniting the culture area of the guanaco hunters under his rule. The outcome of the wars, and of the ecological invasions that preceded and accompanied them, was surely the most complete and surprising transformation of a natural environment by human agency in the history of the world. When one considers the vastness and intractability of the prairie, its hostile soil and its ornery climate; when one remembers the origins of wheat in wild grasses hardly masticable by human jaws and barely digestible by human stomachs; when one considers for how long this near-desert was incapable of sustaining more than its own sparse, indigenous population; when all this is taken into account, the achievement that has made the American Midwest what it is today seems hardly credible. The heroism of the brawny farmers, striding through waving wheatfields, in paintings of the Wisconsin school looks ridiculous to uninformed visitors to the university collection in Madison; but it is profoundly appropriate.

Except for a few conservation parks where the buffalo still roam, the last bit of prairie was put under the plow in the Peace River valley in Alberta in the 1930s. Meanwhile, the success of the prairie experiment, which was in itself a triumph of the transmission of crops and techniques from the Old World to the New, inspired, in its turn, Old World imitators. An American model was already in the mind of Alexis de Tocqueville, when he was charged by his government with the role of adviser on Algerian affairs in the 1840s—when the transformation of the prairie was barely beginning. He understood all too well that America was an empire as well as a democracy, practicing naked aggression to expand at neighbors' expense. All its soil was won by expropriation and bloodshed. Tocqueville believed that the conquest of Algeria, with its narrow but rich coastlands, its vast inland plains, its great open spaces and its untapped resources, would put France in possession of a sort of Old World America—a frontier where the same level of input and achievement could be encouraged among colonists, while the native races were penned in doomed desert reservations.

It was "a promised land, if one didn't have to farm with gun in hand," a prospective "image of Nature cultivated by industry." Philippeville, when Tocqueville first saw it, "looked American" to him, a town in Wild West style, distorted into ugliness by an economic boom. Algiers would become "Cincinnati in Africa." Tocqueville was blindly convinced that "native races," whether in Africa or America, were incapable of civilization. He knew that some of them built cities, practiced sedentary agriculture, possessed writing and, in the Cherokee case, even edited newspapers, but he never allowed these facts to modify his opinion. The best the tribes could hope for was "amalgamation" with their conquerors, not survival on their own. He denounced the cruelty and greed with which Americans oppressed the Indians, but commended policies of equal ruthlessness against the Arabs. He opposed "visible iniquities" for tactical reasons but acknowledged that "we burn harvests, empty silos and seize unarmed men, women and children" as "unfortunate necessities." The proper aim of colonial strategy was "to replace the former inhabitants with the conquering race."

In Algeria, his plan for the country's future was bound to fail. The environment of what was then called the "Great American Desert" was really nothing like the indomitable Sahara. Unlike the American Indians, the tribes of Algeria were irreducible enemies who always had a viable line of retreat. France, with its relatively stable population, could never generate enough emigrants to make Algeria into a convincing metropolitan *département*, while America could fill conquered lands with the demographic surplus of more philoprogenitive societies. Yet Algeria is an example of what America might have become if history had worked out a little differently. Had the Sioux imperial project succeeded, or if the plains had been a bit more hostile to colonization, America, too, might have been a beleaguered seaboard, guarded from the natives of the interior by a broad, highly militarized frontier.

THE BANANA'S TRAJECTORY

After wheat, the second most important crop to have reached America from the Old World is usually said to be rice. The native rice mentioned in the previous chapter should not be cited in refutation: it belongs to a different genus (zizania, not oryza). In colonial times, rice made a vital contribution in areas where wheat failed. Its introduction in Panama in the late sixteenth century and South Carolina in the late seventeenth made those areas viable parts of the Spanish and English empires respectively. It became part of the culinary heritage of much of the Caribbean, especially where Indian labor was introduced by the British, or where slaves were concentrated from parts of West Africa which formerly grew their own kind of native rice. Though this was rather different from the Asian varieties which became predominant in the New World, palates used to either kind could easily adapt to the other. The hallmark—as it were—of Caribbean rice cookery is the combination of rice with beans: this ensures complementarity of proteins and embodies the "mestizo" principle—mixing native ingredients with a colonial intrusion. In the late nineteenth and twentieth centuries, Chinese and Japanese migrants to the Americas formed new markets for rice and introduced new ways of preparing it, such as the glutinous, Japanese-style sweet rice balls now popular as street food in Mexico. Today, the United States is one of the world's major producers of rice, though most of it is exported.

Yet, despite the formidable case that can be made for New World rice, I prefer to give the palm to the banana. Personal prejudice may cloud my judgment on this point. In my youth I spent two years doing research at St. John's College, Oxford. At dinner on Sundays, we wore black tie, often invited ladies, and entertained the visiting preacher who had performed at Evensong. Conversation over dessert in the Senior Common Room rarely flowed easily and had a habit of returning lazily to well-tried topics which would, at least, be new to the preacher. Since bananas always formed part of the dessert—which in England, and especially in Oxford and Cambridge, is an extra course of fruits and sweetmeats served with sweet wines or claret, after the meal and before the coffee—the subject of the history and mythology of the banana could be relied on to recur frequently. Was it the fruit of paradise, as Islamic tradition has it? Where and when was it first cultivated? How diffused? What were the relative histories and merits of the different strains? When the predictability of the topic and the facilities for research are taken into account, it seems strange that we made so little progress in our discussions over so long a time. Still, I have known rather a lot about bananas ever since.

The best candidate for the ancestor of the varieties we eat today grows wild in Southeast Asia. Though known to Europeans in antiquity, bananas were fruits of strong exotic connotations: Greek and Roman botanical lore traced them as far as India. Theophrastus believed that sages gathered under the shade of the banana plant to eat its fruit. Varieties adaptable to almost every tropical and subtropical climate were developed by what we think of as the high Middle Ages; they grew in southern China and many regions of Africa from coast to coast. They were even a garden plant in Moorish Spain, though their cultivation there was not continued by the Christian conquerors. With this exception, the first European cultivators of bananas were colonists of the Canary Islands, where the fruit was well established by the early sixteenth century. That zealous monitor of the arrival of new cultivars in the New World, Gonzalo Fernández de Oviedo, recorded the arrival of the first bananas from the Canaries in 1516. A clue to the variety is contained in the first English description, left to us by Thomas Nichols, a sugar merchant arraigned before the Canarian Inquisition, who published an account of his experiences in 1583. "It is like a cowcumber," he reported, "and best eaten black, when it is sweeter than any confection." Unless Nichols had unusually cloying taste, this suggests that the sour banana was in question—*Musa xparadisiaca* "Dwarf Cavendish"—a variety formerly eaten as a staple in East Africa, where it is presumed to have been introduced in antiquity as a consequence of trade across the Indian Ocean. Rather than the varieties popular in the modern West, where people like to "unzip" sweet, firm bananas and eat them raw, it resembles "plantains"—species of banana suitable only for cooking and common, in the West Indies and parts of East, West and Central Africa, in savory dishes, prepared and served in ways closely similar to yams and cassava. Today, the exotic connotations of the banana have been dispelled. It is one of the world's commonest foodstuffs—second among fruits, in volume of production, only to grapes, most of which go into wine—and it is hard to imagine the day when the greengrocer might say, "Yes! We have no bananas." This is the result of the banana plantations of the Americas. Although most of the world's bananas are produced and consumed in Africa, three quarters of the world trade originates in and around the Caribbean.

THE MIGRATIONS OF MAIZE

In the Columbian Exchange, the New World gave as good as it got. Maize and potatoes were the real treasure of the Indies, for unlike gold and silver, they could be propagated and transplanted. Before the exchange, however, potatoes were still a regional Andean crop, unacceptable elsewhere. Maize had already migrated from its areas of origin in Mesoamerica across most of the Western Hemisphere, to acquire the status of a staple wherever it could be easily grown and of a sacred crop elsewhere. In North America, before the arrival of maize, the crops on which early agricultural experiments were based were native to the region and ways of developing them were worked out on the spot. The confusingly named Jerusalem artichoke was first cultivated—or, at least, "managed"—in its native North American woodlands in the third millennium B.C. Other varieties of sunflower and sumpweed produced oily seeds. Goosefoot, knotweed and maygrass could be pounded for flour. Squashes, which were indigenous to the same region, are exceptionally easy to adapt for agriculture.

These products could only be supplements to a hunting, gathering diet without a starchy staple capable of providing major nutrients in bulk. When such a "miracle crop" of tropical origin arrived, it was virtually ignored for centuries: maize spread into the region from the southwest in the third century A.D. but did not begin to transform the agronomy until about the end of the ninth century, when a new, locally developed variety with a short growing season became available. When it took hold, it was accompanied by the same tyrannies as in other parts of the Americas: collective effort and elites to organize it. Soil had to be prepared in various ways according to the genius of place: earth might have to be ridged or raised; forest might have to be cleared. Surplus food demanded structures of power. Storage had to be administered, stockpiles policed and distribution regulated. Mass labor was mobilized in the service of mound building, fortification, religions of display and the theatrical politics of rulers who demanded high platforms for their rites. Allotments close to the ceremonial centers can be presumed to have produced ritual foods or to have represented personal property; the large communal fields which surrounded them presumably filled a common stockpile with grain and starchy seeds.

Maize cultivation coincided with these developments: that does not mean it caused them on its own. Even agriculturists who (as far as we know) stuck mainly to a diet of native seeds and squashes, and lived in dispersed hamlets and individual farms, developed in ways reminiscent of the maize cultivators. They, too, created large earthwork precincts in geometrically exact shapes, luxurious ceramics and artworks in copper and mica, and what look like the graves of chiefly figures. Nor should it be assumed that the maize miracle was an unmixed blessing even in strictly dietary terms: when it displaced native cultigens, maize did not make people live longer or stay healthier: on the contrary, the exhumed bones and teeth of maize eaters in and around the Mississippi floodplain bear the traces of more disease and more deadly infections than those of their predecessors. When Old World invaders adopted maize, they showed similar reluctance and even worse effects. Slaves fed on it suffered malnutrition through negligent preparation (see above, pp. 35, 48). To the Iroquois, who became dependent on it, maize never lost its foreign flavor: they called wheat and maize by the same name.

It is not therefore surprising that the spread of maize beyond its native hemisphere should have been a slow business. In Europe, which had privileged access to New World agronomy, maize was unsuitable for the climate of much of the best land, and unpalatable to the people of much of the rest. Wherever it went, it was called by names which denoted extraneity: Spanish corn, Guinea corn, Turkey wheat. People rarely knew quite where it came from but they felt its provenance was tainted. It was more suited "for swine than for man" and even today, most European production goes into cattle feed. Most American production goes into the making of corn syrup, and much of the remainder for feed; relatively little is produced for direct human consumption. Gradually its virtues became known and resistance diminished. Maize yields impressively, harvests easily and, provided there is plenty of sunshine, grows at relatively high altitudes compared with wheat. Its period of "takeoff" into widespread, large-scale acceptance was the eighteenth century. It was adopted by hill farmers, bringing new uplands under the plow, in southern and southwestern China at a time of rapidly accelerating population growth. In the Middle East, it became the staple of Egyptian peasants, who grew other grain only to pay their taxes, but it remained a marginal crop in the rest of the region. The politics of the Balkans since the eighteenth century would have been very different without maize, which enabled communities to grow at new altitudes of settlement in the eighteenth century out of the grasp of the Turkish elite. Beyond the reach of tax gatherers, it nourished effectively autonomous settlements, weaning the future political independence of Greece, Serbia and Romania from mountain cradles. Thus in this corner of Europe, an American product really did nurture freedom. By the end of the eighteenth century, an Italian agronomist living near Rimini could write of maize,

> Now my children if you had met in the year 1715, which the old folks have always called the year of the famine, when this foodstuff was not yet used, then you would have seen poor families of peasants go off in winter to feed on the roots of grass to dig up arum roots or as they call it here zago or "snake bread," and cook them and eat them without seasoning and make buns of them. There were even some who chopped up vine shoots with an axe, ground them and made bread. Anyone who could get bread made of acorns or beans was not one of the unfortunate. Finally it pleased God to introduce this foodstuff, here and everywhere. If there are years with little wheat, the peasants can use a food which is basically good and nourishing; and moreover by the grace of God people are beginning to sow certain foreign roots like white truffles, which are called potatoes (and I want to introduce them, here).

POTATOES, SWEET POTATOES

Those words of Battara's suggest that different New World biota spread or stopped together, with interdependent reputations. In China, it was not the potato but the sweet potato that seemed to advance in alliance with maize. As in Europe, the new American foodstuffs rapidly became known in the East but took a long time to win acceptance. Maize appeared in China so quickly after its discovery in America that some scholars insist on an undocumented earlier transmission. Two independent routes seem to have been effective: overland from the west maize was borne as a tribute plant by Turkic frontiersmen and first recorded in 1555; meanwhile it came by sea to Fukien, where a visiting Augustinian saw it cultivated in 1577. It was welcomed as a curiosity, not a serious source of food: it rated no more than a footnote in a standard agricultural compendium of the early seventeenth century. The sweet potato, first reported in Yunnan near the Burmese border in the 1560s, may have come overland from the south. Its flavor had a bad reputation with Han Chinese but it was favored in hill country by immigrants and settlers who were obliged to occupy land previously thought marginal: first in Fukien and later in Hunan. In 1594 it was said to be a governor of Fukien who recommended sweet potatoes when the conventional crops failed. In the eighteenth century, in tandem with maize, the sweet potato transformed vast areas of China. In the 1770s, officials in Hunan, urgently promoting double cropping on rice paddies, advised that the lack of available wasteland for increased output could be compensated by growing maize and sweet potatoes on the hills. In the Yangtze basin, the uplands, formerly covered with forest, were developed for cash crops—indigo and jute—by "shack people" who lived off maize planted on the sunny side of their slopes and potatoes on the shady side. Similar results flowed from the complementarity of these crops in Fukien, Szechuan and Hunan. By the end of the century sweet potatoes had conquered palates sufficiently to be widely sold boiled and roasted by street vendors in Peking. Today, in terms of quantities consumed, maize has overtaken sorghum and even millet as an item of human diet in China. Even here, however, maize and sweet potatoes have only ever been a supplement—not a substitute—for the native staple, rice. They had the effect of extending, not replanting, the cultivated soil. In the rest of the East, their effects were even more limited. India spurned them both and nowhere did sweet potatoes get taken up as in China.

While maize and sweet potatoes conquered China, potatoes established a kind of mastery in Europe. Montignac has designated them "killers" because the genus they belong to also contains deadly nightshade; but, as noted above (see p. 100), if eaten in sufficient quantities, potatoes can supply all the nutrients man needs. For calorific value, they beat all other staples except rice. This was both their blessing and their curse: they could conquer hunger, but the temptation to rely on them exposed whole populations to the threat of famine in the event of crop failure. They were introduced first in the Basque country, then Ireland. Essayed in Belgium in the 1680s during Louis XIV's drive toward the "natural" frontiers of France, they worked their way eastward, supplanting rye as the basic food of a vast swath across the northern European plain to Russia. They were spread by war, for peasants, eluding requisition with the aid of a crop that could be left concealed in the ground, survived on potatoes when other food was in short supply. Eighteenth-century troubles sowed them in Germany and Poland and the Napoleonic Wars took them to Russia, where they conquered a territory Napoleon was unable to subjugate with the entire Grande Armée.

The range of the potato increased with every European war down to and including the Second World War. On its way, it was helped along by savants and monarchs, whose patronage helped dignify a despised vegetable. Count Rumford, as we have seen, fed it to Bavarian workhouse inmates, taking care to have it boiled to pulp in case they recognized and rejected it. Catherine the Great praised it. Marie Antoinette—usually unfairly cast as a promoter of cake for the masses—advertised its merits by wearing potato flowers in her dress. Did the potato "cause" the prodigious growth of Europe's population which began in the eighteenth century? The question is important, since, at its peak, Europe housed a fifth of the world's population, with obvious effects on the sustainability of European empire building. The answer, however, is not easily determined. The rise of population may have caused the rise of the potato, rather than the other way around. Potatoes intruded slowly and patchily. Many potato-less areas experienced population growth. Still, the new tuber certainly fed some of the new people and helped sustain the industrializing urbanizing societies of the nineteenth and twentieth centuries in Germany and Russia. In Ireland its failure in 1845–46 killed a million people, released emigrant labor for the British and North American industrial revolutions and, in total effect, reduced the population of the island by nearly half (see below, p. 204). It can therefore be said to have helped to make possible the new means of production which gave the nineteenth-century West an advantage in competition with the rest of the world.

Without attaining the status of a staple, a world-pervading food of Brazilian provenance was the legume misnamed "peanut." It is 30 percent carbohydrate and up to 50 percent fat and makes a protein- and iron-rich human food—indeed, with a higher proportion of protein by weight than any other crop. It is easy to harvest and fairly versatile in the kitchen. Yet, for elusive reasons, it has always remained marginal in food history. At one extreme, it is undervalued and fed to livestock: the renowned Virginia ham is produced from peanut-fattened pigs. At the other it is treated as a rare delicacy, as in China. Presumably, its route there was by Spanish galleons via the Philippines. It fascinated the Chinese because its subterranean fruit was "born from flowers fallen to the ground" and the seeds resembled silkworm cocoons. Peanuts were ideal for planting in the sandy loams south of the Yangtze and are nutritious enough to have become a staple: but perhaps because of their mysterious generation they remained, in China, a luxury of reputedly magical powers, greeted as "longevity nuts" at banquets in eighteenth-century Peking. Meanwhile, in most of the world they became something of a specialty dish, favored usually as a snack, garnish, confection or sauce. La Condamine carried pocketfuls around to nibble in Quito "asserting that they were the best treasure he had seen in America." In Southeast Asia they achieved a *succès d'estime*, in combination with the piquancy of chili, as the basis of satay. Portuguese ships took them to India and Africa, where they are an important product today, providing most of the world's peanut oil. Half the U.S. crop goes into peanut butter—one of the few genuine survivals of pre-Columbian gastronomy to be widely appreciated in modern America.

THE USES OF SWEETNESS

Cane sugar is, perhaps, the first food to have conquered unaccustomed markets by the power of PR. It was the first of a series of "supply-side" phenomena in the glob-

alizing market of the late Middle Ages and early-modern periods: tropical products which were recommended by their availability and to which European taste-
buds became enslaved. Coffee, tea and chocolate followed where sugar led; but it
was bigger than all of them, partly because it was essential to their success: for,
while none of the peoples who originally infused those beverages necessarily
included sugar in their recipes, it was unusual for European samplers to accept
them unsugared. Sugar was in the vanguard of the "hot drinks revolution" of the
eighteenth century. It is now the world's biggest food product, beating even wheat.

Its own rise, however, was as a culinary additive, independent of the hot beverage triad. The context of the story of the sugaring of European cuisine belongs
rather to the spice boom of Europe's late Middle Ages. At that time, as we have
seen, sugar was an exotic condiment, properly classifiable with pepper, cinnamon,
nutmeg, cloves and mace: a flavor of the Orient which could transmute food and
elevate it out of the ordinary. Transplanted to the New World it rapidly became the
most important item of transoceanic trade. The first mill opened in Hispaniola in
1513. The Brazilian industry was launched by Portuguese enterprise in the 1530s. By
the 1580s three effects were evident. First, Brazil had become the world's major producer and the economies of the sugar islands of the eastern Atlantic (above, p. 156)
went into eclipse. Secondly, the competition for sugar-producing lands was becoming a major cause of imperial rivalry between European states. Finally, the need for
labor in the sugar plantations and mills caused an explosion in the transatlantic
slave trade. Yet the sugar trade was still to experience its greatest revolution, which
would transform it into one of the world's most popular products: the populariza-
tion of the taste for hot sugar-sweetened beverages in Europe.

Coffee arrived in France in 1644 with sieur Jean de la Roque, who brought
some to Marseilles on his return from a visit as ambassador to Constantinople,
along with old porcelain cups of great beauty and small napkins of fine muslin,
embroidered in gold, silver and silk. His habit of drinking it in his Turkish-style
study was thought "a real curiosity." It took "50 years to overcome all the obstacles"
to coffee's general acceptance as a beverage, though the new habit found avant-
garde patrons within a few years. In 1657 Jean de Thevenot noticed that Parisian
aristocrats hired Moorish and Italian coffee makers. Armenian importers and
street brewers popularized it. Francesco Procopio dei Coltelli made it the toast of
his café, which had formerly specialized in cordials, like "sun dew"—fennel, anise,
coriander, dill, caraway, in brandy—and "perfect love liquor." It became the coun-
teropiate of the Rococo West, the potential home-breaker satirized in Bach's
Coffee Cantata. Once the popularity of the new beverage was established the next
stage was transplantation to new lands where Europeans could control the supply.

The great coffee boom of the eighteenth and nineteenth centuries took it to Brazil, to the French islands of the Indian Ocean, and to Santo Domingo, which for a while, until the blacks rebelled and proclaimed the Republic of Haiti in 1802, was the most productive island in the world for coffee and sugar alike. The most enduringly successful of the new coffee lands was Java, where the Dutch introduced the plant in the 1690s, gradually expanded production during the eighteenth century and, in the nineteenth, fought wars to boost production on ever more marginal soils. Peasants were forced to grow unsuitable crops, of which coffee was the chief, in a vicious system. It was denounced in 1860 by Eduard Douwes Dekker, under his pseudonym, Multatuli, in the most famous of Dutch novels, *Max Havelaar, Or, the Coffee Auctions of the Dutch Trading Company*:

> The government compels the husbandman to grow on his land what pleases it. It punishes him when he sells the crop so produced to anyone but it. And it fixes the price it pays him. The cost of transport to Europe, via a privileged trading company, is high. The money given to the Chiefs to encourage them swells the purchase price still further, and . . . since, after all, the entire business must yield a profit, this profit can be made in no other way than by paying the Javanese just enough to keep him from starving, which would decrease the producing power of the nation. . . . It is true that famine is often the outcome of these measures. But . . . merrily flutter the flags . . . on board the ships which are being laden with the harvests that make Holland rich!

Coffee can hardly be called a source of food. Whether chocolate could properly be so called was long a matter of dispute. Early doubts, among Westerners who tried it, are illustrated by a seventeenth-century controversy over its permissibility during fasts. In a work of 1648, which is usually credited with introducing England to the merits of chocolate, Thomas Gage reported the repercussions of this controversy in a remote diocese of New Spain, where the bishop had tried to prevent ladies from refreshing themselves with cupfuls during mass. When excommunication failed, he provoked a riot in the cathedral by ordering the priests to prevent chocolate from being served. When he died mysteriously rumor insisted that a cup of poisoned chocolate was responsible. "And it became afterwards a proverb in that country, 'Beware the chocolate of Chiapa!'"

Though to Gage, who knew chocolate in its natural habitat, it seemed a good, cheap stimulant, he also conveyed its adaptability to a luxury market. He described concoctions mixed with cinnamon, cloves and almonds, which would appeal in Europe, as well as the stews of bitter chocolate and hot chilies which were traditional indigenous recipes. The Lacandona tribe of the Chiapa forest still produce the foaming effect apparent in preconquest depictions by whipping the liquid with a wooden stick. The custom of sweetening it with sugar and vanilla, instead of drinking it bitter or adding the savory and spicy ingredients favored in preconquest recipes, helped the development of a European market, which, for most of the eighteenth century, was supplied chiefly from Venezuela. The elevated status of the beverage in eighteenth-century Europe surrounded the consumption of chocolate with rituals of social differentiation and images of wealth. In Barcelona's ceramics museum, painted tilework of the time in honor of the chocolate cult shows cups of the stuff being offered by bewigged gentlemen, on bended knee, to sumptuously attired ladies, beside the fountains of a pavilioned *hortus conclusus*. It could change from a luxurious beverage to a concentrated source of energy for mass consumption in the West only by a process that would make it eatable as well as drinkable. This was not perfected until the mid-nineteenth century—an episode that belongs to the story of the industrialization of food processing, told in the next chapter. Meanwhile, the shift of the center of production began for reasons quite different from those that had spread coffee growing to new lands in the previous century. It was a fall in demand, as a result of competition from coffee, which led to the decline of the Venezuelan industry and the marketing of cheaper varieties grown in Ecuador. Chocolate is not easy to acclimatize in new environments: it has to be pollinated by midges and, like coffee, demands a hot but shady environment. The problem of finding a location where superior varieties could be cheaply cultivated was solved in 1824, at a time when the Spanish trade was disturbed by the independence struggles of the future South American republics. Portuguese speculators planted it in the former sugar islands of São Tomé and Principe in the Gulf of Guinea. Eventually West Africa became the world's principal chocolate provider, especially after the Gold Coast began to be exploited to supply the greedy English market from the 1920s. Meanwhile, thanks to the expansion of supply, sugary tea, coffee and "cocoa" completed their descent from upper-class exclusivity to become proletarian hunger killers for the labor force of the Industrial Revolution.

THE PACIFIC FRONTIER

The Pacific was the last frontier of the great ocean-borne exchange of foodstuffs. In 1774 a Spanish expedition tried to annex Tahiti. It failed, but left Spanish hogs behind, which first improved, then replaced, the native breed. By 1788, when Captain Bligh arrived on the island, the small, long-legged, long-snouted native pigs had disappeared. In consequence, Tahiti had an advantage in the pork trade which soon transformed the Pacific as a result of two developments: first Captain Cook's perfection of a method of salting pork to keep it edible after a long sea voyage; secondly, the development of Australia as a penal colony. In 1792 George Vancouver shipped eighty live pigs from Tahiti to Sydney in an attempt to create a food source for the convicts; but it proved more economical for Australia to import pork ready salted than to breed pigs. In the first year of the trade, 1802–3, independent Sydney merchants—Australia's first bourgeoisie—handled 300,000 pounds of the meat. By the time the trade waned a quarter of a century later, ten times that amount had changed hands. The muskets that paid for the pork stimulated civil war and turned Tahiti into a monarchy.

Cook, who was responsible for so many more famous initiatives in Pacific history, was also the prophet of pigs and potatoes in New Zealand. His first efforts were resisted by the Maori, who preferred their own food. "All our endeavours for stocking this country with useful animals are likely to be frustrated by the very people we mean to serve." But potatoes were being traded in the north by 1801 and pigs became a trading item by about 1815. Other attempted introductions, such as goats, garlic, cattle and cabbage, failed because they did not fit into traditional Maori agronomy, but potatoes were sufficiently like the kumara or sweet potatoes that had long been familiar on the islands and pigs could be grazed and culled. Cook's shipboard scientist, Johann Reinhold Forster, suffered for his efforts to introduce sheep and goats to the islands, especially when they were billeted in the cabin next to his in an effort to protect them from the weather:

> I was now beset with cattle and stench on both sides, having no other but a thin deal partition full of chinks between me and them. The room offered me by Captain Cook, and which the Master's obstinacy deprived me of, was now given to very peaceably bleating creatures, who on a stage raised up as high as my bed, shit and pissed on one side, whilst five goats did the same afore on the other side.

The expedition succeeded in a series of introductions:

> We have imported goats into Tahiti and laid the foundations of a numerous breed of animals most excellently calculated for the hills occupying the inland parts of this isle. We have left goats, hogs and fowls in various parts of New Zealand, and geese in its southern part. . . . And in all the isles we made presents of garden seeds and planted potatoes in Queen Charlotte's Sound with a good quantity of garlic: so that future navigators may be refreshed in these seas more than they would expect.

The Maori, however, killed the goats Reinhold sent ashore, "which was very provoking to us." During his visit to New Zealand in 1820, Richard Cruise encountered "potatoes and pork, pork and potatoes wherever we went. I began to get tired of pork and potatoes." Eventually, however, in the 1830s, sheep were introduced from Australia for the benefit of New Zealand's white settlers. The land proved ideal for them: the climate favored their fleeces, the salt grazing flavored their flesh. In the 1850s, according to an Otago newspaper, sheep farming presented "visions of quite dazzling wealth." There were eight and a half million of the creatures by 1867.

New Zealand was an outstanding example of what Al Crosby called "New Europes": lands in other hemispheres where the environment resembled Europe's enough for European migrants to thrive, European biota to take root and a European way of life to get transplanted. Even with help from the climate, however, it was not easy to catch reflections of home in such distant mirrors. The strenuous efforts that had to be applied in New South Wales are vividly documented. Take, for instance, the case of James Ruse. He was a pardoned convict who had been a husbandman in Cornwall. In 1789 he received a grant of a farm of thirty acres at Parramata. The "middling soil," it seemed to him, was bound to fail for want of manure. He burned timber, dug in ash, hoed, clod-molded the earth, dug in grass and weeds and left it exposed to sun for sowing. He planted turnip seed "which will mellow and prepare it for next year" and mulched it with his own compost, made from straw rotted in pits. His own labor and his wife's performed the entire job. Success with such untried soils depended on experimentation with varied planting strategies. Early Australia was a strange sort of new Europe at first— made with yams, pumpkins and maize. On the warm coastal lowlands where the first settlers set up, maize did better than the rye, barley and wheat that the founding fleet shipped from England. Firs and oaks were planted but the food trees were more exotic: oranges, lemons and limes grew alongside indigo, coffee, ginger, castor nut. On the outward voyage the fleet acquired tropical specimens, including bananas, cocoa, guava, ipecacuanha, jalap, sugarcane and tamarind. In 1802 "the bamboo of Asia" could be admired in the garden of Government House. The most successful early livestock were introduced from Calcutta and the Cape of Good Hope, which also supplied acclimated fruit trees.

In the long run a European model did prevail but it was primarily a Mediterranean one. Sir Joseph Banks, who equipped the founding expedition, believed that over most of its extent the Southern Hemisphere was about ten degrees cooler at any given latitude than the Northern. He therefore expected Botany Bay to resemble Toulouse and sent over citrus fruits, pomegranates, apricots, nectarines and peaches. "All the vegetables of Europe" fed the convicts in the 1790s but Mediterranean colors predominated in visitors' descriptions. The first governor had oranges in his garden and "as many fine figs as ever I tasted in Spain or Portugal" and "a thousand vines yielding three hundredweight of grapes." Watkin Tench, whose study of the soils was vital to the colony's success—his samples can still be seen, dried to powder, in a Sydney museum—commended the performance of "vines of every sort. . . . That their juice will probably hereafter furnish an indispensable article of luxury at European tables has already been predicted in the vehemence of speculation." He also spotted the potential of oranges, lemons and figs. By the time of a French visit in 1802, peaches were so plentiful that they were used to fatten the hogs. The French commander saw, in the garden at Government House, "the Portugal orange and the Canary fig ripening beneath the shade of the French apple tree." The Mediterranean world also provided the colony with an exportable staple. The first consignment of merino sheep left for New South Wales in 1804. Only five rams and one old ewe survived the journey but these were enough to begin the stocking of the country.

This Australian experience set the pattern for the colonial New Europes of the nineteenth century: "dumb continents" where "the roots are European but the tree grows to a different pattern and design." The North American West, New Zealand and, to a lesser extent, the "Cone" of South America were all settled, displacing the indigenous cultures with dynamic, outward-going and relatively populous economies. All defied their original projectors and developed unpredicted characters of their own—tricks worked by the alchemy of settlement in the crucible of unexperienced environments.

EIGHT

Feeding the Giants

—

Food and Industrialization in the Nineteenth and Twentieth Centuries

There is no feast which does not come to an end.

—CHINESE PROVERB

Food, glorious food,
Canned, packaged and frozen,
Food, glorious food,
Which ones have you chosen?
Soups powdered in plastic bags,
Steaks polished and wooden,
Fish cutlets like Arctic crags,
Air-tight pudden?
Food, glorious food,
Pre-cooked and pre-grated,
Food, glorious food,
De-bloody hydrated . . .

—J. B. BOOTHROYD, *OLYMPIA NOW*

THE INDUSTRIALIZING ENVIRONMENT

When Charles Elmé Francatelli, former maître d'hotel and chief cook to Queen Victoria, published *A Plain Cookery Book for the Working Classes* in 1852, he included some dishes of truly revolting economy. To save money on tea, which he detested anyway, he suggested boiling milk with a spoonful of flour for breakfast: "season it with a little salt and eat it with bread or a potato." He recommended stewed sheeps' trotters for a treat and toast infused in hot water for convalescence. An hour's slow cooking sufficed for cabbage. Tripe he considered "not exactly a cheap commodity for food, yet, as you may feel occasionally inclined to indulge in a treat of this kind, I will give you instructions to cook it in the most economical manner." (In brief, the instructions were: boil in milk for an hour and eat with mustard.) These dishes might have been accessible to the newly emerging urban masses of industrializing Britain and, occasionally, Francatelli mentioned items which, he claimed, could be purchased cheaply in cities. In general, however, the maître's attention was focused on a bygone era of rural aristocracies and peasant dependents. Many of his recipes belonged in an uneasy idyll, spattered by blood from red teeth and claws. "Industrious and intelligent boys," for instance,

> who live in the country, are mostly well up in the cunning art of catching small birds at odd times during the winter months. So, my young friends, when you have been so fortunate as to succeed in making a good catch of a couple of dozen of birds, you must first pluck them free from feathers, cut off their heads and claws, and pick out their gizzards from their sides with the point of a small knife, and then hand the birds over to your mother, who . . . will prepare a famous pudding for your supper.

His idea of "economical and substantial soup for distribution to the poor" was remembered from his days as a country house chef, where he got used to "the charitable custom of distributing wholesome and nutritious soup to poor families living in the neighborhood of noblemen and gentlemen's mansions." The recipe was reminiscent of the old fairy tale of the "stone soup": the cook started with a few old bones, to which vast quantities of meat scraps and vegetables were slowly added.

Even in Francatelli's world, however, the Industrial Revolution was beginning to intrude. He expected at least some of his readers to acquire the kitchen ranges and pots and pans which industrial production was cheapening. These were strictly urban commodities. In the countryside, the hearth was still poor cooks' source of heat, even a couple of generations later, when Flora Thompson described the life of her Oxfordshire village. Nor did the villagers buy meat, like Francatelli's presumed readers. For in Lark Rise, every family kept a pig—acquired as a shoat and anxiously observed for signs of fattening, since a "poor doer" would waste a family's scraps—and each household got a big joint of beef as a gift from the "big house" at Christmas. Back in the city, Francatelli's concern for the economy of his recipes reflected one of the great economic problems of the Industrial Revolution: the hidden costs of concentrating labor, which drove up food prices by increasing demand and making supply more difficult. So leftover pot liquor should be eked out with oatmeal; children would "not require much meat when they have pudding"; fresh bones and ox cheeks figured largely; and "I hope," said Francatelli to his readers, "that at some odd times you may afford yourselves an old hen or cock." Finally, he displayed one of the most insidious signs of industrialization: the rise of the giant food firm. Many of his recipes explicitly boosted the products of Brown and Polson, whose "prepared Indian corn is a most excellent and economical article of food, equal to arrow-root, and will prove, on trial, to be both substantial and nutritive, and also easy of digestion to the most delicate stomachs." This was typical copywriters' language of the time.

The book's endpapers carried advertising that proclaimed the merits of other businesses of the same kind. Colman's mustard was the product of "known skill and improved machinery." In editions printed after 1858, the advertisements stressed medical evidence of the "purity" of the products concerned. This reflected growing public anxiety over an increasingly obvious effect of industrialization: adulteration in patent foods. The new health problems of industrial cities, where infectious disease incubated in the overcrowded, undersanitized environment, were legible between the advertisers' lines. "Be Careful What You Eat" in large letters was the slogan which introduced Borwick's Baking Powder. Robinson's patent groats formed "a popular recipe for colds and influenza." Patent brands of cod liver oil promised to convey "artificially to the lungs of the Consumptive . . . the vital properties of Oxygen without the effort of inhalation." Advertisers also evinced pride in the fact that progress in transport technology made their products widely available. Epps's cocoa was sold not only in London but also by "Grocers, Confectioners, and Druggists in the Country." Colman's mustards "may be obtained of any Grocer, Chemist, or Italian Warehouseman in the kingdom." Francatelli's book, in short, captured the industrialization of food at a transitional moment, where every aspect of the context was being transformed.

For the nature of the market was changing, undergoing what might be called "massification": a vast increase in volume combined with new patterns of concentration which defied existing structures of production and supply. The population of the world, especially the developing world, under the impact of industrialization, was experiencing the early stages of an unprecedented and sustained expansion, demanding equally unprecedented levels of production. In the early nineteenth century, the population of the world probably reached a billion. It rose to 1.6 billion in the course of the century. The birth of the world's six billionth baby was announced in the year 2000. The growth of huge, industrialized and industrializing cities had to be fed by new methods.

In some ways, early in the period, from the time of the introduction of the *levée en masse* in the French Revolutionary Wars, armed forces, on a scale unexperienced in the recent history of Europe, had anticipated the trend. Like cities, these, too, were immense concentrations of people, often located far from the sources of supply. Wartime logistics provided the models and, sometimes, the forges of innovation for the men who devised new ways of producing and supplying food in nineteenth-century Europe. Food factories, for instance, were inspired by the huge production lines which first appeared in state bakeries producing hardtack for navies. The need for campaign provision stimulated the development of canning. Demand for grease for the maintenance of firearms added to the pressure to develop new sources of fat. Margarine was first devised explicitly for the use of the French navy.

Industrialization helped to cause wars: in all the major conflicts of the era in industrializing countries—the American Civil War and the wars of Italian and German unification—centralizing governments in industrializing areas challenged the particularism or autonomy of neighboring, unindustrialized regions. Yet, for most of the European and North American nineteenth century, armies stayed relatively quiescent, fighting only short, limited wars or leaving the industrializing areas for sallies on imperial frontiers. From 1815 to 1914 city growth replaced army growth as the motor of change in Europe. By 1900 nine European cities had more than a million people. The land, where food was produced, lost manpower to the towns, where it was eaten. Most of the population of Britain, by the end of the nineteenth century, had forsaken agriculture for industry and rural for urban life. In the rest of industrializing Europe the same trend was evident. In 1900 two thirds of the inhabitants of St. Petersburg were classified as former peasants. Today, country by country, 2 to 4 percent of people in the "developed" parts of the world remain engaged in agriculture and, at most, 20 percent live in what, for statistical purposes, counts as rural areas.

Towns cannot feed themselves. The result was a potential food gap, which only industrialization could bridge. Therefore, with the enlargement and concentration of markets, food itself became industrialized. Food production got ever more intensive. Processing conformed increasingly to the patterns set by industries producing consumer durables. Supply became mechanized. Distribution was reorganized. Mealtimes shifted with the changing patterns of the working day. Today, and for the last half-century or so, one can even speak of "the industrialization of eating," as food gets "faster" and households rely on dishes prepared outside the home to uniform standards.

PRODUCTION, PROCESSING AND SUPPLY

The first stage of the intensification of food production is documented in the elaborately engraved certificates which eighteenth-century agronomists' societies conferred on "improvers." Increasingly, "scientific" stock breeding and soil management were the most favored activities, followed by introductions of new technology into planting, harvesting, drainage and fertilizing. These achievements were the fodder of the school curricula of my generation. One studied the "Agricultural Revolution" in terms of the heroism of the theorists of new methods and the inventors of new processes: the physiocrats in France, the Reales Sociedades Económicas in Spain, the English Board of Agriculture, the crafters of new high-yielding breeds and strains, the devisers of pumps and seed drills and methods of rotation. Their efforts multiplied the available amounts of potatoes, beets, turnips, clover and alfalfa, increased the availability of winter feed for livestock and slashed the amounts of land left fallow.

Selectively and gradually, farming then became quasi-industrial: there was no standard pattern because conditions were so various. In the "New Europes" created in the colonized grasslands of the Americas and Australasia, the trend was to huge-scale, increasingly mechanized farming and ranching. In parts of old Europe, specialization and consolidation were necessary responses to competition from the New Europes. In the areas of former slave-staffed plantations, a labor crisis followed the abolition of slavery: it was met, in different degrees in different places, by a mixture of mechanization, "coolie" migration and reversion to a more "primitive" pattern of tenure with peasant tenantries and sharecropping. Generally, however, even where traditional patterns of landholding survived the industrial era, as they did in much of continental Western Europe, farming became more and more of a "business" like any other.

Luther Burbank was the most conspicuous farming entrepreneur of the nineteenth century, bringing to his craft the talents of the inventor, investor, publicist and manager. From a small farming background, he started a market garden business in Santa Rosa, California, in 1875, when he was twenty-six years old. In the 1880s he began a series of experiments with new varieties: he was to hybridization what Heliogabulus had been to eating—a dedicated pursuer of wild sensation and huge scale. He delighted in bizarre, eye-catching innovations—a white blackberry, a stoneless plum, a new fruit that was half plum, half apricot—and statistical giantism. He was said to have created a thousand new species, including the Burbank potato, from which that mainstay of the modern table, the Idaho russet, derives. He spoke almost constantly of "working with Nature" but he had an industrialist's zeal for speed of production and scale of output. In his autobiography, he proudly proclaimed that his life was led on "a quantity basis, speeded up." For his thousands of devotees he embodied American ideals. The future guru and multimillionaire "entered Santa Rosa," according to one of his gushing followers, "alone and unknown, with ten dollars, ten potatoes, a few choice books, one suit of clothes and a clean bill of health." He was an apologist for, as well as an exemplar of, American hustle. "We can do anything," he declared, "in America we set our minds and hands to doing."

His renown, however, was equivocal. Was this zealous autodidact "a scientific man of the class of Faraday," as his many admirers claimed, or an undisciplined sciolist—a "plant wizard" or a sorcerer's apprentice? Critics claimed plausibly that his results were obtained by wasteful methods: thousands of plants consigned to the pyre for every experiment that worked. Success was a trick of the statistics: he tried so many hybridizations, some, by the law of averages, were bound to work. For his part, he claimed to be almost infallible and to have a unique gift, a "natural ability" unrivaled among his contemporaries, for identifying useful plants. He became embroiled in the great scientific dispute of his day and, indeed, to some extent, of ours, between orthodox Darwinians, for whom natural selection is a sufficient mechanism to explain everything in evolution, and heretics who insist that random mutations occur.

Burbank himself had no scientific knowledge or instincts. His vocation for gardening, he claimed, began when, at the age of eight, he felt overwhelmed by the beauty and mystery of a green field, warmed by sudden, irrepressible, unseasonal vernal activity amid snow. He favored mystical musings about the "soul of the universe," ignorant speculations on the heritability of acquired characteristics and invocations of "Our Savior, Science." He had a pantheistic, peculiarly personal religion and tended to personify "Mother Nature" as an intelligent force in the world. Sometimes he represented himself as a thief from "Mother Nature's cupboard of marvels." He toyed with eugenics but insisted on the vital importance of nurture. "Probably," he said, "I have used that word 'environment' more often than any other man who ever lived." He exercised, in two respects, a benign influence on the history of food: first, by encouraging successors in the ecological context of species development, and, secondly, by inspiring imitators to develop new species. His example helped to fashion the life-saving new species that later launched the "Green Revolution" (below, p. 206).

Increasingly, in the late nineteenth and twentieth centuries, the capital investment necessary for increased output came from huge industrial companies, which made fertilizers and processed feed. The first chemical fertilizer was invented by

John Lawes, when he dissolved phosphate-rich ore in sulfuric acid in 1842. The process was not much used until the last few years of the century, when phosphate mines began to be discovered and developed on a large scale. Meanwhile, mountains of guano and potash supplied the world's undernourished fields. The real chemical revolution in fertilizer technology came in 1909, when Fritz Haber found a way of extracting nitrogen, the source of nitrate fertilizers, from the atmosphere. His admirers said he had "plucked bread from air."

Ultimately, farms became stages in a sort of conveyor belt: chemical fertilizers and industrially processed feed went in at one end and edible—sometimes barely edible—industrial-scale products came out at the other. The trend approached culmination in 1945, when the "Chicken of Tomorrow" contest was announced in America. Three years later it produced the battery breed. In combination with "growth vitamins" marketed from 1949, and feed laced with antibiotics from 1950, it led rapidly to the forty-thousand-broiler chicken house. By 1954, there were five to six million chicken-breeding businesses in the United States. Some farmers had ten million chicks. Betty MacDonald, a chicken rancher's wife in Washington state, looked back unsentimentally on the old-style "chicken house knee-deep in weasels and blood" where "stupid" chicks would devote themselves to contriving self-immolation in their drinking fountains or under their brooders or "pick each other's eyes out or peck each other's feet until they are bloody stumps." The advocates of the new methods were disingenuous to claim that the chicken came to "cover the globe" because of its unique merits: an undiscerning appetite and its own "refrigeration and heating" supplied by its feather coat. A ruthless new mode of production made chicken the cheap treat of the modern world. In "factory farms" which supplied most of the meat, eggs and dairy products of industrial society in the late twentieth century, animals were treated like machines: anonymous units of production, confined in ergonomically minimal spaces to turn over the maximum amount of output per unit of cost. These practices strained humane sensibilities but comforted stomachs. The latter organs proved the stronger.

The revolution in distribution also sometimes involves inhumane practices, when livestock is transported on the hoof in conditions which torture the creatures. Generally, however, the age of live transportation has been replaced by new techniques, such as rapid, refrigerated conveyance which has made it possible to shift dead carcasses over great distances. Herders in preindustrial and early industrializing societies drove their stock to points of slaughter: the cowboys who fed the rail gangs in the American West from the mid-nineteenth century provided the most strenuous, spectacular and long-range instance in history. Even as they did so, they were contributing to the demise of their own age-old way of life. When the networks were complete the railways carried the live cattle. When refrigeration came in from the 1870s onward, butchered carcasses could be delivered in edible condition over any distance covered by rail. Meanwhile, of course, the revolution in transport affected supplies of less perishable items which could be carried unrefrigerated. Wheat was the most important because of the dual development of railways and wheatlands in the North American prairie in the second half of the nineteenth century. When I was a visiting professor at the University of Minnesota, my balcony in downtown Minneapolis looked out over derelict evidence of this once mighty combination. The empty factories of Pillsbury and General Mills, decorated with fading proclamations of the glories of their flour, were being converted into hotels and apartments. Alongside, the Milwaukee Road railway station, saved from demolition, was undergoing rebirth as an upscale shopping mall. The old trade has shifted from downtown but is still vigorous in relocated, modernized mills, silos and weigh stations. The rails, where they remain unrusted, carry hardly any passengers but are still the arteries of commerce in grain.

In the late nineteenth century, the railroads linked up with steam-powered sea routes. British steam tonnage at sea exceeded that under sail from 1883: ocean routes would never be fully independent of weather, but their dependence on the elements was easing. Minnesota's railroad king, James Hill, whose sole munificence built the marble cathedral of St. Paul, had his own fleet of steamships. They joined the terminals of the fastest railroad across the Rockies with those of the Trans-Siberian Railway, which opened in 1900. The completion of these links was of more than symbolic significance. Land transport could now take bulk cargoes across continents as easily as seas. The great food-producing and consuming belt of the Northern Hemisphere, from Vancouver to Vladivostok, was linked by steam transport. "The flow of trade was no longer governed by Nature." The results included a new form of worldwide specialization, as food no longer had to be produced near the point of consumption. In industrializing areas, agriculture declined. British agriculture virtually collapsed in the last generation of the nineteenth century. All over Western Europe, wheat production was abandoned in the face of cheap long-range imports. The rock-ribbed farmland of New England began its long, slow reversion to forest, as food production shifted west.

Distribution, however, still needed to be local. In the new big-city environments, new ways of shopping evolved. Markets became municipal responsibilities. Until 1846, for instance, the right to hold markets in Manchester was, by tradition and inheritance, a perquisite of the Lords of the Manor, the Mosley family. By the

1830s metropolitan growth made this an equivocal asset. Unrestricted markets in neighboring townships threatened to undermine the value of the family's rights. The difficulty of managing an uncontrollably growing arena was beyond the family's scope and resources. The constant battle for control with the municipal authorities was a drain on the proprietors' energies. "The markets are not such," wrote the historian of the city in 1836, "as a town of great wealth and magnitude might be expected to possess." By the early 1840s Sir Oswald Mosley was willing to sell out for the apparently enormous sum of £200,000. Rationalizing his situation in a heroic style ultimately derived from Caesar's *Commentaries*, he wrote of himself, in the third person, "After many years of unavoidable and anxious litigation in the protection of those manorial rights which he had inherited from his ancestors, he had at length the satisfaction of consigning them to hands which alone are capable of managing them." Thus retreat was romanticized.

Markets built under new municipal dispensation became, in their very structures, monuments to the wonder of industrial technology: palaces of abundance, of crystal walls and roofs, elevated on elegant cast iron arcades. Together with the railway stations, winter gardens and shopping arcades, these were industrializing Europe's equivalents of the aqueducts and agoras of antiquity. Some of the most magnificent examples have disappeared. I hope no one will think mere chauvinism makes me recommend Spain as the land where the survivors are to be seen at their best. The Mercado de la Cebada in Madrid was built in 1870 to be a model for subsequent markets. An irregular glass triangle was erected on columns imported from England and designed by the mayor, Nicolás María Ribero, who had no engineering or artistic background, but a burning ambition to modernize his city. It enclosed five hundred square yards around a central fountain. All Spanish cities have such markets: big ones have several and they remain as remarkable for their contents as their frameworks. "Tucked away in the side streets of Madrid," H. V. Morton found "the most decorous and beautifully arranged markets in the world. They are the sort of ideal market that you might see in a ballet or a musical comedy. . . . Never have I seen fish, fruit, vegetables and meat displayed with a finer sense of the attractiveness of common things."

In rapidly growing towns, markets alone could not meet demand for distribution: they were nodal points which could serve retailers and shoppers who happened to live close to them. Shops and, to a lesser extent, itinerant traders were essential in spanning the spaces between marketplaces and neighborhoods. Grocers, who had formerly specialized in *épicerie* or delicatessen, became general purveyors. In pursuit of the economies of scale achieved by mass production, some of them developed the "chain store" system, led by Thomas Lipton of Glasgow, whose

Home and Colonial Stores were established in the 1870s and 1880s in every major center of population in Great Britain. His "own brand" tea retains a certain international prestige today, when the rest of the business has disappeared. Supermarkets are the paradoxical last stage of this trend: they threaten to engulf other methods of food retailing, combining the scale of the market with the convenience of the shop. For a while, from the 1960s to the 1980s, they tended to get monstrously big and to locate in suburban sites from where shoppers took their purchases home in cars. In the 1990s, however, this trend showed signs of being reversed, as supermarket chains in Europe and a few major metropolitan locations in America moved back to central cities or introduced home deliveries in a reversion to a practice which was once universal among local grocers but had seemed on the point of dying out.

Between the new scale of production in the countryside and the new methods of distribution and supply, the mechanization of processing multiplied the availability of food. Food manufacture imitated other industries: powering production with steam in the nineteenth century, electricity in the twentieth, using mechanized assembly lines and producing a standard product. The story is usually told in terms of heroes, inventors and entrepreneurs who were pioneers of ingenuity and embodiments of the gospel of self-help. Really the processes which brought food manufacture into the factories were more modest, cumulative and imitative. Four products can be selected to illustrate what happened. Three—the chocolate bar, margarine and the meat extract cube—were new inventions of the industrializing age, whereas the industrially generated biscuit was a new version of one of the oldest and most widely eaten of food products, which acquired a new kind of appeal to the senses: a regular, machined geometry, an unmistakable uniformity, and a predictability of consistency and taste, like those of the bar and the cube. These products proclaimed with pride their difference from the handcrafted, individual efforts of the independent artisan.

The most commercially successful biscuits of the nineteenth century came in tins which depicted an idyll. Along a neatly paved street with a quaint, bowfronted shop, elegant officers in Number One dress escorted daintily crinolined ladies. In reality, London Road, Reading, where Joseph Huntley started his biscuit business in 1822, was a mud track where the coach from London stopped on its way west. The coach brought custom virtually to the shop door and diffused patronage along the coaching routes of the realm. The firm quickly built a reputation that made its products sought from London to Bristol and was able to mesh a network of representatives to sell its wares to retailers as far away as Liverpool. But it was an old-fashioned Quaker business, constructed by family connections, run by family members. It was confined in a small, traditional bakery, with the family literally living above the shop. It was technologically primitive, except for the metal boxes made by one of Huntley's sons, which kept the wares fresh. The vision of mass production arrived in London Road with George Palmer, who became a partner in 1846. The idea of industrializing did not, however, spring from George's head: it emerged from context and precedent. Hardtack had long been made by human assembly lines in eighteenth-century dockyards. In 1833 the Royal Navy introduced steam-powered machinery to these establishments for rolling the dough. In the late 1830s, another Quaker, Jonathan Dickson Carr of Carlisle, invented the mechanical biscuit stamp, which enabled numerous biscuits to be cut from a strip of dough with minimal muscle power. To this day, the towns of Reading and Carlisle vie for the honor of having originated mass production of biscuits. Palmer's innovations were modest. He used ovens of an established pattern made for the manufacture of ship's biscuit. For making dough he brought in other inventors' versions of existing technology. He made the process of rolling it reversible, which halved the time taken, as the rollers sped back and forth. His success was due rather to his integrated approach to business—covering marketing and finance as well as production—than to technical ingenuity.

The results of the small increments he and other leading biscuit manufacturers made were, however, spectacular. In 1859 six million pounds of biscuits were produced by the world's three leading manufacturers, all of whom were based in Britain. By the late 1870s the same firms were producing 37 million pounds. The Reading biscuit and the Huntley and Palmer biscuit tin, with its distinctive blue livery, became symbols of the global reach of British industry and imperialism. Lord Redesdale saw the tins used as a portable garden by a Mongolian chieftainess in the 1860s and as altar vessels in a chapel in Ceylon in the 1890s. They were recycled as sword scabbards by followers of the Mahdi, and during the Christianization of Uganda served as containers to preserve Bibles from white ants. The British army which entered Kandahar in 1879 found an advertisement for Huntley and Palmers emblazoned on the bazaar wall. Henry Morton Stanley relied on the biscuits for nourishment in Central Africa and pacified a warlike tribe in what is now Tanzania with some tins as a present. When a naval landing party went ashore at Juan Fernández—Robinson Crusoe's island—in the early 1900s, "all it found there," according to the firm's historian, "was a few goats and—an empty Reading biscuit tin."

Huntley and Palmers had transformed the biscuit. Other industries created foods which were genuinely new to human experience. Chocolate, for instance, was reinvented. From a luxury beverage, it became a solid food with a mass market. To effect this change, it was necessary not only to create mechanized factories for pressing the cocoa bean: such factories existed by the end of the eighteenth century in Barcelona and Bologna but they were still producing an expensive product for the sort of exclusive clientele whom we met as consumers of chocolate in the last chapter. The development of a new product had to await a new cultural climate, a revolution in attitudes. The technology came from continental Europe—from Spain and Italy where cocoa presses were first mechanized; from Holland, where Conrad van Houten created cocoa powder; from Switzerland, where the Caillier and Nestlé families, united by marriage, combined in business to make milk chocolate. But it was English Quaker manufacturers of cocoa who did most to revolutionize tastes. In eighteenth- and early-nineteenth-century England, civil disabilities forced Quakers into business. The chocolate business attracted them particularly, because of cocoa's potential as a temperance beverage. To drive the price and accessibility of their product down to the level of the mass market was an ambition which, for the families like the Frys of York or the Cadburys of Bournville, united God with gain. The chocolate bar was the outcome.

The first true bars, intended for eating, not infusion—not brittle, dry and unmoldable but recognizably of the consistency familiar to every consumer today—were marketed in 1847 by Fry's. They were made of Van Houten's powder, mixed with sugar and cocoa butter. The new product was particularly suited to mass production and its further transformations, over the next 150 years, seemed infinite, as new flavors and textures were contrived by small modifications to the manufacturing process. The entire history of chocolate, from colonial crop to industrialized product, was encapsulated in the fictional chocolate factory, imagined by Roald Dahl, where magically supramodern technology combined with the labor of a tiny race of slaves. Dahl's heroic entrepreneur, Willy Wonka, was inspired by the American chocolate millionaire, Milton Snavely Hershey, whose benevolence as an employer was exceeded only by his munificence as a public benefactor and his genius as a businessman. He was the embodiment of the American dream, rising by perseverance from a string of disasters and bankruptcies. He was still a pushcart peddler in his thirties but, "born with a sweet tooth," as an admiring employee said, "he never stopped making candy." His ascent to greatness began when he opened his chocolate factory on the site of his old family farm in 1904. It grew to include housing, a hospital, a park and a zoo. During the Depression, Hershey kept his workers at work by expanding the amenities of his model community. His most heartfelt philanthropic project was born of personal tragedy: his childlessness inspired him with a vocation as a friend of orphans. "I would give everything I possess," he said of the inmates of his orphanage, "if I could call one of these boys my own." He was so lavish in his benefactions that when he died the sale of his personal effects raised only $20,000. His legacy today includes Hershey Park (a huge Disneyland-style theme park, originally picnic grounds for the chocolate factory's employees), the Milton Hershey School and Medical Center, and the Hershey Hotel, built to the model of a Florentine palazzo, right in the center of Pennsylvania dairy country.

The full effects of the business he launched were not felt for nearly a century after the first bars emerged from his assembly lines. In the Second World War Hershey bars were modified to resist tropical temperatures and a billion bars were issued as rations to help Americans fight successful campaigns in tropical environments. The ecology of cacao had come full spiral when the new conquistadors returned to the tropics with chocolate transformed. Meanwhile, the association between chocolate manufacture and public benevolence began to fade. Chocolate entrepreneurs tended to be radical Protestants—in England, they were almost all Quakers—with fixations about temperance, friendship, brotherly love and thrift. But these qualities were dissipated as firms got big, family traditions vanished and the profit motive took over. In the early days, Hershey supplied chocolate to the fledgling Mars firm in a spirit of comradeship; Hershey's associate, R. Bruce Murrie, was one of the Ms in M&M's. Today, the rivalry of Mars and Hershey is pursued ruthlessly and secretively "bar against bar," according to the only journalist who has been allowed full access to Mars records, in a "chocolate slugfest." Among the present giants of the chocolate industry, only the Mars company, though a formidable enemy in the market, still has, by the general standards of industrial capitalism, exceptional ethical standards. It has never stopped being a family business. Despite a turnover bigger than that of McDonald's, it has never been quoted on the stock exchange and has hardly ever engaged in takeover bids or mergers. Its grimly dedicated and unrestrainedly ambitious patriarch, Forrest Mars, passed on to the present generation, who still run the firm, his fanatical standards of personal austerity, generosity to the workforce and service to the customer: Mars aims to make only a 3 percent return after tax. All employees are "associates" whose remuneration keeps pace with profits. The family's management style is that of a tribal monarchy, but Mars associates earn more than their counterparts in other comparable firms, while the directors earn much less.

A side effect of the industrialization of chocolate was the transformation of the product into something astonishingly different from the form in which it occurred in nature. The power of industry to achieve this sort of metamorphosis fascinated food chemists of the nineteenth century, especially when they turned to the problem of how to present meat to consumers: how to prettify this bloody and elemental source of food. The beauty of butchered carcasses was apparent to still-life painters in the seventeenth and eighteenth centuries and attracted the greatest artists. Studies originally undertaken as exercises in the artistic representation of anatomy became objects of wonder, exposés of the mysteries of creation—even symbols of the Eucharist. When Rembrandt painted a side of beef oozing blood, or Carracci depicted a butcher's shop, with hanging, dripping, glistening joints, and vivid bones and membranes, the beholder had no chance to be repelled. The new romantic sensibilities of the late eighteenth century and the rise of vegetarian propaganda (above, p. 42) changed the way people looked at meat. In the new century the search was on for a way of exploiting the nutrition of meat in an emotionally sanitized form.

The most influential exponent of "animal chemistry," Baron Justus von Liebig, regarded the investigation of the world of meat extracts as an adventure comparable to those of the intrepid explorers of the age, a frontier terrain where

> adventurers of all kinds roam about; and it is on the observations made, and the tales related by these adventurers, during their occasional expeditions or excursions, that the greater part of our knowledge of this district rests. But how few of them have attained so accurate a knowledge, even of the small tract over which they have passed, that those who follow them run no risk of losing their way! It is one thing to travel through a country, and another, very different, to establish a home therein.

He aimed to be at home there himself. He was obsessed by transformation: indeed, he equated it with nutrition, which he defined as the process of changing food substances "into the constituents of organized tissues." Before his researches, the nutritional value of concentrated meat juices, or "osmazone" as some scientists portentously called it, already commanded general respect. Meat bouillon had an honorable history as invalid food. Consommé en gelée rendered the same nourishment in semisolid form and, if enough gelatin was used, could be turned into "portable soup": tablets which fed sick or wounded men in late-eighteenth-century armies and navies. Beef tea—raw meat scrapings infused in hot water—had its advocates. Early in the nineteenth century, François Magendie discovered that foods containing nitrogens contribute to growth. In the 1840s Baron Justus von Liebig believed—until his own experiments disproved it—that nitrogen "formed" flesh. His early efforts focused on squeezing raw meat to produce "the juice of flesh," but this was an uneconomical method, compared with "extraction" by adding water, and produced a liquid with no particularly concentrated nutritive properties. Liebig kept going through his disappointments because he could fore-see the enormous financial rewards of success. Before refrigeration, there was a vast, underexploited surplus of cattle in the Southern Hemisphere and an enor-mous, unsatisfied market in the North. In 1865 Liebig created Oxo to mobilize the former and supply the latter. He steeped raw, pulped beef in water, strained the liquor, boiled it, evaporated it and pressed the residue into cubes. Bovril followed, invented in Canada by John Lawson Johnson in 1874: this was similar, but sold as paste rather than compressed, crumbly cubes. These products were marketed as equivalent to much larger quantities of beef. They drew the ire and fire of the apostles of low-protein diets (above, p. 43): Halliburton described the infusions they yielded as "simply an ox's urine in a cup." Kellogg called them "putrefactive bacteria."

Meat extract is an equivocal product: one can see its usefulness even if one finds the idea repulsive. How margarine survived the context in which it was invented seems much harder to understand. It belongs in the nineteenth-century world—in that brief period of the crisis of fat supplies early in the second half of the century. The want of fat drove European powers into colonial ventures in potential areas of palm oil production. It stimulated the technology of whaling: the industrial whaler equipped with explosive harpoons was introduced in 1865. It encouraged the exploitation of fossil oil, first skimmed out of the ground in Ontario in 1858 and pumped in Pennsylvania in 1859. The crisis in edible fat, how-ever, which was growing ever more acute in industrializing countries, could not be satisfied by these means. By offering a prize for the invention of a "product suitable to replace butter for the navy and the less prosperous classes of society," Napoleon III hoped to solve the problem. The specification was: "this product must be inex-pensive to manufacture and capable of being kept without turning rancid in flavor or smelling strong." Hippolyte Mège-Mouriés, who responded successfully to the challenge in 1869, adopted an approach which seems more magical than scientific. He mixed beef fat with skimmed milk and stirred in a bit of cow's udder. He called the result margarine because he thought its anemic, pinguid sheen resem-bled the small pearls known as *marguerites*.

The result only made a marginal contribution to increasing the exploitable amount of edible fat in the market, and even sophisticated modern variants of the recipe have never produced a substance which can convincingly replace butter, though there are forms of margarine which some pastry cooks prefer for particular recipes. The original margarine did provide a model for the conversion of vegetable oils into butterlike substances, which probably stimulated the development of the oils which are commonly used to make margarine today, such as cottonseed, sunflower and soya. Only big, heavily capitalized enterprises could exploit the invention of margarine, because the business of making it was extremely complicated, demanding a great deal of space and machinery for repeated heating, hydration, precipitation of the fatty acids, hydrogenation, filtering, blending and flavoring.

Still, margarine attracted investment because it could be made from cheap ingredients and sold in bulk. Throughout industrialization, costs were the motor force. Cities and factories were expensive to provision until the output and supply of food adjusted to meet their needs. Under that temporary stimulus, food production outstripped the growth of population. The result, for people privileged to live in industrializing economies, was cheap food. This was not an accident or by-product. It was the conscious strategy of industrializers in every field of endeavor to expand markets by lowering unit prices. In an era of demographic buoyancy it worked. The cheaper the food, the bigger the profits.

FEAST AND FAMINE

At some levels the "Nutrition Revolution" that has accompanied the industrialization of food in the Western world seems a rather trivial affair: a matter of shifts of taste or fashion. Some trends, however, have been sustained over remarkably long periods. The retreat from red meat, for instance, in developed economies has recently attracted much attention and—in the industries concerned—much anxiety, as if it were a new phenomenon. Really, however, it is a historic trend. American beef consumption fell from an annual average of 72.4 pounds per person in 1899 to 55.3 pounds in 1930. This is the sort of change which is easier to document than to explain. Diversification of taste is partly responsible, but so is industrialization, which has made cheaper, more efficient animal proteins available through poultry and fish farming on an industrial scale and, more generally, has concentrated on efficient types of energy conversion, which imply a prejudice in favor of vegetable food sources.

Social changes in the wake of industrialization may also be involved. In the developed world, no trend in the nutrition revolution has been more marked than the equalization of diet between regions and classes. Daily meat consumption in mid-nineteenth-century Paris was double that of Caen, Le Mans, Nantes and Toulon, and between 20 and 40 percent higher than in a range of other cities including Marseilles, Toulouse, Reims, Dijon, Strasbourg and Nancy. Today, these differences have disappeared. The embourgeoisement of shopping—the relentless upmarket march of food shops aimed at the mass market—has been one of the marked features of commonplace social observation of the last couple of generations. Between the two surveys of the life of the poor in his native York which

R. Seebohm Rowntree—scion of another Quaker chocolate-making family—undertook in 1899 and 1935, the working class had, to an amazing degree, closed the nutrition gap which formerly separated them from their employers. He defined most of the families he studied as underfed—but that was because his standards were unrealistically high: he defined adequate nourishment at a level of caloric intake well above the average for all classes. Moreover, his research was distorted by the agenda he shared in common with most professional social scientists at the time: he sought to show that even families on relatively high incomes needed education in nutrition to change their shopping habits. Nonetheless, what is really remarkable about his findings is the fact that whereas the subjects of his earlier study had a monotonous diet with only traces of animal protein on a regular basis, the menus he collected in the 1930s showed that even his poorest families were able to achieve some variety and to include roast beef once a week, fish once a week and another fresh source of animal protein, such as liver or rabbit or sausages, at least twice a week.

Rowntree did, however, find genuine malnutrition among York's unemployed and the city's most abject menials: his lowest category of employed heads of household was represented by a van cleaner, who earned only just enough to feed his family on a standard diet. One of the ironies of the embourgeoisement of recent years is that it has been a cause of heightened suffering for those left out of it. For a while, in the wake of studies like Rowntree's, social-democratic welfare experiments narrowed the "wealth gap." In most of the developed world, it began to grow again in the 1980s, as governments adopted aggressive free market principles to drive on economic growth. To keep up with the Joneses—to sustain, that is, a middle-class type of diet on an "underclass" income—became increasingly hard. The way to eat cheaply and well, if you have a decent larder, stove and cooking pans at home, remains essentially what it has always been: buy seasonal vegetables, abundant potatoes, garlic and onions, pulses and milled but uncooked grains. Use whatever is left over for treats. When Jeffrey Steingarten tested the American government's Thrifty Food Plan, which is intended to enable welfare families to eat adequately on a budget of $3.53 per person per day, he made four remarkable discoveries. First, the average American family spends only marginally more than the poorest families on food prepared at home; so the poorest sector is still in touch with average standards. Second, the government plan aims at "departing as little as possible from the current eating patterns of American families"; in other words, even the poorest are still expected to ape the eating habits of the middle class. The effect is that the suggested meals are sparse and second-rate, whereas a fresh approach, unprejudiced by convention, would produce better, bigger and healthier—as well as more original—meals. Third, the Thrifty Plan had an ideological smack. The menus, wrote Steingarten, "stress the kind of weakly flavored mock-ethnic dishes that American dietitians love and I despise. Green peppers found their insidious way into everything." Steingarten detected a racist assumption underlying the prolific use of collards: the devisers of the Thrifty Plan clearly assumed that most welfare dependents would be black. Finally, the menus were marred by dogmatic nutritionalism. "The recipes expressed a complete catalog of modern nutritional superstitions: salt, cooking oil, and sometimes sugar were reduced to ridiculously small amounts; the turkey was wastefully relieved of its proudest part, its skin; butter was eliminated entirely (even though the transfatty acids in margarine are nearly as dangerous as saturated fat); and milk was always the non-fat dry version, which produced a gray and watery bread pudding." One benefit was that all precooked and convenience foods were eliminated. But not even the poorest people in the privileged West seem able to elude embourgeoisement.

Allowing for such differences in class and income as persist, the big change in Western nutrition has been unremitting overall increase in the average amount people in the developed world eat. The average intake was probably under two thousand calories at the end of the eighteenth century. It is well over three thousand today. Since the exceptional privations of the Second World War, the industrial and postindustrial underclass of the Western world has gone from undernourishment to overnourishment. In the United States and some parts of Northwest Europe, obesity is now a bigger social problem than malnutrition. Fatness is prima facie evidence of social deprivation. As Arthur Odell, General Mills' product development specialist, said in 1978, "You can't sell nutrition. Hell, all people want is coke and pot chips!" The predicament of the overfed West has been depicted most vividly in the cinema, in Marco Ferreri's fascinatingly repulsive *La grande bouffe*, a Sade-like fantasy in which the characters eat themselves to death, or Monty Python's all-devouring character, Monsieur Creosote, who is tipped into death by his last after-dinner mint. But the film-makers' satire was mistargeted: in Western society, the victims of overabundance are likely to be people classified as poor. The very cheapness of food is life-threatening. Most of the world, meanwhile, has not had a chance to contract the diseases of affluence.

For famine, until now, has been the historic counterpart of abundance. A hint of what would happen to the parts of the world omitted from the benefits of industrialization occurred with the Irish potato famine of 1845–49, which caused a million deaths and drove a million migrants overseas, ending Ireland's history as a populous country. Reliance—utter reliance—on a single variety of potato exposed the Irish to destruction by a blight that wiped out the crop. Though the crisis was mismanaged by the imperial government in London, incompetence in famine management was not a peculiarly English, or even a peculiarly imperial vice: similar potato famines devastated Belgium and Finland in 1867–68. Yet the world was genuinely divided, in the industrializing era, into haves and have-nots. While industrializing societies solved their problems of food supply, much of the rest of the world starved.

Outside Europe, North America and a few other lucky locations, the last three decades of the nineteenth century were an age of famine which exceeded all others for mortality and perhaps for every other kind of measurable severity. In the years when the monsoon failed from 1876 to 1878, five million Indians, by the official count, or seven million by an objective estimate, died of famine. The famine that afflicted China at that time was officially "the most terrible disaster in twenty-one dynasties." Equally adverse conditions, associated with a series of El Niño events—the Pacific countercurrent which periodically drenches Peru and spreads droughts around much of the rest of the tropical world—returned toward the end of the 1880s and in the second half of the 1890s. Lake Chad shrank by half. Nile flood levels fell by 35 percent. Estimates of the ensuing mortality range, for example, between about twelve and thirty million in India, twenty and thirty million in China.

Of course the poor are always with us; no agrarian society had ever been immune from periodic famine; and the globally interconnected climate had always wrought havoc in surprising and uncontrollable ways. Nevertheless, the late-nineteenth-century famines did represent a new feature of the history of food: famine was now becoming technically avoidable because of worldwide abundance and globally efficient communications. Nevertheless, it happened and went on happening. Some students have blamed free trade, which made "the price of wheat in Liverpool and the rainfall in Madras . . . variables in the same vast equation of human survival." Imperialism certainly exploited famine and perhaps contributed to its causes. "Europeans," a missionary heard, "track famine like a sky full of vultures." Cetshwayo, the Zulu paramount who tried to defeat the British Empire, thought "the English chiefs have stopped the rain." "Londoners," it has been claimed, "were effectively eating India's bread." If they did not engineer famine, white imperialists at least mismanaged it. Humanitarian sentiment, like food, was plentiful in their countries but they found no ways of turning their surplus of either to practical applications. The view "from the saloon window of the viceregal train" always seemed to obscure the severity of their problems, gravity of their responsibilities and the availability of solutions.

In some respects, of course, imperialism and free trade were beneficial or, at least, equivocal. Cheap iron from Europe had an enormous impact on the food supply of West African peoples, whose indigenous iron industry was ancient but expensive. Before the arrival of European imports, a hoe blade cost a cow and sons had to take turns using the implement. There are, however, two good arguments in favor of indicting imperialism for famine deaths. Earlier, native states had handled exceptionally severe conjunctions of El Niño events relatively well. The ever-normal granaries of the Qing state had coped in 1743–44. In 1661, to the admiration of English observers, the Mughal monarch Aurangzeb "opened his treasury" and saved millions of lives. Moreover, Western countries seemed able to save citizens from hunger when they so wished. The American Midwest suffered as severely as almost any other part of the world from the drought of 1889–90, but relief was well organized and famine deaths were few.

The coexistence of food boom and famine was still the pattern in the late twentieth century: because of inequitable distribution, overproduction and over-feeding in the developed world contrasted with vulnerability to famine elsewhere. For a long time, the problem seemed to get worse. In the 1960s pundits were all convinced that famines would transform the world within a couple of decades. Between 1960 and 1965 the rate of food production in poor countries was half that of population growth. India's reserves in the mid-1960s were "the wheat-fields of Kansas." In 1967 the United States shipped one fifth of its wheat crop to feed India after monsoon failures. But even when emergency famine relief could be efficiently organized—and, usually, what with wars, corruption and ideological rivalries, it could not—it was no long-term solution. The famine trap could only be broken by a revolution in agronomy.

THE LAST PHASE OF THE NEOLITHIC REVOLUTION

"If there was a neolithic revolution," said Fernand Braudel, "it's still going on." The changes introduced at the dawn of farming—specialization, domestication, selective breeding, multiplication of cultigens—have indeed been going on to our own day. Calling the most recent phase the "Green Revolution" makes it sound environmentally friendly. It should really be called the chemical-agricultural revolution because it relies on massive fertilizer campaigns and pesticide programs, or the agroindustrial revolution because it has been backed by huge new industries turning out agrochemicals and farm machinery.

Its great achievements were the "miracle" wheat and rice seeds of the 1960s. Using traditional hybridization techniques, seeds were developed to exploit tropical sunshine. This is because 56 to 59 percent of radiant energy can be utilized near the equator: in the American prairie, the figure is less than 50 percent. The second aim of modern agronomists' efforts was to concentrate on strains which could benefit from fertilizing and weeding, instead of growing straggly in competition with weeds. The range of options and methods was brilliantly summarized in 1916 by the author of one of the most influential textbooks in history, in which Mark Carleton, the chief cerealist of the U.S. Bureau of Plant Industry, set out existing knowledge on the introduction, hybridization and selection of new breeds of grain. At first, before the Second World War, breeders tried to cope with varieties that toppled before harvest by breeding for strength of stem. Then they began to appreciate the properties of Japanese dwarf wheats—produced by breeders long recognized as having "made the dwarfing of wheat an art." Investigations centered on the variety known as Daruma and its descendant, Norin 10, which could transmit its brevity of stature to hybrid offspring. Similarly, work on rice focused on Deegeowoogen, a cross of short rice from Taiwan and Indonesia, which does not fall when fertilized and matures 130 days after planting, regardless of the length of the day: in consequence, more crops can be harvested per year.

In 1961 experimenters produced Gaines—the winter wheat variety which broke all production records on an experimental plot in Washington state. Meanwhile, spectacular progress was being made in experiments with wheat varieties in Mexico, after seven years of frustrating trials, in contrasting environments at the Chapingo station on the rain-fed central plateau and the Sonora station on the irrigated northern coastal plain. Two hundred thousand wheat crosses had been made in Mexico by 1980. Wheat strains developed in Mexico have now colonized the world. This seems a delicious irony from the land that gave the world maize.

As usual with improvements in technology, the developed world actually benefited most. Wheat yields in the United States doubled in little more than twenty-five years thanks to fertilizers and disease-resistant strains. According to figures compiled by some of the leading practitioners and spokesmen of the new agronomy, British farmers in 1977–79 were able to achieve average yields of 13.88 tons per acre, the same as in Mexico's best wheat-growing area, the Yaqui valley, where there was enough sunlight to make the time to harvest only about three fifths of England's. The world's record yield at the time was 32.88 tons per acre, grown intensively on an experimental plot of two hectares in Washington state. At the same time, the average yield in all developing countries in the best year then on record was 3.95 tons per acre. This, however, was double the average for 1950.

When the "miracle" crops were introduced into struggling regions they seemed to have an immediate effect. In India, in the disaster year of 1967, the national harvest was 11.3 million tons, but 16.5 million tons in 1968. When the Filipino "farmer of the year" for 1969 was asked what rice he would plant next year, "I don't know," he replied. "I'm still waiting for a newer variety." In 1970, reversing the gloomy predictions of a few years earlier, the U.N. Food and Agriculture Organization estimated that the earth's agricultural potential would be capable of feeding 157 billion people. Agricultural revolutions in Pakistan, Turkey, India, the Philippines, Kenya and Mexico, it was said, made "earlier agricultural take-offs in the U.S. and Japan seem minor." By the early 1990s, over three quarters of the Third World's grain-growing areas were under the new varieties. In China, the new strains accounted for 95 percent of production.

The Green Revolution deserves to be remembered as one of humankind's greatest achievements: it fed millions who must otherwise have starved. The trouble, however, with most of the problem solving of applied science is that solutions solve old problems but create new ones. The Green Revolution displaced traditional varieties. It threatened biodiversity, which is good for coping with changing circumstances. In Zimbabwe, where two hybrids now account for 90 percent of maize production, an elder told agronomists in 1993,

> You, you are the witches. You are taking us back, you are not making us develop. In times past, my family used not to have problems because I grew the traditional small grains. You are the people who are killing us now, you are taking us back because you are telling us to grow crops that are not proper. Even the fertility that you sell is not good for the small grains. We believe that the Number One crops are the small grains. They are our ancestral spirit, our bank. . . . Ah, you people, you let us throw them away.

This may sound like reactionary fanaticism, but really it reflects a good deal of common sense. Programs of agrarian reform, moreover, often become pretexts for tyranny: land appropriations, bureaucratic compulsion, ruthlessness in dealing with the laggards. "In one Asian country," a U.N. official reported with approval, "the chief of state, explaining his role to a visitor, tapped his finger on the telephone and said: 'Here is the most powerful element in the wheat revolution. When I hear that some staff member is lagging, I pick up the telephone and call the officer involved. He promises action but I tell him, "I don't want promises; I want your return telephone call by tomorrow telling me what you have accomplished."'"

The Green Revolution turned sickly green as the effects of its worst deficiencies became apparent. Because the new crops were designed to work in conjunction with chemical fertilizers and pesticides, they imperiled the ecological balance and the survival of incalculable species of inhabitants of cultivated fields: not just the pests, but the predators who fed on them. Early in the process, in 1961, Rachel Carson published *Silent Spring*. It probably deserves to be ranked among the most influential books ever written. Its apocalyptic vision of songbirds starved into extinction in pesticide-blasted doomscapes recruited hundreds of thousands of people into the ecological movement. Norman E. Borlaug, universally hailed as the scientific "father of the Green Revolution," denounced "vicious, hysterical propaganda" against agricultural chemicals by "scientific halfwits." But more than science was at stake. In England in the 1990s,

> Starting in the autumn, the conventional farmer will spray with a broad-spectrum weedkiller such as Javelin to kill emerging weeds such as grasses, chickweed, pansy, speedwell and red deadnettle. (Pesticides tend to have macho names like Missile, Rapier, Impact and Commando. Chemical companies find that they give the farmer confidence in the product.) Next the crop will receive a dose of Avadex which keeps it free of wild oats into winter. Then, in rapid succession, come methocarb pellets (brand name Draza) to kill slugs and the first spray of insecticide, say Ripcord, to kill aphids.

Ripcord spares ladybirds but is more likely to kill other insects, spiders and fish. That is only the beginning. Conventional farmers will probably spray again with fungicide, herbicide, growth regulator and more insecticide before the year is out. According to the World Health Organization, pesticides had caused a million cases of acute poisoning—most of them agricultural workers—by 1985. The organization attributed twenty thousand deaths to the same cause in 1990. Moreover, chemical fertilizers and pesticides only work on marginal lands with help from irrigation: because of mismanagement of great hydraulic projects in the twentieth century, irrigation has probably led to as much land lost, through erosion and pollution, as gained for agriculture: big dams cause evaporation, salination and "dust bowls." The Green Revolution is still going on but in the long run it looks unsustainable: it relies on technologies which damage the environment and outrage the public.

The world's reliance on the seeds of the Green Revolution is dangerous not only because of the incalculable effects of pesticide profligacy but also because of the risk from rapidly evolving new pests and crop diseases. The most widely canvassed next stage is conversion to genetically modified foods. There is no reason to suppose that these will be other than nutritious, health-giving and efficient. But they are almost as likely as Green Revolution crops to bring unforeseen consequences. Among the foreseeable consequences are the accidental hybridization of non–genetically modified species, with resultant extinctions and the creation of new eco-niches in which new, potentially destructive biota can emerge. Rogue, random effects are always loose in causation. Our sallies in genetic manipulation will be made in tiny portions of the field: mainly in our own species and those we already domesticate. The big battalions in nature will still be those beyond our control. Evolution will still outclass our revolutions as a force for change. Most of the diseases we eliminate, for instance, microbial evolution will replace. Changes we engineer in the species we eat will be like all our previous interventions in the environment: a mixture of solution finding and problem forming. It is not yet clear whether we have the means of escape from the world's food problems or merely a means of multiplying crisis.

In the long run, the world's population will stabilize and perhaps decline. Population alarmism is based on very short-term readings of the statistics. To predict the long-term future one has to take a long look at the past. Population acceleration has always reached a plateau or a turning point whenever it has occurred in the past. Its reversals do not usually depend on "Malthusian checks," though these have been effective at times. Most societies regulate their population increase by modifying marriage customs and exploiting for breeding more or less of their womenfolk's span of fertility as circumstances demand. Prosperity is the world's most effective source of restraint; for there is a fairly direct long-term link between the poor and the philoprogenitive. For what they are worth, some short-term trends are consistent with this analysis. Some of the world's most prosperous countries already have birth rates so low that population is falling or likely to fall and the effect of growing prosperity in areas of historically high birth rates in Asia and South America show trends in the same direction. We can look forward with some optimism to a future in which the world's population can be fed by traditional farming. In the meantime, the benefits of the Green Revolution and of genetic engineering will be useful. At some point, however, the consensus will turn against them and they will have to be reversed. It would be prudent, meanwhile, not to rely on them but rather to adopt further radical innovations only with extreme caution. There is no likelihood of global food shortages in the foreseeable future, nor any danger of famine if we manage distribution properly. There is no need for us to panic into risk.

THE CHIMERA OF PRESERVATION

Freshness in food is the quality hardest to deliver when space opens up between points of production and consumption. It was a problem for city-dwellers in ancient Rome. Seneca described runners, "breathless and shouting," to clear the way as they bore live turbot for gourmets who "cannot taste a fish unless they see it swimming and palpitating in the very dining room." When industrialization multiplied the problems of ensuring fresh supplies, preservation was Western society's first, traditional recourse. Most methods are of great antiquity. As noted above (p. 155), freeze drying, which most people think of as one of the most up-to-date techniques, was perfected as a way of preserving potatoes by early Andean civilizations over two thousand years ago. The technique was elaborate: overnight freezing, then trampling to squeeze out residual moisture, then sun drying, repeated over several days. The durability of frozen food has been known to all Arctic peoples from time immemorial. Wind drying, as suggested above (p. 4), was probably an older technique of preparation than cooking. In every documented period of the history of food, salting, fermenting and smoking appear among recorded preserving techniques.

It is well known, moreover, by trial and error, in almost all societies, that the decay and putrescence of food can be arrested by isolation from the air. Oil seals were used in the storage jars of ancient Mesopotamia. The use of butter or aspic was a favorite device in the European Middle Ages to fill up the cavities in pies and keep the contents from contact with the air. Potted fish and meat are legacies from the same tradition. If potted foods are actually cooked in the pot they will keep for months without refrigeration or added preservatives. In the Middle Ages, tightly coopered, well-seasoned barrels were sought by all long-range navigators to limit bacterial activity. We know very little about the water preservation technology of the period, except that vinegar was used to prolong the life of drinking water on board ship. But the leap to long-range voyaging at the end of the Middle Ages, when Portuguese expeditions to the Indian Ocean tripled earlier records for time spent continuously at sea, would have been impossible without improvements in the design of casks to make them more airtight.

The theory which explains the phenomenon of bacterial suppression, however, was still unknown. The science of food preservation fascinated geniuses of the early scientific revolution. Francis Bacon was the first martyr: he died of an infection contracted while he was experimenting with the "induration" of chicken at low temperatures. In the late seventeenth century Denis Papin's experiments with the preserving properties of boiled sugar inspired Leibniz with the idea of adapting his discoveries to sustain armies in the field. By that date microbial activity had already been revealed by the microscope of Anton van Leeuwenhoek. The commonsense assumption was that the mold and worms that are visibly associated with putrescence generate spontaneously and, like many other life forms on earth, need air to survive.

Yet the problem of explaining how microbes reproduce was actually one of the most profound in science. Archaea, closely followed by the slightly more complex organisms called eukaryotes and prokaryotes—one-celled life forms, the former with, the latter without, nuclei—are the most primitive life-forms on the planet: indeed, for three and a half billion years or so, by most reckonings, these were the only life-forms. As the earth had already existed for between 500 million and one billion years when they appeared, they cannot be said always to have existed. They must have arisen spontaneously at first, by some sort of "chemical accident," before developing the ability to reproduce. Alternatively, the evolutionary process must have been started by an act of divine creation or by some other intervention beyond the realm of science. In the debates of the eighteenth century, though the antiquity of microbes had not been determined, and a theory of evolution had been proposed only in a very rudimentary form, a sense that the very existence of God was at stake—or, at least, the validity of claims about his unique power to create life—invigorated debate about spontaneous generation. As far as we know, there is no case of spontaneous generation in nature. Yet it was a theory much cultivated at the time, especially among free thinkers, until, in 1799, Lazaro Spallanzani observed fission—cells reproducing by splitting—under a microscope. He concluded that microbes did not "appear" from nowhere: they could only multiply in an environment where they were already present.

He demonstrated that if bacteria—or "animalculi," to use the term favored at the time, or "germs," as he called them—were killed by heat before food was sealed, they could not generate spontaneously; the demonstration was imperfect, since he could not show conclusively that the heating was effective in itself: critics claimed that heating worked by somehow depriving the heated substance of air. Nevertheless, the lessons of Spallanzani's experiments for the food industry were clear. Heating and sealing in combination could ensure that food would keep indefinitely. The result was the most important innovation up to that time in the history of food preservation: the rise of canning. The fact that Spallanzani's discovery occurred at a time of war made the application of his work a matter of urgency and utility.

Almost simultaneously—and perhaps merely coincidentally—commercial bottling was introduced into a confectioner's business in Paris by Nicolas Appert, who had been working on the effects of sugar on preservation since about 1780. In 1804 he opened a factory at Massy with fifty workers, and began experiments with tins heated in boiling water, then watched to see whether they showed signs of expansion caused by microbial activity. In practice, most of his output remained confined to glass jars for many years. Meanwhile, he graduated to the use of steam pressure cookers. When, in 1810, he made his process public in a book, he appealed to gourmets and housewives. Really, however, the needs of the army were the paramount consideration. "Appertization" came to mean sterilization by heating. Canning in tinned iron containers, sealed by soldering, began in England at about the same time. Appert switched to them in 1822. They were not, at first, entirely reliable. Sir John Franklin's expedition in search of the Northwest Passage failed, and all the members perished, not, perhaps, because of cold but because of botulism—ironically, in an environment so cold that exposed food naturally kept fresh while lethal bacteria bred in the expedition's cans. On the other hand, some cans from the 1820s have been found to contain still edible food.

At first, the industry was chiefly concerned with supplying the armed services; but a few products soon achieved a certain éclat with the wider public. The first was sardines, canned in Nantes in the 1820s. By 1836 Joseph Colin's firm was producing 100,000 cans annually. By 1880 50 million tins of sardines were emerging yearly from canneries on the west coast of France. In terms of volume of production, milk was probably the next most important product of the early industry. Gail Borden began canning milk in America in time to supply Union armies in the Civil War. The great interest of these products was that they acquired properties and flavor which distinguished them from their fresh forms: sardines acquired succulence and a grainy consistency; canned—popularly "condensed"— milk, which was sugared to assist preservation, had distinctive sweetness and a thick consistency.

Canning, in effect, was a method of cooking, not just preserving. Grimod de La Reynière, the great gourmet, early food guru and disseminator of Appert's bottling process, declared bottled petits pois to be as delicious as those eaten in season. He was wrong. They are different and, in their way, better. The lengths to which Three Men in a Boat went to enjoy canned pineapple supply one of the legendary episodes in English comic literature. Their dog escaped "merely with a flesh wound" as, using the mast as a weapon,

> We beat it out flat; we beat it back square; we battered it into every form known to geometry—but we could not make a hole in it. Then George went at it, and knocked it into a shape so strange, so weird, so unearthly in its wild hideousness, that he got frightened and threw away the mast. Then we all three sat round it

on the grass and looked at it. There was one great dent across the top that had the appearance of a mocking grin.

The peculiar quality which made this bootless, booty-less battle seem worthwhile was the "thought of the juice." Jules Gouffré, one of the most famous chefs of the nineteenth century, was devoted to the pursuit of individual creativity, but he had high praise for the tenderness of canned petits pois, and the aftertaste of tinned salmon terrine.

I should declare my interest. I like fresh food. I like the modifications made by frankly transforming preservation methods. I do not like old food which masquerades as fresh. Therefore I do not like freezing or irradiation. The justification for these processes is claimed to be that they do not impair, or barely impair, flavor. Pressure cooking in a space filled with steam at 120 degrees for at least fifteen minutes kills microbes and spores: it also kills a lot of the taste and texture of many foods. Steaming or boiling deals with most microbes and as far as we know, all pathogenic ones, but leaves spores that germinate as the liquid cools. So second and even third boilings are necessary: failure to observe this requirement was one of the reasons why Spallanzani's efforts were imperfect. After two or three boilings most green vegetables have been done to death. Obviously, none of these methods suited the scientists and entrepreneurs who sought a way of preserving food without changing it. Milk is a special case: it can be pasteurized—heated, that is, to seventy degrees—without much noticeable effect on its flavor. This kills enough germs to delay souring. Ultraheat treatment is exposure to a four-second blast of vigorous boiling followed by rapid cooling. Milk so treated will keep for months but many palates reject the claim that the quality is unaffected. Chemical preservation is risky. In the late nineteenth and early twentieth centuries, Borax was added to most preserved fish and meat, and used to prolong the shelf life of dairy products; now it is reclassified as a poison and forbidden. Chemical suppression of bacteria seems bound to affect the flavor of food, even if it does no further harm.

Irradiation is extremely effective as a method of preservation. Only one known microbe survives gamma rays, but the idea is revolting and it is impossible to believe that the delicacy, aroma and gustatory impact of the food are unaffected either by the irradiation process or by the long shelf life to which irradiated items are condemned. Any method of preservation which delivers food disguised as fresh, months after emergence from the field or slaughterhouse, seems repugnant. Traditionally preserved foods are changed by the process; so no subterfuge is involved; in some respects they are changed for the better. It would be a sacrifice to eat only pickled, fermented, dried, potted or smoked, sugar-preserved and salted foods but as long as they do not altogether supplant fresh articles they are an enhancement of life. Others, like cheese and sauerkraut, rely on their own bacterial allies to suppress others which cause decay: a cheese is an ecosystem and in the veins of Roquefort or Stilton you can see the battlegrounds of rival bacteria, friendly and malignant. In line with the maxim "Il faut vivre pour manger et ne pas manger pour vivre," preserving should not be for its own sake, but, like cooking, should be practiced to produce an effect delightful in itself. While genuinely fresh food is abundant, what is gained by misrepresenting as fresh food which lingers after processing, like an embalmed corpse, supine, lifeless and commendable only because of the absence of stench?

Freezing supplied the least offensive answer to the problems of the search for preservation without alteration. From 1806, Boston traders conducted extensive commerce in enormous blocks of Arctic ice, towed to destinations all over the Atlantic world. In 1851 the first refrigerated rail car, cooled by natural ice, brought butter from Ogdensburg, New York, to Boston. Ice, however, remained, in most of the world, an expensive commodity, which could never be the basis of industrial freezing: there would never be sufficient ice nor low enough temperatures. The solution was the compressed-gas cooler, perfected in Australia in the 1870s primarily for the brewing industry—but its wider usefulness was obvious in a hemisphere with a large meat surplus and nowhere nearby to export it to. The first long-range shipment of frozen meat is generally said to have been made in 1876 by the SS *Paraguay* from Argentina to France at minus thirty degrees Celsius. Australia's first shipment to London was made in 1880.

The impact was enormous: meat became relatively cheap and abundant in the industrial world. Yet this was a modest effect in comparison with what followed in the third and fourth decades of the twentieth century. Clarence Birdseye, having observed Inuit cookery in the Arctic, invented cellophane wrapping, which made it possible to freeze food more quickly while it was fresh. He also introduced a waxed cardboard wrapper that did not dissolve when thawed. This "marvellous invention" by man "wrought a miracle which . . . may change the whole course of food history." So said General Foods' copywriters in their first advertisement for Birdseye "Frosted Foods." Cole Porter included cellophane in his list of "the tops," along with a summer night in Spain, the National Gallery and Garbo's salary. By 1959 Americans were spending $2.7 billion annually on frozen foods, including half a billion on ready-prepared meals of the "heat and serve" variety. Birdseye had opened the way to a further stage of industrialization: the industrialization not just of production, processing and supply, but of eating.

An hour before the migrants' train arrived in Chicago they began to notice the smell.

> It was an elemental odour, raw and crude; it was rich, almost rancid, sensual and strong. There were some who drank it in as if it were an intoxicant; there were others who put their handkerchiefs to their faces. The new emigrants were still tasting it, lost in wonder, when suddenly the car came to a halt, and the door was flung open, and a voice shouted—"Stockyards!"

The scene that greeted the travelers in Upton Sinclair's novel *The Jungle* was emblematic of the way food processing had aped and accompanied industrialization. Sinclair made it sound like hell. The smoke from the stockyards "might have come from the center of the world." Twenty thousand head of livestock moaned. Flies blackened the air in Beelzebub's abattoir. It was

> the greatest aggregation of labor and capital ever gathered in one place. It employed 30,000 men. It supported directly 250,000 people in its neighborhood, and indirectly it supported nearly half a million. It sent its products to every country in the civilized world, and it furnished the food for no less than thirty million people!

It made food of old and crippled cattle, covered with boils. "When you plunged your knife into them they would burst and splash foul-smelling stuff into your face. . . . It was such stuff as this as made the 'embalmed beef' that had killed several times as many United States soldiers as all the bullets of the Spaniards." Dead rats were shoveled into the meal with the other floor sweepings. "There were things that went into the sausage in comparison with which a poisoned rat was a tidbit."

Industrialization bred impurity, corruption and adulteration. But in the industrial era, more industrialization was the only admissible solution. In the late nineteenth century food science became obsessed with purity and the course of development in the food industries was directed toward products that would be uniform, predictable and safe. All the old priorities of traditional cuisines were supplanted: pleasure, individuality, cultural identity. Farsighted food producers realized that purity legislation, by driving up unit costs, would favor economies of scale and bring more business to the heavily capitalized reaches of the industry. Hygiene was a selling point, which would enhance any brand.

The Cleanliness King of the late nineteenth century was one of the sector's biggest moguls. Henry J. Heinz of Pittsburgh was intended for the Lutheran ministry but he found his real vocation peddling his parents' surplus garden produce from the age of eight. He learned about the salability of purity in the 1860s, while still in his teens, hawking garden horseradish in clear glass bottles, which exposed the product to the buyers' eyes. At the end of that decade, he was gathering recipes for pickle in his notebooks: data on walnut catsup and a vegetable pickle he called "chow-chow" featured alongside analyses of cleaning fluid and horse colic cure. One hundred fifty biblical quotations were interspersed. After bankruptcy in 1875 he diversified into a range of pickles, expanded into canning and used packaging and advertising to turn Heinz into one of the biggest businesses in Pittsburgh—the capital of America's steel industry. He already made more than sixty products when he coined the slogan "57 Varieties," but he felt drawn to the number, apparently for "occult reasons" during a visionlike experience on a New York elevated train.

He built a factory in the Romanesque style, with a vast auditorium where stained glass windows recorded Heinz's philosophy: the superiority of management over labor and capital. An employee who joined the firm in 1888 for five cents an hour on a ten-and-a-half-hour day could enjoy a free uniform, medical and dental treatment, and a daily manicure (if she handled food). She had the use of a dressing room with hot showers, a pool, a gym, a roof garden, a reading room and a dining room with an Orphenion and a hundred pictures on the walls. For treats, she could have occasional rides in the parks in the firm's wagonettes, lectures, recitals, free courses in dressmaking, millinery, cookery, drawing, singing and citizenship, and four dances a year at which "Mr. Heinz stayed on the balcony, waving down at us." Members of her family could join her at the annual Christmas Party, when Mr. Heinz shook Santa by the hand, and the annual outing to a local beauty spot, when three special trains conveyed up to four thousand revelers. The founder's rewards included a "baronial castle in Pittsburgh's most opulent neighborhood" with a bathroom mural that showed a life-size nude naiad with conches at her lips and feet, and a formidable private museum of art. He did not perhaps merit the cognomina of "prophet" and "pioneer" bestowed on him after his death, but he had made purity pay.

Mechanization was hallowed by the rhetoric of purity "untouched by human hand." In combination with industrial-scale food production, uniformity filleted out flavor. In pasteurized cheese originality and individuality are boiled out. The balance of microbial activity, which trades danger for flavor, is destroyed. Apple varieties which work best in the mass market are those which look attractive: big and glossy, like witches' gifts. Fruit is sold immature to increase its shelf life.

Some fruits survive freezing without much sacrifice of flavor: others, such as strawberries and bananas, are ruined by the experience. Parallel with the war against impurity, the modern food industry has exploited health scares to produce "phony foods." The search for salable substitutes for sugar and butter has become a food industry grail quest. Together with salt, sugar and butter form an unholy trinity, anathemized by fashionable dietary orthodoxy. None of them deserves the obloquy flung by health scaremongers. Like most foods, they are good for you in normal quantities. Salt has a seriously adverse effect on the blood pressure of a small minority of people—8 percent in America, where the statistics are probably most reliable. Though saturated fats, including butter, are statistically associated with heart disease, normal consumption rates do no harm except to the small numbers of people who have exceptionally high cholesterol (above, p. 53–4). Sugar contributes no more to disorders for which it is commonly blamed—such as fatness, hyperactivity and bad teeth—than other fermentable carbohydrates; most people probably eat no more than is good for them, without having to be restrained by officious dietitians and nutritionists. The idea that health generally is served by ingestion of laboratory concoctions such as artificial sweeteners, margarines and sucrose polyester is offensive to brain and palate alike. Untargeted health advice on these matters from governments and health education agencies does no good, except to vested interests. In the long run, it subverts rational public health policy by inducing a cry-wolf mentality and discrediting health campaigns generally. In consequence, people probably take less notice of official advice about hygiene, smoking and sexual behavior—all of which genuinely are important.

The willingness of the public to accept ersatz foods is surprising, but, if indefinitely extended, it could inspire nightmares. "Textured" soya products already imitate meat: why, if one rejects meat, should one want a vegetable textured to feign it? Hi-lysine corn, which adds the essential amino acid in which traditional corn is deficient, has been brokered as a potential way of replacing meat with a cheap alternative protein source. Perhaps the ultimate mockery is to make food from microbes. They are organic, malleable and so plentiful as to be inexhaustible. Some have already been exploited for the purpose. Chlorella is made from mass-cultured algae and, allegedly, is good for cakes, biscuits and ice cream. The cyanobacterium spirulina can be sun-dried and nibbled as a biscuit: it had a certain faddish following in the 1980s. The microbiologist J. R. Postgate reported that

a process was developed in the 1970s in the USA for growing mushroom mycelium on meat residues (apparently about three quarters of the material handled by a modern slaughterhouse is thrown away), but I do not know what became of it. Mushroom soup? . . . No doubt chlorella biscuits and methano-burgers will one day be a delicious meal that one will take for granted; as one reconstitutes one's dehydrated Château Latour (esters specially blended to repro-duce that greatest of years, 1937), one may wonder at the barbarian habits of one's ancestors who grew large animals, killed them and actually ate their flesh.

Meanwhile, it is not clear whether industrially processed food delivers the promises of hygiene its advocates made for it in the last century. When foods are mass-produced, one mistake can poison a lot of people. Life after cooking carries serious health hazards. Every time prepared food is unfrozen, or ready-meals reheated, an eco-niche opens for microbial infestation. Listeria proliferate in refrigerators. In 1988 a new strain of salmonella appeared in chickens. This was almost certainly the result of the abuse of antibiotics in livestock feed. With a rapidity few biochemists could forecast, bacteria respond to antibiotics by adapt-ing successfully, exchanging genetic material and emerging in new, resistant forms. A salmonella outbreak at a trade exhibition buffet in May 1990 affected 100 out of 150 guests. Chicken drumsticks had been delivered partially frozen, then placed in a fridge, cooked next day, coated in egg and breadcrumbs, placed in a freezer for two days, defrosted for three and a half hours, deep-fried, left to cool, then refrig-erated for three hours and reheated before serving. Joints cooled overnight affected hundreds of children in the same school in incidents a year apart. At about the same time, there were reports of a case where wedding guests were poisoned by an antibiotic-resistant staphylococcus identical to the strain in the nasal mucus and septic spots of the person who sliced the turkey and ham. The hazards of imper-fect hygiene in food processing are obvious; but microbial mutations are always threatening to outflank vigilance and outstrip science. In 1964 a typhoid outbreak in Aberdeen claimed four hundred victims before the cause was traced. A new strain of typhoid bacteria, invulnerable except to chlorine, infected cans which had escaped the chlorine rinse usually applied to cool the cans down after heating. The beef had in turn left traces of the infection on the blade of a mechanical slicer, which then infected other meat.

Industrialized eating has, at best, equivocal implications for health. It is surely corrosive of society—at least, of lines of continuity in the pattern of family life which has become traditional in the modern West: the focus for family life which the warmth and aromas of the kitchen provide; the fraternity of the shared meal. In one respect, the power of industrialization to change family feeding habits is apparent to everybody who has experienced it: mealtimes have adjusted to new patterns of work. Soup has become "of the evening" in modern France. In America and Britain, the four-meal day has long been over. Lunch has almost disappeared in favor of daytime snacking and evening "dinner." That British institution—*le fifoclock*, when "everything stops for tea"—has vanished. Even in Germany and Italy—lands that lunch—the main meal has to be taken in office cafeterias to save time in the working day. In Spain, one can hardly imagine the national culture surviving if mealtimes were disturbed: in the 1920s, the dictatorship of General Primo de Rivera was doomed when he planned to "modernize" Spanish mealtimes in line with the industrial working day by instituting "fork lunch at 11 A.M." In Spain today the needs of the modern economy are met by two recourses: the *día intensivo*, which enables people to work continuously from 8:00 A.M. to 3:00 P.M. before retiring for a traditional family meal, and the cell phone, which means that lunchers can stay in touch with the rest of the world during the extended afternoon lunch break.

Family life could survive in its traditional form, no doubt, even if families normally ate together only once a day. Even that, however, seems increasingly unlikely. In 1887, Edward Bellamy's *Looking Backward* appeared. In his socialist utopia there were no homes with kitchens. Instead, people ordered their dinners from menus printed in newspapers and ate them together in huge and solemn but comfortable people's palaces: though supplied by private enterprise, such eateries have now, in the form of fast food outlets, materialized. People still eat, ever less regularly, at home but mealtimes are atomized; different family members choose to eat different things at different times.

It is comforting to reflect that fast food is not in itself a new phenomenon. Hot ready-to-eat meals have served the urban poor in almost every city dwelling culture in history. Flats in ancient Rome rarely had any cooking space or apparatus on the premises: people bought their meals ready-made from vendors. On the streets of Becket's London public kitchens were open day and night for food to suit all purses, selling game, fish and poultry roasted, fried or boiled. In Paris in the thirteenth century you could buy boiled and roast veal, beef, mutton, pork, lamb, kid, pigeon, capon, goose; spiced pasties filled with chopped pork, chicken or eel; tarts filled with soft cheese or egg, hot waffles and wafers, cakes, pancakes, simnels and tarts, hot mashed peas, garlic sauce, cheese of Champagne and Brie, butter, hot pasties. In the fourteenth century, Piers Plowman heard the vendor's cry: "Hot pies, hot! Good piglets and geese! Go dine, go!"

In some ways, nothing seemed to have changed by 1928, when the *Ladies' Home Journal* boasted, as if announcing a historical "first," that "there are few things except soft-boiled eggs that you can't buy almost ready to eat today." Nevertheless, there are obvious differences between what might be called the fast food of tradition and the convenience eating of today. The street vendors of antiquity and the Middle Ages were for the most part small, artisanal, human-scale enterprises, providing local services to supply households with the means of common meals. The fast food industry today is dominated by the products of industrial processing, designed to be eaten "on the fly" or in front of the television or computer screen. Instead of a bond, meals are becoming a barrier. "Convenience" enjoys a higher priority than civilization or pleasure or nourishment. Surveys regularly claim to show that people know processed food tastes worse than fresh. They also believe that it is less nutritious. Yet they are willing to make the sacrifices for convenience.

The victims have chronicled and endured this revolution with spine-chilling sangfroid. During the Second World War, the columnist Eleanor Early promised her readers, "The day is coming when a woman can buy a boiled dinner and carry it home in her purse . . . when you'll serve the girls a bridge luncheon with dehydrated meat and potatoes . . . and custard made with powdered eggs and powdered milk for dessert." In 1937 Dick and Mac McDonald opened their drive-in restaurant in San Bernardino: this was the closest thing to conveyor-belt eating the Industrial Revolution had yet produced. From 1948, they began to eliminate plates and cutlery at mealtimes—the reversal of one of the long-sought, hard-won achievements of civilization, which customers have accepted unprotestingly. Their fifteen-cent hamburger was the enfleshment of food-Fordism. In 1953 a "research lunch" served to President Eisenhower in Beltsville, Maryland, featured powdered orange juice, "potato chip bars," whey cheese spread, "dehydrofrozen peas," hormone- and antibiotic-fed beef and pork and lowfat milk.

This was the era when the novelty value of foreign food was beginning to have an impact in the American market. Its first triumphs were modest, for the McCarthy era was no time to risk outrageously un-American eating: spaghetti with meatballs was admissible, and chop suey or chow mein—a wartime concoction, for which Heinz advertised a recipe using their cream of mushroom soup. Nor did foreign forces halt the advance of fast food. According to a magazine which appeared in 1978,

> Foreign and ethnic foods are all the rage these days. . . . To make something German don't hire a German cook, just give your roast beef a topping of German-style sauerkraut, that is, canned sauerkraut with some caraway seeds added. Mix oregano, basil and garlic with canned tomatoes, add chicken, and you have an unusual Italian hero sandwich. For Chinese add one or more of: ginger, anise seed, garlic, onions, red pepper, fennel seed, cloves or cinnamon.

Today Burger King has managed to keep up a challenge to McDonald's by promising and delivering a "complete meal in fifteen seconds": to be fair to them, one should add that in 2000, Burger King launched a new publicity campaign with the slogan "It just tastes better"—implicitly, than McDonald's product. This is not a claim I feel I want to test. Nor do I take comfort from the rise of "fusion food," which is widely regarded as evidence that the food market today is animated by a taste for the inventive and exotic. On the contrary, this new style of cuisine seems to me drearily representative of the trends of our times. Fusion food is Lego cookery. Only the revolution in availability makes it possible to mix and match elements delivered—often in processed form—to a kitchen which resembles an assembly point. Analogy with the automobile and computer "factories" where nothing is really made but parts are assembled after delivery from wherever in the world they can be most cheaply produced. More people can get more variety than ever before; yet they seem willing to forgo the privilege in favor of cheap, standard products.

For people who think cooking was the foundation of civilization, the microwave, as suggested in Chapter 1, is the last enemy. Tad's restaurant in the 1960s served complete frozen dinners in plastic skins, which customers defrosted at tableside microwaves. That was a gimmick which, happily, failed to catch on, perhaps because the microwave is best suited to that public enemy, the solitary eater. The communion of eating together is easily broken by a device that liberates household denizens from waiting for mealtimes. In alliance with pret-a-porter meals the microwave makes possible the end of cooking and eating as social acts. The first great revolution in the history of food is in danger of being undone. The companionship of the campfire, cooking pot and common table, which have helped to bond humans in collaborative living for at least 150,000 years, could be shattered.

Nevertheless, despite all the minatory signs that have accompanied the industrial era of Western history, there are good reasons to be optimistic about the future of food. The industrial era is over or ending. Between them, the innovations in production, processing and supply have encouraged the gradual emergence of a globalized marketplace, dominated by gigantic corporations and multinationals. This has been a new phenomenon in the history of food, but not, so far, one which really shows signs of engrossing the whole world of food: that is a fantasy of the biggest capitalists and the fiercest anticapitalists. An artisanal reaction is already under way. Local revulsion from pressure to accept the products of standardized taste has stimulated revivals of traditional cuisines. Even McDonald's and Coca-Cola make adjustments to regional tastes and cultural prejudices, modifying their recipes, adjusting their presentation. Identity is reasserting itself as a big element in consumers' prejudices: foods are what marketers call "necktie" products—striped with the insignia of the eater's self-perception, his community or country or class. In prosperous markets, the emphasis is shifting from cheapness to quality, rarity and esteem for artisanal methods. As we have seen, food industries made money by lowering prices in an era of demographic buoyancy: that era is over in the developed West. As the currently industrializing parts of the world catch up, the same shift will become characteristic there, too. The fantasy of a world fed from toothpaste tubes and packets of powder will be like all the other modernist fantasies which have been falsified by history: the socialist utopias, the cyberocracies, the nuclear-powered society, the Corbusier cities, the world of the Jetsons. The future will be much more like the past than the pundits of futurology have foretold. The priorities of fast food already seem as outmoded as Futurism or Vorticism: they belong to an already bygone era, which was exhilarated by the novelties of speed. The fifteen-second hamburger will join the fifteen-cent hamburger: consigned to the dustbin of history. American palates, which have swallowed so much trash in the interests of efficiency, have largely rejected instant coffee. This fastidiousness may be a sign for the future as much as a survival from the past.

Despite the conquests of the standard products, food remains an art and some contemporary food culture in the developed world shares features associated with postmodernism in other arts. The internationalization of the palate and the rise of fusion cookery reflect multiculturalism. "Noneating"—forms of behavior in the twilight of the table, such as fad dieting and fashionable anorexia—is to food what, say, the silence of John Cage is to music or *The Blair Witch Project* is to cinema. Bulimia is ironic eating, where excess and obsession meet: the sufferer gorges in secret and induces vomiting. The Campbell's soup can has become a postmodernist icon. This is a double irony, because canned foods no longer seem to be the fists of the food giants: they have lost any sense of mechanist menace they might once have had in competition with fresh foods. They have become part of an old-fashioned, comforting repertoire of home cooking, defying the quick-frozen, irradiated or instantly infused alternatives. Indeed, that is exactly how Campbell's advertises them. The fashionable cult of the raw is not a reversion to savagery, but a rebellion against processing, a rejection of the industrial idea of "freshness."

Postmodern persnicketiness is a healthy reaction against greed and ecological arrogance. In the overnourished West, to eat well is to eat less. Rational exploitation of nature has to stop short of despoliation. We have been turning too much of the planet into too much food: wasting resources, endangering species. Fussiness and "foodism" are methods of self-protection for society against the deleterious effects of the industrial era: the glut of the cheap, the degradation of the environment, the wreckage of taste. The organic farming movement, which abjures battery breeding and chemical fertilizers and pesticides, is making a surprising impact on the market, when one considers that its products are, from the consumers' point of view, differentiated chiefly by extra cost. The Prince of Wales, who is one of the movement's most eloquent spokesmen and most exemplary practitioners, feels defensive about conventional farmers' dismissal of "muck and magic eccentrics" and "well-meaning . . . doom-mongers hankering after a pre-industrial, Arcadian past." But the excesses of industrialism need to be reversed. Reason and instinct are combining irresistibly to reverse them. The role of the next revolution in food history will be to subvert the last.

Notes

PREFACE

xi *neglect it*: Anne Sebba, "No Sex, Please, We're Peckish," *Times Higher Education Supplement,* February 4, 2000.

CHAPTER 1: THE INVENTION OF COOKING

2 *"some sorcery"*: E. Clark, *The Oysters of Locmariaquer* (Chicago, 1964), p. 6.

2 *"like candy"*: K. Donner, *Among the Samoyed in Siberia* (New Haven, 1954), p. 129.

2 *"fancy cannot grasp"*: W. S. Maugham, *Altogether* (London, 1934), p. 1122.

3 *harnessing flame*: W. C. McGrew, "Chimpanzee Material Culture: What Are Its Limits and Why?," in R. Foley, ed., *The Origins of Animal Behaviour* (London, 1991), pp. 13–22; J. Goudsblom, *Fire and Civilisation* (Harmondsworth, 1994), pp. 21–25.

4 *oven for seeds*: Vergil, *Georgics* II, v. 260; C. Lévi-Strauss, *From Honey to Ashes: Introduction to a Science of Mythology,* ii (London, 1973), 303.

5 *"in the preparations"*: B. Malinowski, *Magic, Science and Religion and Other Essays* (London, 1974), p. 175.

5 *hot stones*: C. Lévi-Strauss, *The Raw and the Cooked* (London, 1970), p. 336.

5 *"nature and society"*: Ibid., p. 65.

5 *"honorable cooked rice"*: E. Ohnuki-Tierney, *Rice As Self: Japanese Identities Through Time* (Princeton, 1993), p. 30.

5 *and their anniversaries*: J. Hendry, "Food As Social Nutrition: The Japanese Case," in M. Chapman and H. Macbeth, eds., *Food for Humanity: Cross-Disciplinary Readings* (Oxford, 1990), pp. 57–62.

6 *"eating of beef"*: C. E. McDonaugh, "Tharu Evaluations of Food," in Chapman and Macbeth, *Food for Humanity,* pp. 45–48, at p. 46.

6 *to the warriors*: A. A. J. Jansen et al., eds., *Food and Nutrition in Fiji,* 2 vols. (Suva, 1990), ii, 632–34.

6 *demonize these enemies*: G. A. Bezzola, *Die Mongolen in abendländischer Sicht* (Berne, 1974), pp. 134–34.

7 *"for all that"*: J. A. Brillat-Savarin, *The Philosopher in the Kitchen,* tr. A. Drayton (Har-

mondsworth, 1970), p. 244. (I generally prefer this translation to the more commonly cited *The Physiology of Taste*, tr. M. F. K. Fisher (New York, 1972).

7 *"off his nose"*: L. van der Post, *First Catch Your Eland: A Taste of Africa* (London, 1977), p. 28.

7 *"makes the ears bleed"*: Ibid., p. 29; L. van der Post, *African Cooking* (New York, 1970), p. 38.

8 *inside their vulvae*: J. G. Frazer, *Myths of the Origins of Fire* (London, 1930), pp. 22–23.

8 *almost every culture*: G. Bachelard, *Fragments d'un poétique du feu* (Paris, 1988), pp. 106, 129.

8 *fire are unknown*: See the symposium on the subject in *Current Anthropology*, xxx (1989); Goudsblom, *Fire and Civilisation*, pp. 16–23.

8 *"use of fire"*: A. Marshak, *Roots of Civilisation* (London, 1972), pp. 111–12; A. H. Brodrick, *The Abbé Breuil, Historian* (London, 1963), p. 11.

8 *"wild boar"*: H. Breuil, *Beyond the Bounds of History: Scenes from the Old Stone Age* (London, 1949), p. 36.

9 *"crackling"*: C. Lamb, *A Dissertation upon Roast Pig* (London, n.d.[1896]), pp. 16–18.

9 *"to dress it"*: Ibid., pp. 34–35.

9 *hominid foragers*: Goudsblom, *Fire and Civilisation*, p. 34.

10 *"or knives and forks"*: Ibid., p. 36.

11 *insoluble problem*: D. L. Jennings, "Cassava," in N. W. Simmonds, ed., *Evolution of Crop Plants* (London, 1976), pp. 81–84.

12 *"under the ashes"*: Quoted in P. Camporesi, *The Magic Harvest: Food, Folklore and Society* (Cambridge, 1989), pp. 3–4; variant version in G. Bachelard, *The Psychoanalysis of Fire* (London, 1964), p. 15.

12 *apply it to cooking*: C. Perlès, "Les origines de la cuisine: l'acte alimentaire dans l'histoire de l'homme," *Communications*, xxxi (1979), pp. 1–14.

12 *blacken and smoke*: P. Pray Bober, *Art, Culture and Cuisine: Ancient and Medieval Gastronomy* (Chicago, 1999), p. 78.

13 *"all was roasted"*: Trans. E. V. Rieu (Harmondsworth, 1991), p. 43.

13 *on tree trunks*: F. J. Remedi, *Los secretos de la olla: entre el gusto y la necesidad: la alimentación en la Cordoba de principios del siglo XX* (Cordoba, 1998), p. 208.

13 *cook food on*: C. Perlès, "Hearth and Home in the Old Stone Age," *Natural History*, xc (1981), pp. 38–41.

14 *sticks together*: H. Dunn-Meynell, "Three Lunches: Some Culinary Reminiscences of the Aptly Named Cook Islands," in H. Walker, ed., *Food on the Move* (Totnes, 1997), pp. 111–13.

14 *with stone*: C. A. Wilson, *Food and Drink in Britain from the Stone Age to Recent Times* (London, 1973), p. 65.

14 *Ireland alone*: M. J. O'Kelly, *Early Ireland* (Cambridge, 1989).

15 *"usually feasted on it"*: J. H. Cook, *Longhorn Cowboy* (Norman, 1984), p. 82.

16 *on a dagger*: C. Perry, "The Horseback Kitchen of Central Asia," in Walker, ed., *Food on the Move*, pp. 243–48.

17 *"what they wanted"*: S. Hudgins, "Raw Liver and More: Feasting with the Buriats of Southern Siberia," in Walker, *Food on the Move*, pp. 136–56, at p. 147.

17 *in wrestling:* Trans., Rieu, pp. 274–76.

17 *"cultural object":* C. Lévi-Strauss, *The Origin of Table Manners* (London, 1968), p. 471.

18 *from c 6,000 B.C.:* A. Dalby, *Siren Feasts: A History of Food and Gastronomy in Greece* (London, 1996), p. 44.

18 *"or technical skill":* H. Levenstein, *Revolution at the Table* (New York, 1988), p. 68.

19 *over half:* C. Fischler, "La 'macdonaldisation' des moeurs," in J.-L. Flandrin and M. Montanari, eds., *Histoire de l'alimentation* (Paris, 1996), pp. 858–79, at p. 867.

CHAPTER 2: THE MEANING OF EATING

21 *"like gluttony":* "Gluttony," *Sunday Times*, December 31, 1961, quoted in C. Ray, ed., *The Gourmet's Companion* (London, 1963), p. 433.

22 *"visited the houses":* E. Ybarra, "Two Letters of Dr. Chanca," *Smithsonian Contributions to Knowledge*, xlviii (1907).

22 *"should be tastier":* B. de Sahagún, *Historia de las Cosas de la Nueva España* (Mexico City, 1989), p. 506.

22 *"sepulchre of human flesh":* A. R. Pagden, *The Fall of Natural Man* (Cambridge, 1982), p. 87.

22 *"the last fingernail":* Ibid., p. 83.

23 *"my own eyes":* H. Staden, *The True History of His Captivity*, 1557, M. Letts, ed. (London, 1929), p. 80.

23 *human butcher meat:* Pagden, *Fall of Natural Man*, p. 85.

23 *"at a most doleful rate":* P. Way, "The Cutting Edge of Culture: British Soldiers Encounter Native Americans in the French and Indian War," in M. Daunton and R. Halpern, eds., *Empire and Others: British Encounters with Indigenous Peoples, 1600–1850* (Philadelphia, 1999), pp. 123–48, at p. 134.

23 *"over other food":* J. Hunt, *Memoir of the Rev. W. Cross, Wesleyan Missionary to the Friendly and Feejee Islands* (London, 1846), p. 22.

23 *open to question:* W. Arens, *The Man-Eating Myth* (New York, 1979); G. Obeyeskere, "Cannibal Feasts in Nineteenth-Century Fiji: Seamen's Yarns and the Ethnographic Imagination," in F. Barker, P. Hulme and M. Iversen, eds., *Cannibalism and the Colonial World* (Cambridge, 1998), pp. 63–86.

24 *Arawak hosts:* Quoted in L. Montrose, "The Work of Gender in the Discourse of Discovery," in S. Greenblatt, ed., *New World Encounters* (Berkeley, 1993), p. 196.

24 *anthropophagous appetites:* Pagden, *Fall of Natural Man*, p. 83.

24 *human flesh:* G. Williams, ed., *The Voyage of George Vancouver, 1791–5*, 4 vols. (London, 1984), ii, p. 552.

24 *"around at night":* A. Rumsey, "The White Man As Cannibal in the New Guinea Highlands," in L. R. Goldman, ed., *The Anthropology of Cannibalism* (Westport, 1999), pp. 105–21, at p. 108.

24 *named after him:* A. W. B. Simpson, *Cannibalism and the Common Law* (Chicago, 1984), p. 282.

25 *came to call:* All these kinds of cannibalism, especially "revenge cannibalism," are well

attested at intervals in Chinese history, too. See K. C. Chang, ed., *Food in Chinese Culture* (New York, 1977).

25 *feed off the dead*: *Memoirs of Sergeant Burgogne, 1812–13* (New York, 1958).

25 *the "custom of the sea"*: Simpson, *Cannibalism and the Common Law*, passim.

25 *"brains of his apprentice"*: Ibid., p. 132.

25 *an open boat*: Ibid., p. 145.

25 *eaten by the others*: Way, "The Cutting Edge of Culture," p. 135.

26 *those who died*: P. P. Read, *Alive* (New York, 1974).

27 *"to eat mutton"*: On these texts see F. Lestringant, *Le Huguenot et le sauvage* (Paris, 1990) and *Cannibalism* (London, 2000).

27 *"their game"*: D. Gardner, "Anthropophagy, Myth and the Subtle Ways of Ethnocentrism," in Goldman, *Anthropology of Cannibalism*, pp. 27–49.

27 *in their culture*: T. M. Ernst, "Onabasulu Cannibalism and the Moral Agents of Misfortune," in Goldman, *Anthropology of Cannibalism*, pp. 143–59, at p. 145.

27 *and the Pacific*: P. R. Sanday, *Divine Hunger: Cannibalism As a Cultural System* (Cambridge, 1986), p. x.

27 *lost warriors*: Ibid., p. 6.

27 *at work*: Ernst, "Onabasulu Cannibalism," p. 147.

27 *nonrenewable in nature*: Sanday, *Divine Hunger*, p. 69; A. Meigs, "Food As a Cultural Construction," in *Food and Foodways*, ii (1988), pp. 341–59.

28 *cycle of fertility*: Sanday, *Divine Hunger*, pp. 72–82.

28 *nine hundred stones*: R. A. Derrick, *A History of Fiji*, 2 vols. (Suva, 1957), p. 22.

28 *"symbolizing dominance"*: Sanday, *Divine Hunger*, p. 21.

29 *"cooked men"*: Sahlins, quoted in ibid., p. 22. See P. Brown and D. Tuzin, eds., *The Ethnography of Cannibalism* (Wellington, 1983).

29 *"better than savages"*: N. J. Dawood, ed., *Arabian Nights* (Harmondsworth, 1954), p. 45.

30 *at harvest time*: A. Shelton, "Huichol Attitudes to Maize," in Chapman and Macbeth, *Food for Humanity*, pp. 34–44.

30 *fear the fire*: S. Coe, *America's First Cuisines* (Austin, 1994), p. 10.

31 *but for salvation*: W. K. Powers and M. M. N. Powers, "Metaphysical Aspects of an Oglala Food System," in M. Douglas, ed., *Food in the Social Order: Studies of Food and Festivities in Three American Communities* (New York, 1984), pp. 40–96.

31 *conservation measure*: M. Harris, *Good to Eat: Riddles of Food and Culture* (London, 1986), pp. 56–66.

32 *"very dirty and loathsome"*: Quoted in M. Douglas, *Purity and Danger* (London, 1984), p. 31.

32 *pig and camel*: Ibid., p. 55.

32 *infant a cough*: Jansen, *Food and Nutrition in Fiji*, pp. 632–34.

32 *food will die*: Douglas, *Purity and Danger*, p. 155.

32 *cling to the womb*: Sahagún, *Historia*, p. 280.

33 *"men more attentive"*: Brillat-Savarin, *Philosopher in the Kitchen*, pp. 92–93.

33 *Paleolithic cave:* T. Taylor, *The Prehistory of Sex* (London, 1996), p. 87.

34 *fennel for colitis:* Flandrin and Montanari, *Histoire de l'alimentation*, p. 72.

34 *melon and millet:* C. Bromberger, "Eating Habits and Cultural Boundaries in Northern Iran," in S. Zubaida and R. Tapper, eds., *Culinary Cultures of the Middle East* (London, 1994), pp. 185–201.

34 *strong spices:* E. N. Anderson, *The Food of China* (New Haven, 1988), pp. 187–90.

34 *pumpkin and papaya:* A. Beardsworth and T. Keil, *Sociology on the Menu* (London, 1997), p. 128.

35 *treatise of antiquity:* quoted in Flandrin and Montanari, *Histoire de l'alimentation*, p. 261.

35 *from sewer water:* Galen, *De bonis malisque sucis*, A. M. Ieraci Bio, ed. (Naples, 1987), pp. 6, 9.

35 *for the elderly:* Galen, *Scripta minora*, eds. J. Marquardt, I. E. P. von Müller and G. Helmreich, 3 vols. (Leipzig, 1884–93) ("De sanitate tuenda," c. 5).

36 *"rotted to the roots":* S. de Champlain, *Voyages*, W. L. Grant, ed. (1907), pp. 33–42.

37 *suited to it:* F. López-Ríos Fernández, *Medicina naval española en la época de los descubrimientos* (Barcelona, 1993), pp. 85–163. The quotations from Lind (*A Treatise of the Scurvy*, 1753, facsimile ed. [Edinburgh, 1953]) in the following two paragraphs are quoted from this work.

38 *"plenty of it":* Ibid., pp. 109–11.

38 *"lunacy, convulsions":* G. Williams, *The Prize of All the Oceans* (London, 2000), pp. 45–46.

39 *"days fit for duty":* J. Lind, *A Treatise of the Scurvy* (Edinburgh, 1953), p. 148; López-Ríos Fernández, *Medicina naval española*, pp. 106–7.

39 *recommendation was deleted:* M. E. Hoare, ed., *The Resolution Journal of Johann Reinhold Forster*, 4 vols. (London, 1981–82), iii, 454.

39 *come to hand:* P. LeRoy, *A Narrative of the Singular Adventures of Four Russian Sailors Who Were Cast Away on the Desert Island of East Spitzbergen* (London, 1774), pp. 69–72.

40 *"drinking water":* J. Dunmore, ed., *The Journal of Jean-François de Galaup de la Pérouse*, 2 vols. (London, 1994), ii, 317, 431–32.

40 *up and about:* M. Palau, ed., *Malaspina '94* (Madrid, 1994), p. 74.

40 *reached Valparaiso:* Vancouver, *Voyage*, pp. 1471–72.

41 *moral health, too?:* S. Nissenbaum, *Sex, Diet and Debility in Jacksonian America: Sylvester Graham and Health Reform* (Westport, 1980).

41 *"did not continue":* C. F. Beckingham et al., eds., *The Itinerario of Jerónimo Lobo* (London, 1984), pp. 262–63.

41 *"feed luxuriously":* Quoted in C. Spencer, *The Heretics' Feast: A History of Vegetarianism* (London, 1993), p. 100.

42 *"invigorating diet":* *Wealth of Nations* (1784), iii, 341. See also K. Thomas, *Man and the Natural World* (London, 1983).

42 *"human blood":* Henry Brougham, quoted in T. Morton, *Shelley and the Revolution in Taste* (Cambridge, 1994), p. 26.

42 *competition between species:* G. Nicholson, *On the Primeval Diet of Man* (1801), ed. R. Preece (Lewiston, 1999), p. 8.

42 *"matter for corruption":* Ibid., p. 33.

42 *"rice husks will be"*: C. B. Heiser, *Seed to Civilization: The Story of Food* (Cambridge, 1990), p. 85.

42 *sacred texts*: J. Ritson, *An Essay on Abstinence from Animal Food as a Moral Duty* (1802).

43 *"other motives"*: P. B. Shelley, *A Vindication of Natural Diet* (London, 1813); ed. F. E. Worland (London, 1922).

43 *tree of Eden*: Morton, *Shelley and the Revolution*, p. 136.

43 *"sufficient nourishment"*: Ibid., p. 29; M. Shelley, *Frankenstein* (Chicago, 1982), p. 142.

44 *virgin soil*: Nissenbaum, *Sex, Diet and Debility*, p. 6.

44 *"this is evil"*: Ibid., p. 127.

44 *he called Granula*: Ibid., pp. 151–52.

44 *with roughage*: Levenstein, *Revolution at the Table*, p. 93.

44 *"unscientific feeding"*: E. S. Weigley, *Sarah Tyson Rorer: The Nation's Instructress in Dietetics and Cookery* (Philadelphia, 1977), p. 37.

45 *"of the stomach"*: Ibid., pp. 125, 138.

45 *"city or country"*: Ibid., p. 61.

45 *recycled leftovers*: Ibid., pp. 2, 63, 139.

45 *potato around it*: Ibid., p. 48.

46 *laboratory science*: Levenstein, *Revolution at the Table*, p. 87.

46 *"life and work"*: Ibid., p. 88.

46 *"juices of the body"*: A. W. Hofmann, *The Life-work of Liebig* (London, 1876), p. 27.

46 *"concentrated form"*: Ibid., p. 31. Henry Chavasse thought children should be protected from vegetables. *Advice to Mothers on the Management of Their Offspring* (1839), quoted in S. Mennell, "Indigestion in the Nineteenth Century: Aspects of English Taste and Anxiety," *Oxford Symposium on Food and Cookery, 1987: Taste: Proceedings* (London, 1988), pp. 153–66.

47 *"chew the residue"*: Brillat-Savarin, *Philosopher in the Kitchen*, p. 304.

47 *"an old vinegar-barrel"*: J. H. Salisbury, *The Relation of Alimentation and Disease* (New York, 1888), p. 94.

47 *tear and digest meat*: Ibid., pp. 145–48.

48 *"meat if desired"*: Ibid., pp. 97–98, 127, 135, 140.

48 *"'on every jar'"*: Levenstein, *Revolution at the Table*, p. 41.

48 *until the 1930s*: Ibid., p. 149.

48 *unhealthy food doles*: D. A. Roe, *A Plague of Corn: The Social History of Pellagra* (Ithaca, 1973); E. H. Beardsley, *A History of Neglect: Health Care for Blacks and Millworkers in the Twentieth-Century South* (Knoxville, 1987).

48 *"white-flour bread"*: Ibid., p. 155.

48 *Cream of Wheat*: Ibid., p. 159.

49 *"Grapefruit-juice Diet"*: H. Levenstein, *Paradox of Plenty: A Social History of Eating in Modern America* (Oxford, 1993).

49 *the Duchess of Windsor*: Ibid., pp. 11–12.

49 *"fat rolls off"*: B. G. Hauser, *The Gayelord Hauser Cookbook* (New York, 1946).

49 *"improperly balanced"*: L. R. Wolberg, *The Psychology of Eating* (London, 1937), p. x.

49 *"Greenland Eskimo"*: Ibid., pp. 36–38.

50 *"into his mouth"*: Ibid., p. 18.

50 *produced by rotting*: P. M. Gaman and K. B. Sherrington, *The Science of Food* (Oxford, 1996), p. 102.

50 *"high natural levels"*: Levenstein, *Paradox of Plenty*, p. 21.

50 *"The oomph vitamin"*: Ibid., p. 22.

50 *U.S. Food Agency*: Ibid., p. 64.

51 *"kill more Japs"*: Ibid., pp. 69, 71, 75–76, 95.

51 *colitis and dysentery*: R. McCarrison, *Nutrition and Health* (London, n.d.), p. 18.

51 *Kikuyu neighbors*: Ibid., pp. 23, 51, 75, 78.

52 *weight equally*: J. LeFanu, *Eat Your Heart Out: The Fallacy of the Healthy Diet* (London, 1987), pp. 56–61.

52 *according to Jolan Chang*: J. Chang, *Zest for Life: Live Disease-Free with the Tao* (Stockholm, 1995).

52 *"forces" restored*: Ibid., p. 23.

52 *"all the same"*: G. B. Bragg and D. Simon, *The Ayurvedic Cookbook* (New York, 1997).

52 *"the effects are amazing"*: U. Lecordier, *The High-Sexuality Diet* (London, 1984), pp. 17–23.

52 *"for many centuries"*: H. C. Lu, *The Chinese System of Using Foods to Stay Young* (New York, 1996), p. 27.

52 *"eat brain"*: J.-M. Bourre, *Brainfood* (Boston, 1990), pp. 57–65.

53 *increased cholesterol*: Jansen, *Food and Nutrition in Fiji*, ii, pp. 554–69.

53 *button mushrooms*: Lu, *Chinese System of Using Foods*, p. 9.

53 *"tea prevents scurvy"*: Ibid., pp. 10–18.

54 *"non-alcoholic punch"*: "The British Are Digging Their Own Graves with Their Teeth," *Northants Chronicle and Echo*, quoted in LeFanu, *Eat Your Heart Out*, p. 21.

54 *no weight gain at all*: Ibid., pp. 28–29.

54 *high cholesterol counts*: H. L. Abrams, "Vegetarianism: An Anthropological-Nutritional Evaluation," *Journal of Applied Nutrition*, xii (1980), 53–87.

54 *foraging cultures*: L. L. Cavalli-Sforza, "Human Evolution and Nutrition," in D. N. Walcher and N. Kretchmer, eds., *Food Nutrition and Evolution: Food As an Environmental Factor in the Genesis of Human Variability* (Chicago, 1981), p. 2.

CHAPTER 3: BREEDING TO EAT

55 *"Water Buffalo"*: Quoted in F. T. Cheng, *Musings of a Chinese Gourmet* (London, 1962), p. 73.

55 *"lobster and foie gras"*: Flandrin and Montanari, *Histoire de l'alimentation*, p. 776.

56 *plenty of meat*: D. Brothwell and P. Brothwell, *Food in Antiquity* (London, 1969), p. 67.

56 *for invalids*: P. J. Ucko and G. W. Dimbleby, eds., *The Domestication and Exploitation of Plants and Animals: A Survey of the Diet of Early Peoples* (Baltimore, 1998).

56 *heart of Boston*: Clark, *Oysters of Locqmariaquer*, pp. 39–40.

56 *today's equivalents*: Brothwell and Brothwell, *Food in Antiquity*, p. 64; J. G. Evans, "The Exploitation of Molluscs," in Ucko and Dimbleby, *Domestication and Exploitation* (London, 1969), pp. 479–84.

57 *tuna bones*: Dalby, *Siren Feasts*, p. 38.

57 *Mesolithic middens*: G. Clark, *World Prehistory in New Perspective* (New York, 1977), pp. 113–14.

57 *natural oyster beds*: Clark, *Oysters*, p. 39; M. Toussaint-Samat, *History of Food* (London, 1992), p. 385.

58 *bigger game*: Flandrin and Montanari, *Histoire de l'alimentation*, p. 41.

58 *crop failure*: K. V. Flannery, "Origins and Ecological Effects of Early Domestication in Iran and the Near East," in Ucko and Dimbleby, *Domestication and Exploitation*, pp. 73–100.

59 *developed together*: T. Ingold, "Growing Plants and Raising Animals: An Anthropological Perspective on Domestication," in D. R. Harris, ed., *The Origins and Spread of Agriculture and Pastoralism in Eurasia* (London, 1996), pp. 12–24; H.-P. Uepermann, "Animal Domestication: Accident or Intention," in ibid., pp. 227–37.

59 *were encouraged*: W. Cronon, *Changes in the Land: Indians, Colonists and the Ecology of New England* (New York, 1983), pp. 49–51.

60 *"whole race to degenerate"*: C. Darwin, *The Variation of Animals and Plants Under Domestication*, 2 vols. (London, 1868), ii, 207–9.

61 *"It was gorgeous"*: J. M. Barrie, *The Admirable Crichton*, Act 3, Scene 1.

62 *"meat I wanted"*: Lévi-Strauss, *Raw and the Cooked*, p. 82.

62 *animals into traps*: T. F. Kehoe, "Coralling: Evidence from Upper Paleolithic Cave Art," in L. B. Davis and B. O. K. Reeves, eds., *Hunters of the Recent Past* (London, 1990), pp. 34–46.

62 *vitamin C*: S. B. Eaton and M. Konner, "Paleolithic Nutrition: A Consideration of Its Nature and Current Implications," *New England Journal of Medicine*, cccxii (1985), 283–89; S. B. Eaton, M. Shostak and M. Konner, *The Stone-Age Health Programme* (London, 1988), pp. 77–83.

64 *to their enemies*: O. Blehr, "Communal Hunting As a Prerequisite for Caribou (Wild Reindeer) As Human Resource," in Davis and Reeves, *Hunters of the Recent Past*, pp. 304–26.

64 *hungry for fat*: B. A. Jones, "Paleoindians and Proboscideans: Ecological Determinants of Selectivity in the Southwestern United States," in Davis and Reeves, *Hunters of the Recent Past*, pp. 68–84.

64 *a one-ton lizard*: J. Diamond, *Guns, Germs and Steel: The Fates of Human Societies* (London, 1997), p. 43.

65 *dance could begin*: L. van der Post, *The Lost World of the Kalahari* (London, 1961), pp. 234–40.

65 *killing grounds*: J. C. Driver, "Meat in Due Season: The Timing of Communal Hunts," in Davis and Reeves, *Hunters of the Recent Past*, pp. 11–33.

66 *"they are thirsty"*: G. Parker Winship, ed., *The Journey of Coronado* (Golden, 1990), p. 117.

67 *to live on*: L. Forsberg, "Economic and Social Change in the Interior of Northern Sweden, 6,000 B.C.–1,000 A.D.," in T. B. Larson and H. Lundmark, eds., *Approaches to Swedish Prehistory: A Spectrum of Problems and Perspectives in Contemporary Research* (Oxford, 1989), pp. 75–77.

67 *a surprising appetite*: Donner, *Among the Samoyed*, p. 104.

67 *six hundred strong*: R. Bosi, *The Lapps* (New York, 1960), p. 53.

67 *to winter quarters*: A. Spencer, *The Lapps* (New York, 1978), pp. 43–59.

68 *two thousand reindeer*: P. Hadjo, *The Samoyed Peoples and Languages* (Bloomington, 1963), p. 10.

68 *with his teeth*: Donner, *Among the Samoyed*, p. 106.

68 *it to the corral*: J. H. Cook, *Fifty Years on the Old Frontier* (Norman, 1954), pp. 14–18.

68 *Native American populations*: N. D. Cook, *Born to Die: Disease and New World Conquest, 1492–1650* (Cambridge, 1998), p. 28.

68 *"exchange genes"*: J. McNeil, *Something New Under the Sun* (London, 2000), p. 210.

69 *two stomachs*: R. J. Adams, *Come an' Get It: The Story of the Old Cowboy Cook* (Norman, 1952), quoted in A. Davidson, *The Oxford Companion to Food* (Oxford, 1999).

70 *a domestic breed*: See Diamond, *Guns, Germs and Steel*, pp. 168–75.

70 *on capture*: G. C. Frison, C. A. Reher and D. N. Walker, "Prehistoric Mountain Sheep Hunting in the Central Rocky Mountains of North America," in Davis and Reeves, *Hunters of the Recent Past*, pp. 218–40.

71 *unused to it*: M. Harris, *Good to Eat: Riddles of Food and Culture* (London, 1986), pp. 131–32.

73 *previous centuries combined*: McNeil, *Something New Under the Sun*, p. 246.

73 *zero in 1980*: Ibid., pp. 248–51; L. P. Paine, *Down East: A Maritime History of Maine* (Gardiner, 2000), pp. 118–33.

74 *the tide falls*: Jansen, *Food and Nutrition in Fiji*, i, 397.

75 *usual habitat*: Toussaint-Samat, *History of Food*, pp. 326–27.

CHAPTER 4: THE EDIBLE EARTH

76 *"vanish completely"*: Trans. William Radice (London, 2000).

77 *"'feed like princes'"*: Brillat-Savarin, *Philosopher in the Kitchen*, pp. 243–44.

78 *gather them wild*: Leo Africanus, quoted in M. Brett and E. Femtress, *The Berbers* (Oxford, 1996), p. 201.

80 *farming came about*: A. B. Gebauer and T. D. Price, "Foragers to Farmers: An Introduction," in *The Transition to Agriculture in Prehistory* (Madison, 1992), pp. 1–10.

80 *"period of civilisation"*: Darwin, *Variation of Animals and Plants*, i, 309–10.

80 *"in New York"*: Diamond, *Guns, Germs and Steel*, pp. 14–22.

81 *"seas of wild rice"*: C. A. Reed, ed., *Origins of Agriculture* (The Hague, 1977), p. 370.

81 *ninth millennium B.C.*: J. R. Harlan, "The Origins of Cereal Agriculture in the Old World," in Gebauer and Price, "Foragers to Farmers," pp. 357–83, 363.

82 *more tyranny*: M. N. Cohen and G. J. Armelagos, *Paleopathology at the Origins of Agriculture* (New York, 1984), pp. 51–73.

82 *way of life*: L. R. Binford, "Post-Pleistocene Adaptations," in S. R. Binford and L. R. Binford, eds., *New Perspectives in Archaeology* (Chicago, 1968), pp. 313–41; M. D. Sahlins, "Notes on the Original Affluent Society," in R. B. Lee and I. DeVore, eds., *Man the Hunter* (Chicago, 1968), pp. 85–88; *Stone Age Economics* (Chicago, 1972), especially pp. 1–39.

82 *"work as hard"*: J. R. Harlan, *Crops and Man* (Madison, 1992), p. 27.

82 *be highly toxic*: T. Bonyhady, *Burke and Wills: From Melbourne to Myth* (Balmain, 1991), pp. 137–39, 140–41.

83 *"living conditions"*: J. R. Harlan, *Crops and Man* (Madison, 1992), p. 27.

83 *"'cut wheat'"*: Ibid., p. 8.

85 *climatic prerequisites*: V. G. Childe, *Man Makes Himself* (London, 1936); *Piecing Together the Past* (London, 1956).

85 *experimentation with plants*: C. O. Sauer, *Agricultural Origin and Dispersals* (New York, 1952).

85 *and grazing herds*: R. J. Braidwood and B. Howe, eds., *Prehistoric Investigations in Iraqi Kurdistan* (Chicago, 1960).

85 *food sources were few*: K. Flannery, "The Origins of Agriculture," *Annual Reviews in Anthropology*, ii (1973), 271–310.

85 *"human communities"*: E. S. Anderson, *Plants, Man and Life* (London, 1954), pp. 142–50.

85 *where people lived*: C. B. Heiser, *Seed to Civilization: The Story of Food* (Cambridge, Massachusetts, 1990), pp. 14–26.

85 *existing foodstuffs*: Binford and Binford, eds., *New Perspectives in Archaeology*; M. Cohen, *The Food Crisis in Prehistory* (New Haven, 1977).

85 *as a cause*: B. Bronson, "The Earliest Farming: Demography As Cause and Consequence," in S. Polgar, ed., *Population, Ecology and Social Evolution* (The Hague, 1975).

86 *supplies are secure*: B. Hayden, "Nimrods, Piscators, Pluckers and Planters: The Emergence of Food Production," *Journal of Anthropological Research*, ix (1953), 31–69.

86 *kind of conviviality*: B. Hayden, "Pathways to Power: Principles for Creating Socioeconomic Inequalities," in T. D. Price and G. M. Feinman, eds., *Foundations of Social Inequality* (New York, 1995), pp. 15–86.

86 *religious response*: Harlan, *Crops and Man*, pp. 35–36.

87 *to tell apart*: S. J. Fiedel, *Prehistory of the Americas* (New York, 1987), p. 162.

87 *varieties of beans*: G. P. Nabhan, *The Desert Smells Like Rain: A Naturalist in Papago Indian Country* (San Francisco, 1982); *Enduring Seeds: Native American Agriculture and Wild Plant Conservation* (San Francisco, 1989).

87 *"when planted"*: B. Fagan, *The Journey from Eden: The Peopling of Our World* (London, 1990), p. 225.

87 *without husking*: D. Rindos, *The Origins of Agriculture: An Evolutionary Perspective* (New York, 1984).

88 *loss of the main crop*: K. F. Kiple and K. C. Ornelas, eds., *The Cambridge World History of Food*, 2 vols. (Cambridge, 2000), i, 149.

89 *"supply trains"*: C. I. Beckwith, *The Tibetan Empire in Central Asia: A History of the Struggle for Great Power Among Tibetans, Turks, Arabs and Chinese During the Early Middle Ages* (Princeton, 1987), p. 100.

90 *"be abundant"*: A. Waley, *The Book of Songs Translated from the Chinese* (London, 1937), p. 17.

90 *trees and scrub*: D. N. Keightley, ed., *The Origins of Chinese Civilization* (Berkeley, 1983), p. 27.

90 *occasional rhinoceros*: K. C. Chang, *Shang Civilization* (New Haven, 1980), pp. 138–41.

91 *ground in Shansi*: Waley, *Book of Songs*, p. 24.

91 *"pink-sprouted and white"*: Ibid., p. 242.

91 *over the ruins:* K. C. Chang, *Shang Civilization* (New Haven, 1980).

91 *indigenous to China:* Te-Tzu Chang: "The Origins and Early Culture of the Cereal Grains and Food Legumes," in Keightley, ed., *Origins of Chinese Civilization*, pp. 66–68.

92 *carried home:* W. Fogg, "Swidden Cultivation of Foxtail Millet by Taiwan Aborigines: A Cultural Analogue of the Domestica of Serica Italica in China," in Keightley, *Origins of Chinese Civilization*, pp. 95–115.

92 *the millet stocks:* Waley, *Book of Songs*, pp. 164–67.

92 *the mountains in 664:* K. C. Chang, "Origins and Early Culture," p. 81.

92 *monitored and destroyed:* K. C. Chang, *Shang Civilization*, pp. 148–49. The paragraphs on millet in China are derived from F. Fernández-Armesto, *Civilizations* (London, 2000), pp. 251–53.

92 *until the nineteenth:* A. G. Frank, *ReOrient: Global Economy in the Asian Age* (Berkeley, 1998); J. Goody, *The East in the West* (London, 1996); F. Fernández-Armesto, *Millennium* (London, 1995; rev. ed., 1999).

93 *third millennium* B.C.: I. C. Glover and C. F. W. Higham, "Early Rice Cultivation in South, Southeast and East Asia," in Harris, *Origins*, pp. 413–41.

93 *wore skins:* H. Maspero, *China in Antiquity* (n.p., 1978), p. 382.

94 *maize cultivation:* D. W. Lathrap, "Our Father the Cayman, Our Mother the Gourd," in C. A. Reed, ed., *Origins of Agriculture* (The Hague, 1977), pp. 713–51, at 721–22.

94 *second millennium* B.C.: Coe, *America's First Cuisines*, p. 14.

94 *"habits of life":* Darwin, *Variation of Animals and Plants*, i, 315.

95 *tempted to conquest:* Fernández-Armesto, *Civilizations*, p. 210.

96 *"in companionable villages":* P. Pray Bober, *Art, Culture and Cuisine: Ancient and Medieval Gastronomy* (Chicago, 1999), p. 62.

96 *surrounding bracts:* Heiser, *Seed to Civilization*, p. 70.

97 *farmed plant:* M. Spriggs, "Taro-Cropping Systems in the South-east Asian Pacific Region," *Archaeology in Oceania*, xvii (1982), 7–15.

98 *nine thousand years ago:* J. Golson, "Kuku and the Development of Agriculture in New Guinea: Retrospection and Introspection," in D. E. Yen and J. M. J. Mummery, eds., *Pacific Production Systems: Approaches to Economic History* (Canberra, 1983), pp. 139–47.

98 *a few days:* Heiser, *Seed to Civilization*, p. 149.

99 *shrines and nurseries:* D. G. Coursey, "The Origins and Domestication of Yams in Africa," in B. K. Schwartz and R. E. Dummett, *West African Culture Dynamics* (The Hague, 1980), pp. 67–90.

99 *New Guinea:* J. Golson, "No Room at the Top: Agricultural Intensification in the New Guinea Highlands," in J. Allen et al., eds., *Sunda and Sahul* (London, 1977), pp. 601–38.

99 *earliest anywhere:* J. G. Hawkes, "The Domestication of Roots and Tubers in the American Tropics," in D. R. Harris and G. C. Hillman, eds., *Foraging and Farming* (London, 1989), pp. 292–304.

100 *"else to eat":* J. V. Murra, *Formaciones económicas y políticas del mundo andino* (Lima, 1975), pp. 45–57.

100 *"good to drink":* J. Lafitau, *Moeurs des sauvages amériquains, comparés aux moeurs des premiers temps*, 2 vols. (Paris, N. D.), i, 100–101.

CHAPTER 5: FOOD AND RANK

102 *four hundred oysters at a sitting*: M. Montanari, *The Culture of Food* (Oxford, 1994), pp. 10–11.

102 *hallowed by risk*: Ibid., pp. 23, 26.

103 *"scorpion-fish"*: Quoted in Dalby, *Siren Feasts*, pp. 70–71, translation modified.

103 *and so on*: M. Girouard, *Life in the English Country House* (New Haven, 1978), p. 12.

103 *above subsistence level*: B. J. Kemp, *Ancient Egypt: Anatomy of a Civilization* (London, 1989), pp. 120–28.

104 *"will have departed"*: Fernández-Armesto, *Civilizations*, pp. 226–27.

104 *were served*: Flandrin and Montanari, *Histoire de l'alimentation*, p. 55.

104 *"the platter itself"*: Montanari, *Culture of Food*, p. 22.

104 *the broken bits*: O. Prakash, *Food and Drinks in Ancient India from Earliest Times to c. 1200 A.D.* (Delhi, 1961), p. 100.

104 *wafers and cakes*: T. Wright, *The Homes of Other Days: A History of Domestic Manners and Sentiments in England* (London, 1871), p. 368. See also J. Lawrence, "Royal Feasts," *Oxford Symposium on Food and Cookery, 1990: Feasting and Fasting: Proceedings* (London, 1990).

104 *walk to a waddle*: H. Powdermaker, "An Anthropological Approach to the Problems of Obesity," *Bulletin of the New York Academy of Medicine*, xxxvi (1960), in C. Counihan and P. van Esterik, eds., *Food and Culture: A Reader* (New York, 1997), pp. 203–10.

105 *out in sweat*: S. Mennell, *All Manners of Food* (Oxford, 1985), p. 33. On Louis XIV's eating habits, see B. K. Wheaton, *Savouring the Past: The French Kitchen and Table from 1300 to 1789* (London, 1983), p. 135.

105 *jug of water*: Brillat-Savarin, *Philosopher in the Kitchen*, pp. 60–61.

105 *"reward of pleasure"*: Ibid., p. 133.

106 *"'baked in the ashes'"*: A. J. Liebling, *Between Meals: An Appetite for Paris* (New York, 1995), p. 6.

106 *"somewhat forgotten"*: *The Warden* (London, 1907), pp. 114–15.

107 *"having too much"*: Levenstein, *Revolution at the Table*, pp. 7–14.

108 *"when I go there"*: *New Yorker*, 1944, quoted in J. Smith, *Hungry for You* (London, 1996).

109 *unit of weight*: W. R. Leonard and M. L. Robertson, "Evolutionary Perspectives on Human Nutrition: The Influence of Brain and Body Size on Diet and Metabolism," *American Journal of Human Biology*, vi (1994), 77–88.

109 *"but not us"*: J. Steingarten, *The Man Who Ate Everything* (London, 1997), p. 5.

109 *few leaves at one side*: M. F. K. Fisher and S. Tsuji in S. Tsuji, *Japanese Cooking: A Simple Art* (Tokyo, 1980), pp. 8–24.

110 *"on a silver bowl"*: I. Morris, ed., *The Pillow-Book of Sei Shonagon* (Harmondsworth, 1967), pp. 69, 169.

110 *"dried beans"*: L. Frédéric, *Daily Life in Japan at the Time of the Samurai, 1185–1603* (London, 1972), p. 72.

110 *"eating and drinking"*: Captain Golownin, *Japan and the Japanese, Comprising the Narrative of a Captivity in Japan*, 2 vols. (London, 1853), ii, 147.

110 *"their game"*: R. Alcock, *The Capital of the Tycoon: A Narrative of a Three Years' Residence in Japan*, 2 vols. (London, 1863), i, 272.

111 *club for foreigners*: J. Street, *Mysterious Japan* (London, 1922), pp. 127–28.

111 *recapture its spirit*: S. Tsuji, *Japanese Cooking*, pp. 8–14, 21–22.

111 *fat and water*: Bober, *Art, Culture and Cuisine*, pp. 72–73.

111 *good for stomachache*: Flandrin and Montanari, *Histoire de l'alimentation*, p. 72.

111 *"most its own"*: A. Waley, *More Translations from the Chinese* (New York, 1919), pp. 13–14, quoted in Goody, *Cooking, Cuisine and Class* (Cambridge, 1982), p. 112; translation modified.

112 *clotted cream and cheese*: Athenaeus, *The Deipnosophists*, iv, 147, trans. C. B. Gulick, 7 vols. (London, 1927–41), ii (1928), pp. 171–75.

112 *taken indecorously*: A. Waley, *The Book of Songs* (New York, 1938), x, 7–8.

112 *ever creative tension*: Goody, *Cooking, Cuisine and Class*, p. 133.

113 *"sea-urchin at a glance"*: Juvenal, Satire 4, 143.

113 *scattered with pearls*: T. S. Peterson, *Acquired Tastes: The French Origins of Modern Cuisine* (Ithaca, 1944), p. 48.

114 *flamingos' tongues*: C. A. Déry, "Fish As Food and Symbol in Rome," in Walker, ed., *Oxford Symposium on the History of Food* (Totnes, 1997), pp. 94–115, at p. 97.

114 *nausea in their readers*: E. Gowers, *The Loaded Table: Representations of Food in Roman Literature* (Oxford, 1993), pp. 1–24, 111.

114 *white wine*: Montanari, *Culture of Food*, p. 164.

114 *"between their legs"*: O. Cartellieri, *The Court of Burgundy* (London, 1972), pp. 40–52.

114 *"persecuted by the Turks"*: Ibid., pp. 139–53.

115 *what they had eaten*: D. Durston, *Old Kyoto* (Kyoto, 1986), p. 29.

115 *"nature provides them"*: J.-C. Bonnet, "The Culinary System in the *Encyclopédie*," in R. Forster and O. Ranum, *Food and Drink in History* (Baltimore, 1979), pp. 139–65, at p. 143.

116 *pepper and knot grass*: Hu Sihui, *Yinshan Zhengyao—Correct Principles of Eating and Drinking*, quoted in Toussaint-Samat, *History of Food*, p. 329.

116 *"as an art"*: Gowers, *Loaded Table*, p. 51.

116 *fragment of Alexis*: Dalby, *Siren Feasts*, p. 122.

116 *"got me there"*: Antiphanes, quoted in ibid., p. 113; translation modified.

117 *improving foie gras*: L. Bolens, *Agronomes andalous du moyen age* (Geneva, 1981).

117 *"than my thumb"*: Brillat-Savarin, *Philosopher in the Kitchen*, pp. 54–55.

118 *dumb barbarian*: Steingarten, *Man Who Ate Everything*, p. 231.

118 *his resentment*: F. Gómez de Oroxco, in M. de Carcer y Disdier, *Apuntes para la historia de la transculturación indoespañola* (Mexico, 1995), pp. x–xi.

118 *"founded upon elegance"*: Montanari, *Culture of Food*, p. 58.

121 *"rose red"*: M. Leibenstein, "Beyond Old Cookbooks: Four Travellers' Accounts," in Walker, *Food on the Move*, pp. 224–29.

121 *scented with sandalwood*: Wright, *Homes of Other Days*, pp. 360–61.

121 *grape must*: Bober, *Art, Culture and Cuisine*, p. 154.

121 *the Middle Ages:* J. Goody, *Food and Love: A Cultural History of East and West* (London, 1998), p. 131.

122 *"Cicero of the potato":* Bonnet, "Culinary System," pp. 146–47.

122 *assuaged without them:* See also Goody, *Food and Love,* p. 130.

122 *Catherine de Medici ill:* Peterson, *Acquired Tastes,* pp. 109–10.

123 *behind barriers:* J.-R. Pitte, *Gastronomie française: histoire et géographie d'une passion* (Paris, 1991), pp. 127–28.

123 *were in print:* Ibid., p. 129.

123 *"had no heart":* Wright, *Homes of Other Days,* p. 167.

124 *"at the beginning":* Dalby, *Siren Feasts,* p. 25.

124 *"life and death":* A. Beardsworth and T. Keil, *Sociology on the Menu* (London, 1997), p. 87.

124 *aside for alms:* Montanari, *Culture of Food,* p. 86.

124 *"gets the straw":* Camporesi, *Magic Harvest,* p. 95.

124 *"refined people":* Ibid., p. 119.

124 *honey wine in Ethiopia:* Goody, *Cooking, Cuisine and Class,* p. 101.

124 *cooked in champagne:* J.-P. Aron, "The Art of Using Leftovers: Paris, 1850–1900," in Forster and Ranum, *Food and Drink in History,* pp. 98–108, at pp. 99, 102.

125 *"the fodder of man":* Camporesi, *Magic Harvest,* pp. 80–81, 106.

125 *sumptuary laws:* Peterson, *Acquired Tastes,* p. 92.

125 *"soaked in water":* Dalby, *Siren Feasts,* p. 64.

125 *"clandestine delights":* Camporesi, *Magic Harvest,* p. 90.

126 *barley bread:* Montanari, *Culture of Food,* p. 31.

126 *"White bread and often!":* Ibid., p. 51.

126 *to lose caste:* Forster and Ranum, *Food and Drink in History,* p. x.

126 *grains selected:* Prakash, *Food and Drinks,* p. 100.

126 *seventeenth-century France:* Peterson, *Acquired Tastes,* pp. 84–88.

126 *"roast chicken":* Montanari, *Culture of Food,* p. 57.

127 *patriotic preference:* J. Revel, "A Capital's Privileges: Food Supply in Early-Modern Rome," in Forster and Ranum, *Food and Drink in History,* pp. 37–49, at pp. 39–40.

127 *mechanical press:* Montanari, *Culture of Food,* p. 143.

127 *"has no scales":* Dalby, *Siren Feasts,* p. 200.

127 *"twice a week":* John Byng, quoted in J. P. Alcock, "God Sends Meat, but the Devil Sends Cooks, Or, a Solitary Pleasure: The travels of the Hon. John Byng Through England and Wales in the Late XVIIIth Century," in Walker, *Food on the Move,* pp. 14–31, at p. 22.

127 *"personnes aisées":* M. Bloch, "Les aliments de l'ancienne France," in J. J. Hemardinquer, ed., *Pour une histoire de l'alimentation* (Paris, 1970), pp. 231–35.

127 *sixty cents:* Remedi, *Los secretos de la olla,* p. 81.

128 *any of them:* B. Díaz del Castillo, *Historia verdadera de la conquista de la Nueva España,* ed. J. Ramírez Cabañas, 2 vols. (Mexico, 1968), i, 271.

128 *lords' feasts*: T. de Benavente o Motolinia, *Memoriales*, ed. E. O'Gorman (Mexico, 1971), p. 342.

128 *tomatoes and squashes*: F. Berdan, *The Aztecs of Central Mexico: An Imperial Society* (New York, 1982), p. 39.

128 *"relatives and friends"*: Sahagún, *Historia*, pp. 503–12.

129 *"China brier"*: P. P. Bober, "William Bartran's Travels in Lands of Amerindian Tobacco and Caffeine: Foodways of Seminoles, Creeks and Cherokees," in Walker, *Food on the Move*, pp. 44–51, at p. 47.

129 *"south of the Sahara"*: Goody, *Food and Love*, p. 2.

130 *nuts or leaves*: Goody, *Cooking, Cuisine and Class*, pp. 40–78.

CHAPTER 6: THE EDIBLE HORIZON

132 *"consumer conservatism"*: M. Douglas, ed., *Food in the Social Order: Studies of Food and Festivities in Three American Communities* (New York, 1984), p. 4.

133 *"horseman's weight"*: Quoted in Goody, *Food and Love*, p. 134.

133 *"bad meat eatable"*: R. Warner, *Antiquitates Culinariae* [1791], quoted in Goody, *Cooking, Cuisine and Class*, p. 146.

134 *the dishes were identical*: Levenstein, *Paradox of Plenty*, p. 45.

134 *White House kitchen*: Ibid., p. 140.

134 *"no schmier"*: Liebling, *Between Meals*, pp. 8, 16, 131.

135 *versus unsweet*: R. Barthes, "Towards a Psychology of Contemporary Food Consumption," in Forster and Ranum, *Food and Drink in History*, pp. 166–73.

135 *limit waste*: M. L. De Vault, *Feeding the Family: The Social Organization of Caring As Gendered Work* (Chicago, 1991).

135 *"seldom horse"*: Dalby, *Siren Feasts*, p. 21.

135 *"bits you can't eat"*: Menander, quoted in ibid., p. 21.

136 *"eating anything"*: Archestratus, quoted in ibid., p. 159.

136 *to be repatriated*: Jansen, *Food and Nutrition in Fiji*, ii, 191–208.

136 *to them repulsive*: Levenstein, *Revolution at the Table*, p. vii.

136 *"sight of bread"*: Quoted in Coe, *America's First Cuisine*, p. 28.

136 *"such a thing"*: Ibid., p. 126.

136 *"eating our food"*: F. Fernández-Armesto, *The Empire of Philip II: A Decade at the Edge* (London, 1998).

138 *fried chicken*: S. Zubaida, "National, Communal and Global Dimensions in Middle Eastern Food Cultures," in Zubaida and Tapper, *Culinary Cultures of the Middle East*, pp. 33–48, at p. 41.

139 *"make with olive oil"*: A. de Bernáldez, *Memorias del reinado de los Reyes Católicos*, ed. A. Gómez-Moreno and J. M. Carriazo (Madrid, 1962), pp. 96–98.

140 *recipe books*: A. E. Algar, *Classical Turkish Cooking* (New York, 1991), pp. 57–58.

141 *rose to 1,370*: Ibid., p. 28.

144 *classic bredie*: Van der Post, *African Cooking*, pp. 131–51.

145 *baboons and monkeys*: Darwin, *Variation of Animals and Plants*, i, 309.

145 *"very excellent"*: Elisha Kane, medical officer in Franklin relief expedition, 1850, quoted in Levenstein, *Paradox of Plenty*, p. 228.

146 *boiled snake and black rice*: A. Lamb, *The Mandarin Road to Old Hue* (London, 1970), p. 45.

147 *"methods of preparation"*: G. West and D. West, *By Bus to the Sahara* (London, 1995), pp. 79, 97–100, 149.

147 *"economic exile"*: Goody, *Food and Love*, p. 162.

147 *nineteenth-century North America*: Cheng, *Musings of a Chinese Gourmet*, p. 24.

148 *the "stranger effect"*: F. Fernández-Armesto, "The Stranger-Effect in Early-Modern Asia," *Itinerario*, xxiv (2000), 8–123.

149 *wheat for baking*: Hermippus, quoted in Dalby, *Siren Feasts*, p. 105.

149 *"by its products"*: Brillat-Savarin, *Philosopher in the Kitchen*, p. 275.

151 *"traded there"*: H. A. R. Gibb and C. F. Beckingham, eds., *The Travels of Ibn Battuta*, A.D. 1325–1354, 4 vols. (London, 1994) iv, 946–47.

152 *agent for Portugal in Amsterdam*: J. Israel, *The Dutch Republic and the Hispanic World* (Oxford, 1982), pp. 25, 45, 92, 123–24, 136, 203, 214, 288–89.

152 *without this inducement*: M. Herrero Sánchez, *El acercamiento hispano-neerlandes, 1648–78* (Madrid, 2000), pp. 110–25.

154 *easily gulled*: F. Fernández-Armesto, *Columbus* (London, 1996), p. 87.

154 *"meat, fruits"*: E. Naville, *The Temple of Deir el Bahari* (London, 1894), pp. 21–25; Fernández-Armesto, *Civilizations*, pp. 224–26.

154 *"extraordinary character"*: Agatharchides of Cnidus on the Erythraean Sea, ed. S. M. Burstein (London, 1989), p. 162.

155 *India and Ceylon*: L. Casson, "Cinnamon and Cassia in the Ancient World," in *Ancient Trade and Society* (Detroit, 1984), pp. 224–41; J. I. Miller, *The Spice Trade of the Roman Empire* (Oxford, 1969), p. 21.

155 *outside the empire*: Miller, *Spice Trade*, pp. 34–118; Dalby, *Siren Feasts*, p. 137.

155 *poet put it*: Dalby, *Siren Feasts*, p. 137.

157 *fifteenth century*: C. Verlinden, *Les Origines de la civilisation atlantique* (Paris, 1966), p. 167–70.

157 *a remote age*: F. Fernández-Armesto, *Before Columbus* (Philadelphia, 1987), p. 198.

157 *"we do of sugar"*: J.-B. Buyerin, *De re cibaria* (Lyon, 1560), p. 2.

161 *Western expense*: A. Reid, *South-east Asia in the Age of Commerce*, 2. vols. (New Haven, 1988–93), i, 277–303; F. Fernández-Armesto, *Millennium* (London, 1999), pp. 303–9.

CHAPTER 7: CHALLENGING EVOLUTION

163 *"tired of"*: A. Davidson, ed., *The Oxford Companion to Food* (Oxford, 1998), s.v.

164 *"the only god is love"*: Philibert Commerson in 1769, quoted in R. H. Grove, *Ecological Imperialism: Colonial Expansion, Tropical Island Edens and the Origins of Environmentalism, 1600–1860* (Cambridge, 1996), p. 238.

164 *abundance was spectacular*: E. K. Fisk, "Motivation and Modernization," *Pacific Perspective, i* (1972), 21.

165 *preserved in vinegar*: Dalby, *Siren Feasts*, p. 140.

165 *plant in antiquity*: Ibid., p. 87.

165 *introduction to Britain*: C. A. Dery, "Food and the Roman Army: Travel, Transport and Transmission (with Particular Reference to the Province of Britain)," in Walker, *Food on the Move*, pp. 84–96, at p. 91.

166 *lived off them*: McNeil, *Something New Under the Sun*, p. 210.

167 *"on the environment"*: Grove, *Ecological Imperialism*, p. 93.

167 *meaning testicle*: Coe, *America's First Cuisines*, p. 28.

168 *to Montezuma's zoo*: Ibid., p. 96.

168 *the Irish*: C. T. Sen, "The Portuguese Influence on Bengali Cuisine," in Walker, *Food on the Move*, pp. 288–98.

169 *Red Sea origin*: McNeil, *Something New Under the Sun*, p. 173; F. D. Por, "Lessepsian Migration: An Appraisal and New Data," *Bulletin de l'Institut Océanique de Monaco*, no. spéc. 7 (1990), pp. 1–7.

170 *in other continents*: Fernández-Armesto, *Civilizations*, pp. 93–109.

170 *"dense population"*: *The Prairie* (New York, n.d.), p. 6.

171 *fed imported livestock*: A. W. Crosby, *Ecological Imperialism: The Biological Expansion of Europe* (Cambridge, 1986.)

171 *"seasoned bread"*: P. Gerhard, "A Black Conquistador in Mexico," *Hispanic American Historical Review*, viii (1978), pp. 451–59.

171 *were their mainstays*: C. M. Scarry and E. J. Reitz, "Herbs, Fish, Scum and Vermin: Subsistence Strategies in Sixteenth-Century Spanish Florida," in D. Hurst Thomas, ed., *Columbian Consequences*, ii: (Washington, 1990), pp. 343–54.

172 *construction materials*: W. Cronon, *Nature's Metropolis: Chicago and the Great West* (New York, 1991).

173 *"conquering race"*: A. de Tocqueville, *Writings on Empire and Slavery*, ed. J. Pitts (Baltimore, 2001), p. 61.

175 *the Indian Ocean*: F. Fernández-Armesto, *The Canary Islands After the Conquest* (Oxford, 1982), p. 70.

176 *on the spot*: B. D. Smith, "The Origins of Agriculture in North America," *Science*, ccxlvi (1989), 1566–71.

176 *pounded for flour*: B. Trigger and W. E. Washburn, eds., *The Cambridge History of the Native Peoples of the Americas*, i (Cambridge, 1996), 162.

177 *their predecessors*: G. Amelagos and M. C. Hill, "An Evaluation of the Biological Consequences of the Mississippian Transformation," in D. H. Dye and C. A. Cox, eds., *Towns and Temples Along the Mississippi* (Tuscaloosa, 1990), pp. 16–37.

177 *same name*: Lafitau, *Moeurs des sauvages amériquains*, i, 70.

178 *nurture freedom*: Fernández-Armesto, *Millennium*, p. 353.

178 *"introduce them here"*: Battara's *Prattica agraria* (1798), i, 95, quoted in Camporesi, *Magic Harvest*, p. 22.

179 *as in China*: Fernández-Armesto, *Millennium*, p. 353.

180 *population growth*: M. Morineau, "The Potato in the XVIIIth Century," in Forster and Ranum, *Food and Drink in History*, pp. 17–36.

180 *"seen in America"*: Juan de Velasco, quoted in Coe, *America's First Cuisines*, p. 38.

181 *Italian coffee makers*: J. Leclant, "Coffee and Cafés in Paris, 1644–93," in Forster and Ranum, *Food and Drink in History*, pp. 86–97, at pp. 87–89.

181 *"perfect love liquor"*: Ibid., p. 90.

182 *"Holland rich"*: Tr. R. Edwards (Harmondsworth, 1987), pp. 73–74 (punctuation modified).

182 *"'chocolate of Chiapa'"*: T. Gage, *The English-American his Travail by Sea and Land*, (1648), p. 7.

183 *wooden stick*: S. D. Coe, *The True History of Chocolate* (London, 1996), p. 65.

183 *Gulf of Guinea*: Ibid., p. 201.

183 *the Industrial Revolution*: J. Goody, "Industrial Food: Towards the Development of a World Cuisine," in Counihan and van Esterik, *Food and Culture*, pp. 338–56; S. W. Mintz, "Time, Sugar and Sweetness," in ibid., pp. 357–69.

184 *into a monarchy*: E. S. Dodge, *Islands and Empires: Western Impact on the Pacific and East Asia* (Minneapolis, 1976), pp. 137–39.

184 *"other side"*: Ibid., p. 233.

184 *"they would expect"*: Ibid., p. 409.

185 *"provoking to us"*: Ibid., p. 418.

185 *"pork and potatoes"*: J. Belich, *Making Peoples: A History of the New Zealanders* (Auckland, 1996), pp. 145–46.

185 *performed the entire job*: F. Crowley, *A Documentary History of Australia*, i (1980), pp. 10, 24, 32.

186 *"French apple tree"*: A. Frost, cited in F. Fernández-Armesto, *Millennium* (London, 1996), pp. 641, 747. See now A. Frost, *Sir Joseph Banks and the Transfer of Plants to and from the South Pacific* (Melbourne, forthcoming, 2002).

186 *unexperienced environments*: Fernández-Armesto, *Millennium*, pp. 640–41.

CHAPTER 8: FEEDING THE GIANTS

187 *"to an end"*: Quoted in Cheng, *Musings of a Chinese Gourmet*, p. 147.

187 *"bread or a potato"*: C. E. Francatelli, *A Plain Cookery Book for the Working Classes* (London, 1977), p. 16.

188 *eat with mustard*: Ibid., pp. 44–45.

188 *"for your supper"*: Ibid., p. 22.

189 *in patent foods*: J. M. Strang, "Caveat Emptor: Food Adulteration in Nineteenth-Century England," *Oxford Symposium on Food and Cookery, 1986: The Cooking Medium: Proceedings* (London, 1987), pp. 129–33.

189 *in the kingdom*: Ibid., pp. 13–19, 31–32, 89.

192 *launched the "Green Revolution"*: L. Burbank, *An Architect of Nature* (London, 1939), pp. 1, 5, 27, 32, 34, 41; F. W. Clampett, *Luther Burbank, "Our Good Infidel"* (New York, 1926), pp. 21–22; K. Pandora, in *American National Biography*.

193 *"bread from air"*: McNeil, *Something New Under the Sun*, p. 24.

193 *battery breed*: Levenstein, *Revolution at the Table*, p. 109.

193 *ten million chicks*: W. H. Wilson and A. J. Banks, *The Chicken and the Egg* (New York, 1955), p. 10.

193 *"bloody stumps"*: B. MacDonald, *The Egg and I* (Bath, 1946), pp. 65, 115.

193 *feather coat*: Wilson and Banks, *Chicken and the Egg*, p. 38.

194 *"governed by Nature"*: C. Wilson, in F. H. Hinsley, ed., *New Cambridge Modern History*, xi (Cambridge, 1976), 55.

195 *"managing them"*: R. Scola, *Feeding the Victorian City: The Food Supply of Manchester, 1770–1870* (Manchester, 1992), pp. 159–62.

195 *"of common things"*: H. V. Morton, *A Stranger in Spain* (London, 1983), p. 130.

195 *marketplaces and neighborhoods*: J. Burnett, *Plenty and Want: A Social History of Diet in England from 1815 to the Present Day* (London, 1966), p. 35.

197 *mass production of biscuits*: Goody, *Cooking, Cuisine and Class*, pp. 156–57.

197 *"biscuit tin"*: T. A. B. Corley, *Quaker Enterprise in Biscuits: Huntley and Palmers of Reading, 1822–1972* (London, 1972), pp. 52–55, 93–95.

198 *cocoa butter*: Coe, *True History of Chocolate*, p. 243.

199 *only $20,000*: S. F. Hinkle, *Hershey* (New York, 1964), pp. 8–15.

199 *earn much less*: J. G. Brenner, *The Chocolate Wars: Inside the Secret World of Mars and Hershey* (London, 1999), pp. 9, 20, 42, 47–59.

200 *"home therein"*: J. Liebig, *Researches on the Chemistry of Food* (London, 1847), p. 2.

200 *"organized tissues"*: Ibid., p. 9.

201 *"putrefactive bacteria"*: Levenstein, *Revolution at the Table*, pp. 107–108.

201 *"smelling strong"*: Quoted in Toussaint-Samat, *History of Food*, p. 221.

202 *in 1930*: Levenstein, *Revolution at the Table*, p. 194.

202 *have disappeared*: R. Mandrou, "Les comsommations des villes françaises (viandes et boissons) au milieu du XIXe siècle," *Annales*, xvi (1961), 740–47.

203 *twice a week*: R. S. Rowntree, *Poverty and Progress: A Second Social Survey of York* (London, 1941), pp. 172–97.

204 *"bread pudding"*: Steingarten, *Man Who Ate Everything*, p. 37.

204 *"coke and pot chips!"*: Levenstein, *Paradox of Plenty*, p. 197.

205 *"twenty-one dynasties"*: M. Davis, *Late Victorian Holocausts: El Niño Famines and the Making of the Third World* (London, 2000), pp. 4–5, 111.

205 *35 percent*: B. Fagan, *Floods, Famines and Emperors: El Niño and the Fate of Civilizations* (London, 2000), p. 214.

205 *thirty million in China*: Davis, *Late Victorian Holocausts*, p. 7.

205 *"human survival"*: Ibid., p. 12.

205 *"full of vultures"*: Ibid., p. 139.

205 *"stopped the rain"*: Ibid., p. 102.

205 *"eating India's bread"*: Ibid., p. 26.

205 *availability of solutions:* Ibid., p. 146.

206 *using the implement:* Goody, *Cooking, Cuisine and Class*, pp. 60–61.

206 *millions of lives:* Davis, *Late Victorian Holocausts*, pp. 283, 286.

206 *monsoon failures:* L. R. Brown, *Seeds of Change: The Green Revolution and Development in the 1970s* (London, 1980), pp. xi, 6–7.

206 *"still going on":* F. Braudel, "Alimentation et categories de l'histoire," *Annales*, xvi (1961), 723–28.

207 *breeds of grain:* M. Carleton, *The Small Grains* (New York, 1916).

207 *strength of stem:* H. Hanson, N. E. Borlaug and R. G. Anderson, *Wheat in the Third World* (Epping, 1982), pp. 15–17.

207 *harvested per year:* Heiser, *Seed to Civilization*, p. 88.

207 *coastal plain:* Hanson, *Wheat in the Third World*, pp. 17–19, 31.

207 *by 1980:* Ibid., p. 40.

207 *disease-resistant strains:* Heiser, *Seed to Civilization*, p. 77.

207 *average for 1950:* Hanson, *Wheat in the Third World*, pp. 6, 15.

207 *16.5 million tons in 1968:* Ibid., p. 48.

208 *"newer variety":* Ibid., p. 23.

208 *"seem minor":* Brown, *Seeds of Change*, p. ix.

208 *95 percent of production:* McNeil, *Something New Under the Sun*, p. 222.

208 *"throw them away":* quoted in J. Pottier, *Anthropology of Food: The Social Dynamics of Food Security* (Cambridge, 1999), p. 127.

208 *""you have accomplished"'":* Hanson, *Wheat in the Third World*, p. 107.

209 *"scientific halfwits":* Levenstein, *Paradox of Plenty*, p. 161.

209 *"to kill aphids":* H. R. H. The Prince of Wales and C. Clover, *Highgrove: Portrait of an Estate* (London, 1993), p. 125.

209 *in 1990:* McNeil, *Something New Under the Sun*, p. 224.

211 *"dining room":* *Quaestiones Naturales*, Book 3, Chapter 18.

211 *in the field:* G. Pedrocco, "L'industrie alimentaire et les nouvelles techniques de conservation," in Flandrin and Montanari, *Histoire de l'alimentation*, pp. 779–94, at p. 785.

213 *sterilization by heating:* A. Capatti, "Le gout de la conserve," in ibid., pp. 795–807, at p. 798.

213 *west coast of France:* Goody, *Food and Love*, p. 160.

213 *eaten in season:* Capatti, "Le gout de la conserve," p. 799.

214 *"thought of the juice":* (London, 1957), pp. 116–17.

214 *tinned salmon terrine:* Capatti, "Le gout de la conserve," p. 801.

215 *cookery in the Arctic:* Toussaint-Samat, *History of Food*, p. 751.

215 *"heat and serve" variety:* Levenstein, *Paradox of Plenty*, pp. 107–8.

216 *"Stockyards":* *The Jungle* (Harmondsworth, 1965), p. 32.

216 *"thirty million people":* Ibid., p. 51.

216 *"rat was a tidbit":* Ibid., p. 163.

217 *made purity pay*: R. C. Alberts, *The Great Provider: H. J. Heinz and His 57 Varieties* (London, 1973), pp. 7, 40, 102, 11, 130, 136–41; *A Golden Day: A Memorial and a Celebration* (Pittsburgh, 1925), pp. 17, 37.

218 *in the 1980s*: J. R. Postgate, *Microbes and Man* (Cambridge, 1992), pp. 139–40, 146, 151.

219 *"ate their flesh"*: Ibid., pp. 238–40.

219 *reheated before serving*: Gaman and Sherrington, *The Science of Food*, pp. 242, 244–46.

219 *infected other meat*: Postgate, *Microbes and Man*, p. 68.

220 *modern France*: J. Claudian and Y. Serville, "Aspects de l'evolution recente de comportement alimentaire en France: composition des repas et urbanisation," in Hemardinquer, *Pour une histoire de l'alimentation*, pp. 174–87.

220 *culture in history*: M. Carlin, "Fast Food and Urban Living Standards in Medieval England," in M. Carlin and J. T. Rosenthal, eds., *Food and Eating in Medieval Europe* (London, 1998), pp. 27–51, at p. 27.

220 *"Go dine, go"*: Ibid., pp. 29, 31.

220 *"eat today"*: Levenstein, *Revolution at the Table*, p. 163.

221 *"for dessert"*: Ibid., p. 106.

221 *lowfat milk*: Ibid., p. 113.

221 *cream of mushroom soup*: Ibid., pp. 122–23.

221 *"cloves or cinnamon"*: *Fast Service* magazine, 1978, quoted in Levenstein, *Paradox of Plenty*, p. 233.

222 *to test*: Levenstein, *Revolution at the Table*, p. 227.

222 *tableside microwaves*: Ibid., p. 128.

224 *"Arcadian past"*: Highgrove, pp. 30, 276.

Index

ABOUT THE AUTHOR

Felipe Fernández-Armesto is a Professorial Fellow of Queen Mary, University of London, and a member of the Modern History Faculty at Oxford University. He is the author of thirteen books, including *Millennium: A History of the Last Thousand Years* and *Civilizations: Culture, Ambition, and the Transformation of Nature*.

Having just savored *Near a Thousand Tables*, feast on these other great works by world-renowned historian Felipe Fernández-Armesto.

Civilizations
Culture, Ambition, and the Transformation of Nature

A wide-ranging display of dazzling scholarship, *Civilizations* is a brilliant exploration of the nature of civilization in which Fernández-Armesto compares societies through their relationships to climate, geography, and ecology.

"This is a history that highlights not warfare but farming, fishing, hunting, and herding.... Stupendously informative and elegantly written, *Civilizations* is an embarrassment of riches."

—*The Boston Globe*

Millennium
A History of the Last Thousand Years

This *New York Times* notable book is an ambitious, absorbing, and boldly conceived 1,000-year world history that covers every civilization on the planet from Asia to Europe to the Americas and back again.

"Felipe Fernández-Armesto has accomplished a herculean task... a pleasure to hold and read....I was left wanting to go back and read it all again."

—*The New York Times Book Review*

Available in paperback wherever books are sold

For more information about Felipe Fernández-Armesto and his books, visit www.simonsays.com